THE
FINAL
TEST

The Uncertain Future of
Cricket's First-Class Game

HUW TURBERVILL

BLOOMSBURY SPORT
LONDON · OXFORD · NEW YORK · NEW DELHI · SYDNEY

BLOOMSBURY SPORT
Bloomsbury Publishing Plc
50 Bedford Square, London, WC1B 3DP, UK
Bloomsbury Publishing Ireland Limited
29 Earlsfort Terrace, Dublin 2, Ireland

BLOOMSBURY, BLOOMSBURY SPORT and the Diana logo are trademarks of
Bloomsbury Publishing Plc

First published in Great Britain 2025

A catalogue record for this book is available from the British Library

Library of Congress Cataloguing-in-Publication data has been applied for

ISBN: HB: 978-1-3994-1752-5; eBook: 978-1-3994-1751-8

2 4 6 8 10 9 7 5 3 1

Typeset in Bembo Std by Deanta Global Publishing Services, Chennai, India
Printed and bound in Great Britain by Clays Ltd, Elcograf S.p.A.

To find out more about our authors and books visit www.bloomsbury.com
and sign up for our newsletters
For product safety related questions contact productsafety@bloomsbury.com

The Final Test is part...

Looking at how Test cricket is being consumed by T20...

Why somebody like me cannot move with the times like others can...

An attempt to appreciate or at least understand the allure of franchise cricket...

But more than anything ... a love letter to the Test game

CONTENTS

INTRODUCTION

*'Cricket fans seem to divide into three, in the
sport's own version of the culture wars.'*

The final Test match of the English summer is like Janus, the Roman
god with two faces. The cricket season is still alive (just) … but
the unforgiving winter beckons. The match is traditionally held at
The Oval in South London, England's oldest Test ground, an olive
oasis amid a concrete jungle. It is a magnificent occasion. It is often
memorably moving, with great England players retiring and overseas
stars appearing in this country for the last time. The 2022 Test, the
third and final one of the series against South Africa, had even
greater poignancy, with the death of Her Majesty The Queen having
occurred on the opening day.

Before the news broke, the band came out on to the outfield and
were about to play 'God Save the Queen', but rain forced them to
beat a retreat into the pavilion, and sadly it was not played.

The Queen had been born at the start of the 1926 English cricket
season. England had regained the Ashes from Australia that year, the

only one of the five Tests to end in a positive result coming at The Oval. She acceded to the throne in 1952. England beat India 3–0 that summer. That year she was introduced to the sides during the second Test, at Lord's. The only match that ended in a draw was the final one. At The Oval. Eighty-six per cent of all men's Test matches had been played during her 70-year reign, the other 14 per cent having been played before she came to the throne.

I could not help feeling that her passing might be seen as a metaphor for the demise of the longer game. Yes, I know that people have been writing its epitaph since one-day cricket started in the 1960s; speculation was reaching a frenzy now, though. It did not help that the South Africans gave the impression that they did not want to be there, as they meekly folded to a crushing nine-wicket defeat.

The death of the Queen. The potential death of Test cricket…

I am desperately trying not to be reactionary and despairing at the damage being done to what I love. I try to stay on civil terms with the young, liberal clique who now dominate the press box, the domain of sports journalists. But Test cricket does seem to be in mortal danger. First they are coming for the 50-over game. Then the five-day. Twenty20 (T20) is growing like Japanese knotweed. White-ball tournaments – mainly T20 and T10 – are not only sprouting in traditional cricket hotbeds, but now also even places like Saudi Arabia have expressed an interest … although the reasons for that seem less about runs and more about funds.

It is easy to see a future, in 20 years' time, of T20 saturation, fuelled by the fanaticism of Indian fans for the format, specifically the Indian Premier League (IPL), with possibly the Ashes surviving only as a biannual Ryder Cup-style event. A novelty. If that.

The table overleaf from *The Cricketer*, May 2024 shows the rise of One-Day Internationals (ODIs) from 1970/71, and then T20 internationals (T20Is) in the 2000s. If, like me, you are fearful that T20 will smother everything else, we can only dread to think what the table will look like in 2030 and 2040. It is difficult to see that the modern thirst for instant gratification will recede in the coming years. We are 'time-poor' and the trend has only been going in one direction for some time. Indeed, the prophesised leisure boom of the 21st century never really happened.

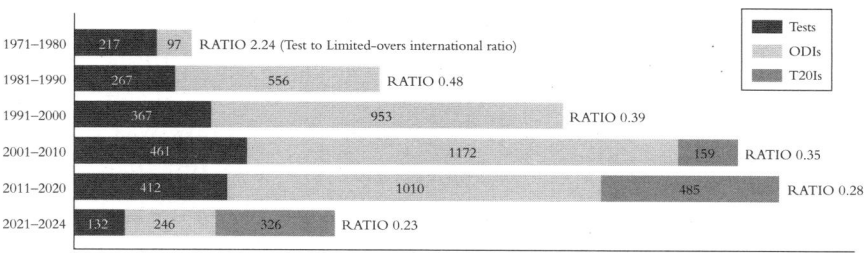

Figure 0.1: Format breakdown decade by decade since 1971 (*The Cricketer*)

After all, the 2023 men's Ashes was concertinaed into a tiny window that slammed shut before the school holidays, allowing The Hundred, a competition that lauded Australia cricket writer Gideon Haigh has described as a '10th-rate IPL knock-off', to hog it. 'I couldn't believe the schedule when I saw it,' the former Australia fast-bowling great, Glenn McGrath, told *The Cricketer*. 'We need to protect Test cricket better, not squash series like this.'

The moneymen behind the T20 franchise fiesta barely try to conceal their vision. 'We can make Test cricket work if we make it more of an event,' said Manoj Badale, lead owner of the IPL outfit Rajasthan Royals. 'We should have it at the same time every year, played between a small set of nations that can actually afford it, and Lord's becomes like a Wimbledon.' I believe that he was actually attempting to mollify us Test fanatics. Two Test matches in a fortnight of the English summer at the most, though? Well … how generous of him…

Rob Lynch was at it, too, shortly before leaving his job as chief executive of the Professional Cricketers' Association (PCA) – the players' union in England and Wales – to become Marylebone Cricket Club's new director of cricket and operations. The New Zealander, who briefly kept wicket for Auckland, also suggested that the Ashes could become like the Ryder Cup, and cricketers would become like golfers, travelling the world with their caddies (kit people). He was only being honest, I suppose, but it sounded grisly.

The players who have benefitted most from T20 play a similar tune. It reminds me of the question the fictitious comic television host Mrs Merton (Caroline Aherne) posed to Debbie McGee in *The Mrs Merton Show*: 'What first attracted you to the millionaire, Paul Daniels?' England white-ball captain Jos Buttler was actually trying to be constructive about the Test game, probably, but his comments in the spring of 2024 were clunky and could easily be misconstrued. 'Test cricket is very traditional and cricket started with that as the only format,' he said. 'It has 150 years of history behind it and tradition. T20 cricket only started in 2003, so people who love all the history and records prefer it, but I'll tell you what: the kids on TikTok and Instagram aren't watching Test cricket. I hope that T20 and The Hundred is the way they can then learn to love Test cricket. If they love The Hundred and say, "I really enjoyed watching Ben Stokes" and then Mum or Dad says, "Well, you can see him for four or five days if you want in Test cricket," that can be the great introduction for the younger generation into Test cricket.' I am not sure I share Buttler's faith, however.

The game has 'democratised', said the former England captain, Sir Andrew Strauss, seemingly glorying in the T20's growth across the globe, at the expense of Test cricket. He was extolling the virtues of the free market, fitting for a man who gives pep talks to the Conservative Party. Look what happens when that 'money talks' doctrine goes unchecked, though, like the selling of school playing fields in the 1980s – that was a huge stake hammered into state-school cricket, one that it will probably never recover from. The hilarious BBC comedy *Not the Nine O'Clock News* had a funny joke about America being so late for the last two World Wars that they wanted to be especially early for the next one. Strauss seemed a bit like that with the 'High-Performance Review' into English cricket that he delivered in 2022. He was late embracing T20. Cynics might say that it appears that Strauss wants, therefore, to be the first to be accepting when it extinguishes everything else. He was one of England's greatest captains: in conjunction with the hard-nosed, driven Zimbabwean Andy Flower as coach, he led them to one of their finest triumphs in Australia, the Ashes series victory in 2010/11, and by the following summer the 'Andocracy', as it became known, had taken England to No. 1 in the Test rankings. Strauss had not been bitten by the T20 bug at that stage; he tried to stop Kevin Pietersen et al. playing in the IPL in a move that saw him compared with King Cnut. As an administrator, he was the architect of England's extraordinary 2019 World Cup win as hosts, only four years after their farcical 2015 campaign in Australasia. Like Fox Mulder (who wanted to believe in aliens), I wanted to believe (in Strauss). But as the chair of the England and Wales Cricket Board's

Performance Cricket Committee, he cut to the chase: he advocated the bare minimum of domestic four-day/red-ball games (10 per club per summer in the County Championship), and a subsequent white-ball overload. He is clearly now one of those who feel that there is no point fighting the future. He upset the county fans even more on Sky by wheeling out the lazy trope about 'one man and his dog' watching Championship matches during that South Africa Test at The Oval in 2022. This is the competition in which he cut his teeth, of course, and although his incredible dedication and preparation, which put others to shame, has been chronicled memorably in a book by his Middlesex teammate David Nash, the comment was still galling. In the end, his High-Performance Review was not fully implemented because Strauss did not take county chiefs, members and supporters with him. His 'Poll Tax moment'…

Cricket fans seem to divide into three, in the sport's own version of the culture wars: traditionalists who refuse to accede territory – 'a reduction from 14 rounds of County Championship matches a summer over my dead body'; pragmatists who want to 'act now to future-proof a healthy balance'; and progressives who say: 'Just let global forces take their course.'

Former England one-day captain Eoin Morgan, who led the national team to that famous 2019 triumph (and also played for Middlesex), told me, 'You only get the right answer if you ask the right question, which is: "Where will the game be in 10 years?" There is a danger that cricket will follow football and go down the club/Champions League route.' I wonder if he really meant to use the word 'danger'… I am sure in his mind the word is 'inevitability'.

That Strauss did not even speak to all the counties about his High-Performance Review, published in September 2022, seemed odd. The document was reminiscent of Tony Blair's attempts to freeze Ken Livingstone out of the race to be Mayor of London in 2000. It stated optimistically (or should that be 'realistically' when you consider the dogma of administrators who crave get-rich-quick schemes?): 'The Hundred is committed through to 2028, and is a clear best vs best competition,' as if its status was non-negotiable. There is too much cricket, it says, but it was disingenuous – it did not point out that, unlike Australia, England and Wales has two T20-type competitions for its elite professionals – the Blast, which the 18 counties play in, and The Hundred, with its eight new 'city'/regional teams, who took to the field for the first time in 2021. As the old saying goes, 'Never commission a report until you know its findings.'

Former England captain Mike Gatting's stance was more constructive and emollient (well, it pleased me more, anyway). He told *The Cricketer* (August 2023):

> I want to keep Test cricket at the forefront. My time on the MCC [Marylebone Cricket Club] World Cricket Committee is winding down. It's been great, working with the much-missed Shane Warne, having such insight from the likes of Sourav Ganguly, Brendon McCullum, Kumar Sangakkara, Ricky Ponting and so many more. I'd like us to put something on the table: a framework. Test cricket is worth saving for the IPL [Indian Premier League] as much as anything, the quality of players. India have a responsibility, as England and Australia did in the early days, to keep the game safe. We've never had so much money in the game. We should be happy, but it's making people blind. India makes 80–90 per cent of the money, but the formula needs adjusting as countries are struggling.

To someone like me brought up on county cricket, the IPL seems like it is being played on another planet. I lived in Suffolk, so my nearest county ground was Essex. In the school holidays I often stayed with my grandfather, who lived in Sussex and took me to Hove. Yes, there were wooden benches, and quaint pavilions, and players in whites, and picnics of cheese in pitta, ham rolls, Golden Wonder crisps and tea in flasks. India's premier tournament has loud outfits, team names that seem to pay homage to whisky and cigarette brands; there are dancing girls (despite feminism) and pyrotechnics (in spite of climate concerns). English cricketers cannot wait to leave the county sides that developed them for the rucksack of rupees on offer, and of course it is easy to see why. But it still seems disloyal... What about the County Championship? What about your mates? What about the devoted followers who have watched you develop? Former England all-rounder Andrew Flintoff wrote:

> I played for Chennai in the IPL in 2009 ... I remember standing in the middle of the field, in a yellow kit, and my body was sore and hurting ... I just couldn't put everything on the line for Chennai.

In doing so he spoke for many of us. But things seem to have moved on (he is now head coach of the Northern Superchargers men's side in The Hundred). The argument seems to have been lost. One of his successors as an England all-rounder, Sam Curran, has become a global superstar, thanks to the IPL, even if he has not really nailed down a place in any of the three England formats – certainly not the Test or 50-over teams. He has even been awarded an MBE.

There is Australia's Big Bash, which began in 2011/12, occupying the Christmas/New Year slots that had so gloriously been taken up by international cricket not long before. There were the Sixers, the Stars and Renegades. What about Test cricket? What about the wonderful World Series Cup, which featured Australia and usually two others, including England, every four years? The Big Bash expanded in 2018/19, then contracted in 2023/24, a rare example of dilution of the T20 product – an acknowledgement that maybe, just for once, the goose that laid the golden egg had been over-farmed. In October 2023 Cricket Australia announced that it recorded a $16.9m loss in 2022/23, despite hosting the 2022 T20 World Cup.

Why has it all gone so wrong since one of the most exciting winters of my life, the 1986/87 Ashes tour, following Gatting's men down under? Pyjama cricket, Australia v England, packed crowds, under lights, with Richie Benaud, Tony Greig, Bill Lawry and Chappelli (Ian Chappell) commentating, and Daddles the Duck doddering across the screen. I saved my pennies and backpacked around Australia in 1994/95, and even though England were abject, and the announcer played *The Muppet Show* theme as Mike Atherton's men warmed up, and England lost to Zimbabwe and Australia's 2nd XI, it was still an amazing experience. But 28 years later … only 10,406 turned up to watch the third ODI between Australia and England (B) at the Melbourne Cricket Ground (MCG) in November 2022: a travesty. Buttler's men should have been on an open-top bus in London after winning the T20 World Cup in Australia a short time before, not being made to switch formats instantly for an encounter that did not even have International Cricket Council (ICC) Super League points at stake. 'Today was the day the music died cricket-wise,' the presenter Johnny Barran said to me. 'Lots of people are talking about how to keep bilateral cricket relevant and this series is a good example of how not to do that,' said Buttler. Moeen Ali described England's schedule as 'horrible'. Surely enough is enough. It is time that current and past cricketers had more say in scheduling, rather than lawyers and businesspeople.

West Indies cricket was another favourite thing of my childhood, another key component of that 1986/87 winter in Australia. Now there is the Caribbean Premier League, undoubtedly their prime product after Cricket West Indies reduced their regional competition: instead of the six island sides playing each other home and away, there are eight sides playing home or away – seven rounds of matches instead of 10. Needs must; I get that. Former West Indies Cricket Board chief executive Johnny Grave said that they had little choice, and argued that they spend more in relative terms than other countries, with hundreds of miles of travel needed between the islands. It just seemed another lurch towards a world comprising exclusively of T20 and T10 – or, as they call the latter in the Caribbean, the 6ixty (as in the number of balls in an innings), though.

Take also South Africa's Test side. They were due to play only 28 Tests from 2023–2027, compared to England's 43. They sent what looked like a B or even a C side to New Zealand in the spring of 2024 so that their best players would not miss their T20 tournament. Former Australia batting great Steve Waugh slammed the move, saying: 'If I was New Zealand I wouldn't even play the series. I don't know why they're even playing. Why would you when it shows a lack of respect for New Zealand cricket?' Former South Africa wicket-keeper and coach Mark Boucher was also unimpressed:

> If I was New Zealand cricket, I would be quite disappointed. ...
> I do think that we in South Africa need to sit down, have a hard look at ourselves at the scheduling and find a way to make it right.

Although they were not even playing in the series, Pat Cummins and Steve Smith also raised concerns over Test cricket and T20 franchise clashes. On the South Africa tour to New Zealand, Smith said: 'That's not really what you want to see. Ultimately, it's their decision as a board around what is important to them. But it is not ideal.' Australia's captain Cummins added: 'It is disappointing ... It is weird, because in Australia Tests are so strong. The crowds are great ... But it does feel like there is [sic] probably fewer countries than five or 10 years ago that are really putting all their resources into international cricket.'

In 2022, South Africa also cancelled a one-day international series in Australia, imperilling their 2023 50-over World Cup place, to ensure that their players were ready for the domestic T20.

Is all that progress for the better of the game? I think not. 'South Africa have only two more Tests this year [West Indies at home], and don't have a three-match Test series now for two years,' their former batting great Gary Kirsten told me in early 2023. 'We have gone from four- and five-Test series to three even when I was playing, and now to two. There is no way that you can build or sustain a Test cricket system when your national team is playing so little,' he continued. 'The international cricket community needs to look very quickly at how to make Test cricket sustainable and say: "How do we sustain Test cricket across all Test-playing nations so that there is a real interest to make it work?"'

He went on: 'Somehow, we need to make Test cricket a viable proposition for all Test-playing nations, otherwise we will end up watching three international teams – Australia, England and India – playing Test cricket against each other. It is really tough for the smaller Test-playing nations to rely on the Test game to survive – it is just not going to happen.'

Boucher was South Africa's coach in the 2022 series in England. The Oval Test was his last in charge. 'I love Test cricket to bits,' he said. 'I think it is the truest form of the game and one that we really need to look after and take care of. I think the heads in cricket need to get together and we need to find a way of thinking how we can play more Test cricket. Because it's exciting, especially with the way the game is being played now. You seldom have draws.' He added, 'The game has maybe moved forward because of T20 cricket, the guys are playing shots that they would never usually play. It is attacking and it is a nice game to watch at the moment. The more we see it, the better it will be for everyone.' It is hugely doubtful that their warnings will be heeded, however. The SA T20 is the thing over there now. The South African authorities are so keen on it that they gave tickets away dirt-cheap in its inaugural year in 2023, while neglecting the international team.

There is also the Pakistan Super League, the Bangladesh Premier League, the (Sri) Lanka Premier League, the Super Smash in New Zealand, the International League T20 (United Arab Emirates), Nepal's Everest Premier League and the county Blast/The Hundred in England and Wales. Even countries like the US, with their

Major League Cricket, are signing English players in the heart of our summer. Former England batsman Jason Roy left Surrey and went there for the inaugural edition in 2023, in Texas and North Carolina. He scored 54 runs for Los Angeles Knight Riders at an average of 18 runs per game. He was reportedly paid £150,000: a fraction under £2778 a run. Nice work if you can get it.

Saudi Arabia are also eyeing a slice of the pie. They might only be ranked 32nd in the ICC rankings at the time of writing, but you can guarantee that the wages that they offer will exceed everyone else's if their Saudi Pro (football) league is anything to go by. The nation's crown prince, Mohammed bin Salman, said he 'doesn't care' about accusations of sportswashing.

Test cricketers are being targeted by Indian Premier League owners for all-year-round contracts, allowing them to play short-form tournaments for Indian-owned franchises in the West Indies, the UAE and elsewhere. In fact, with the news that India had landed a spacecraft on the Moon, I wondered if an IPL offshoot would be set up there… Now that one truly would be out of this world.

And yet … am I being too harsh? Too reactionary? The Victor Meldrew of the cricket world?

Embrace the hegemony of T20, or resist it? That is the great existentialist dialectic that all cricket followers should be wrestling with. Stick or twist.

Why do some people accept change, and others resist it? The most obvious examples are conservatism v liberalism; Brexit v Remain; Trumpian Republicanism v Democratism; those who hit the streets of England in the summer of 2024 to rail against immigration v those who work to help refugees. Why, whenever there is societal revolution rather than evolution, do some people laud it in the name of progress, and others try to repel it? Is it in our genes, or is it how we have been brought up – nature v nurture? Is it people virtue-signalling to show that they are trendy, accepting and tolerant? Are resistors too stubborn? Is racism – conscious or subconscious – at work? Or snobbery? I am in the traditional bracket when it comes to cricket. Am I backward? Are cricket writers who give administrators a sedan-chair ride 'client journalists'? Part of a 'chumocracy'?

In the first chapter I will try to open my mind…

1

HOW PEOPLE LEARNED TO STOP WORRYING AND LOVE T20

'Cricket is now played and watched by more people than ever before. And the game itself – the one we see played out with a bat and ball, whether over 100 balls a side or five days – has never been so enthralling.'

Oh, that introduction was awfully negative, wasn't it? Maybe it is time to look on the bright side of life. The British satirical magazine *Private Eye* has poked fun at cricket's administrators for trying to turn cricket into an equivalent of football. They may be on to something. The FIFA rankings – sponsored by Coca-Cola, that quintessence of commercialism – rank the football-playing nations from one to 207. At the time of writing, Argentina, the 2022 World Cup winners, are at the summit, with San Marino at the bottom. Right, I am now going to play devil's advocate. There is no reason why cricket could not have something similar. Already, records for T20I matches include *all*

nations, not just the Test-playing ones. As I write this, Nepal's Kushal Malla has the record for the fifth-highest score in T20 internationals, behind four players of Test-playing nations: Australia's Aaron Finch, who has the first- and third-highest scores; his compatriot Glenn Maxwell, who has the fourth-highest; and Hazratullah Zazai of Afghanistan, who has the second-highest. Malla's unbeaten 137 came for Nepal against Mongolia at the Hangzhou Cricket Ground, Pingfeng Campus Cricket Field, in September 2023. Tying with him, although he was dismissed, was Zeeshan Kukikhel of Hungary, who made goulash of Austria at the Seebarn Cricket Centre, Lower Austria, in June 2022. Of course, the bowling was not in the same league as that of England, when Finch made the third-highest score (156) at the Rose Bowl, Southampton, in August 2013. But that is not the point, say the globalists. It is a level playing field – the democratisation, of which Strauss spoke.

The *Telegraph*'s Tim Wigmore described this as 'cricket's golden age' in an article for *The Cricketer* magazine (August 2023). 'Cricket is now played and watched by more people than ever before,' he wrote. 'And the game itself – the one we see played out with a bat and ball, whether over 100 balls a side or five days – has never been so enthralling.' Afghanistan's Rashid Khan, Wigmore wrote, is 'Exhibit A. T20 leagues have created a global free market for talent. Here, a player's passport does not matter; what matters is what qualities they bring to a team.'

In England and Wales, one can also see a T20 pyramid structure developing in domestic cricket, involving the 18 first-class counties, perhaps also even involving the 21 National (former Minor) Counties. England and Wales Cricket Board (ECB) chief executive Richard Gould likes such a model, although those obsessed with 'elite' eight-team tournaments look likely to thwart him. Spread the talent. Perhaps it would have consisted of four divisions: a premier league of nine counties, a second tier with the same number, then two regional groups of 10 and 11 counties. The National Counties would be in these lower tiers at the start, but in theory they could rise to the top. They could do, to use a football analogy, 'a Wrexham' – the North Wales football club that returned to the Football League and is now climbing up it, following their buy-out by Hollywood actors Ryan Reynolds and Rob McElhenney.

It is an efficient model. From April to September the teams could have played T20 matches in midweek and at weekends. The danger, of course, is if the modernists have their way there would hardly be any first-class cricket, save for some sort of trial, for the aforementioned 'Ashes redux' redesign; the 50-over game would be no more.

Would it be so bad? T20 is still cricket – a gripping contest between bat and ball. It is a neat format, fun to play and enjoyable to watch. Twenty overs, four per bowler. Takes about three hours. You still have time to play yourself in (in the first 10 overs, anyway). Then superb entertainment. Sixes aplenty. The shots … wow! Ramps and scoops, and reverse sweeps. Artful bowling. No two balls the same. Slower ones. Yorkers. Slow bouncers. Knuckle balls. Cutters. Wizardry. But why must T20 be at the expense of everything else? Why should it kill Test cricket, that colourful, quirky, five-act phenomenon that has enchanted millions for nearly 150 years?

When people say T20 is like baseball, eyes roll, and rightly so … although… There is an article as I type this on the BBC website entitled 'IPL: The batting blitz turning cricket into baseball' commenting on the 'six-hitting festival' that was the 2024 tournament. I was sitting in the Metropole Hotel in Brighton with fellow cricket lover Sean Gardner after a cracking first day's play between Sussex and Glamorgan at Hove in May 2023. The baseball highlights on BT Sport were on in the bar. I have nothing against baseball. I know that it has a lot of British followers. It looks a fun game. If I were American, I am sure I would like it. The highlights of the baseball week, however, were a showreel ostensibly of shots over what we would call long-on and midwicket. An occasional strike would go over long-off. Surely it is impossible to argue that T20 is more aesthetically pleasing than Test cricket?

One winter Sunday I was scrolling on my phone when I spotted on Instagram that Somerset batsman Tom Banton had posted a showcase of his strokeplay in the nets as he prepared for a T10 tournament: 80–90 per cent of the shots were him clearing his front leg and whacking over midwicket and long-on. Coincidentally, in a separate post underneath, a fan had posted a video of Ian Bell playing a mesmerising cover drive that went for four for England in a Test match. My impression is that most shots in T20 matches are played on the leg side. I asked the stats gurus CricViz about this. They kindly looked into it and reported back that actually the balance of shots to leg over off is 'only' 54 per cent to 46. Perhaps that is not as big a deficit as I thought, but to me it is still significant. More than 52/48, certainly, but perhaps let us not go there…

T20 does not allow for the epic, either. The format that is most at risk is the 50-over game. In T20, could you get an innings like the one Australia's Glenn Maxwell played against Afghanistan at Mumbai's Wankhede Stadium in the 2023 50-over World Cup in India? Maxwell had a back injury, was crippled by cramp in his legs, and was also recovering from concussion after falling out of a golf buggy (yes, really), but his eye-hand co-ordination was so good, his arms were so powerful, that he just stood there swatting balls into the stands as if he was launching free T-shirts to spectators. Australia had slumped to 91 for 7 in pursuit of 292, but Maxwell struck 201 not out from only 128 balls, his innings including 10 sixes.

Then there are the pitches in T20. They are generally as flat as Californian highways. India coach Rahul Dravid, one of the finest batsmen of all time, hit the nail on the head. Criticising the ICC for marking down pitches that offered too much assistance to bowlers during that same tournament, he said: 'If you want to only see 350-run matches and rate only those wickets as good, then I disagree with that. You have to see different skills on display as well. If we wanted to only see fours and sixes being hit, then we have T20 for that.'

There can be people who love the county game, have fond memories of Ian Botham and Viv Richards raining sixes down on spectators at Taunton; Imran Khan running down the hill to hit batsmen on the head at Hove; Graham Gooch biting the left shoulder of his shirt to stay upright, whipping seamers through mid-on at Chelmsford; Graeme Hick, bolt upright, spanking it to all parts of wondrous Worcester under the gaze of the captivating cathedral… We do not give up what we love so easily. Then there are people who might say: 'All that was great, but things move on. T20 on the global franchise stage is where it is at now. History is bunk. Bring on the future.' Take Kevin Pietersen's declaration on X: 'The old guard … keep saying T20 is sh*te and we want more Tests. What they don't realise is that kids have zero interest in Tests. … My greatest format is Tests. … But I've moved with the times…' (Conveniently, he overlooks the fact that Test cricket still makes up the lion's share of the ECB's agreement with Sky TV.)

Some of us feel and take pleasure from nostalgia, some of us do not. I confess to being sentimental but have friends who are absolutely not. I wonder if the way I look back on Test and county cricket in the 1980s is illusory. I am indebted to the great cricket/sportswriter Duncan Hamilton for introducing me to the Portuguese word, *saudade*. It means longing for past happiness. The Victorians thought nostalgia was a disease. Clearly, too much of it can be a bad thing. In this book I intend to go on a journey to recall what I loved about cricket, what I still adore, why people want wholesale change, and why other people, including myself, fear it.

2

TESTING THOUGHTS

'Huw, you will be here at The Oval Test in 20 years…'

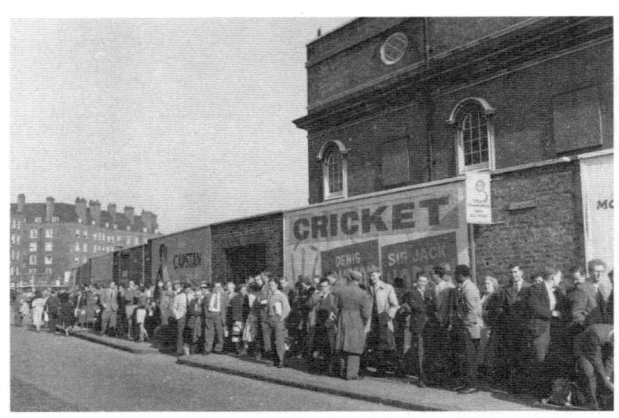

There was no play on the first day of that third and final Test between England and South Africa at the Kia Oval in September 2022. Rumours began to circulate about Her Majesty's death in the morning, and confirmation sadly arrived at teatime. I was meeting a friend that evening, and as I sat in a pub in Clapham waiting for him, and as the alcohol, and the rhythm of the unremitting rain, started to magnify my melancholy, my thoughts turned to my parents, who had both died in the last three years. While they would have been sad, they would also have enjoyed the poignant review of the Queen's reign, the backdrop to their lives.

The cricket finally got underway on the second morning – the show must go on! – and a ridiculously short game followed, befitting of the T20 era. South Africa were bowled out for 118 in 36.2 overs. Bizarrely, England faced exactly the same number of overs and balls, making only 158. It felt like an opportunity spurned. South Africa did not fare a great deal better second time around, however, making 169 in 56.2 overs, and England romped to victory, by nine wickets. The batting was often rash and ugly, impatient and wasteful. Frankly, it was not a great advert for the Test game, and if I was looking for evidence that the future of the long game was assured, I did not find it. Amid the frenzy I explored the media centre, asking writers and commentators, 'Where do you see Test cricket being in 20 years' time?' Here's what they had to say to me.

Nasser Hussain, former England batsman and captain, now Sky commentator:

I've been hearing about the demise of Test cricket for 30 years or more. We are lucky in England to have such passionate supporters of the format. We have had sell-outs, big last-day crowds, in part thanks to the transformation in the England side under captain Ben Stokes and coach Brendon McCullum. The crowds have loved it. I fear that in certain parts of the world Tests are a bit duller and fans are not so keen. It would be a shame if we just had England, Australia and India... You need a build-up to an Ashes series, for expectation to grow; you would not want it played every year. So I do fear for the format globally: the ICC and the individual nation boards need to ensure cricket [all formats] is for all. Franchises are signing individuals up, however, and stars like Trent Boult [of New Zealand] are calling time on their international careers prematurely. So there are alarm bells. Players are also changing thanks to T20; there is less emphasis on keeping the ball out, so we are seeing quicker Tests. But don't write Test cricket off yet.

Scyld Berry, former longstanding cricket correspondent of the *Telegraph*, now a columnist:

Test cricket is killing itself; specifically the International Cricket Council's Future Tours Programmes. Not the 'Big Three': India, Australia and England. They will be playing four- and five-Test series in the future. They will be all right ... they always are. It is the two-Test series, being played by all the other countries... If you say, 'It is a two-Test series', you are proclaiming the fact that it is utterly unimportant. What happens in reality? A touring team flies in, a week at most ahead of the first Test. They play a two- or three-day warm-up, often among themselves. They go into the first Test completely unacclimatised. They lose easily, and so the only question that remains is 'Will they rally to draw the series 1–1, or will it be 2–0?' And as soon as people become aware that the Test series has started, it is over. Utterly undramatic. Did Shakespeare write *Hamlet* in two acts?

He did not, Scyld. And to take the metaphor further, most of Shakespeare's plays have five acts – like a Test match has five days.

Richard Thompson, chair of the England and Wales Cricket Board, was chair of the dominant county, Surrey. As such, he was a major proponent of the 18-county system, and a supporter of Test cricket. Each Test match they hosted made about £50m for Surrey County Cricket Club. As chair of the ECB, he had to take a more holistic view:

> Our domestic season is actually quite short compared to other countries'. I do not want to diminish the red-ball competition, the County Championship. For me, it is the gold standard. It is where you make history, where you define your career. But you need to ensure that what red-ball cricket you are playing – and I think we kind of get fixated on volume and not schedule – there has to be a schedule and a rhythm to the season that I have not experienced in 12 years.

Pat Pocock, who took 1399 first-class wickets for Surrey, and 67 Test wickets for England:

> It's been proven over the last 50 years that you cannot make county cricket pay for itself – but there have been two 'golden geese' in that time. In 1968/69 you had the introduction of the Sunday League (40 overs per innings) where more people watched on that day than the rest of the week put together. You also had the introduction of overseas players. County cricket plays two vital roles: it gives a format that you can build a county club membership around – you cannot build a members' club around

T20. County cricket also allows players to acquire a technique for Test cricket... You cannot learn this. Therefore, without county cricket, there will not be any Test matches. Over the next 20 years, so much depends on the management. With Richard Thompson as ECB chair we have given ourselves the best chance, but his term, at present, is only for five years. Having just won a Test match and series so decisively as we have [against South Africa in 2022], then I think it is a perfect time to ask this question. The bowling departments have bulldozed their way throughout the series, but, long term, this is not what the cricketing public want, regardless of who wins! On my last England tour, David Gower's tour of India 1984/85, we were in the middle of a Test match and four senior and experienced English supporters came up to me in the hotel one evening and said, 'Pat, this was the best day's cricket we have seen for years.' I asked why. They said, 'When we watch cricket, we want to see fast bowlers bowling fast with the new ball. We then want to see quality spinners bowling at quality batsmen.' Phil Edmonds and I had bowled all day, every day and the Indians had many fine, quality batsmen. They said, 'We love to see the tussle of the competition that exists in such a duel.' Therefore, when good spin bowlers do not bowl, not only does the team suffer from the lack of wickets, but the public are starved of what many regard as the best part of the game to watch.

Nick Hoult, the *Daily Telegraph* cricket correspondent:

I think that there will still be six Tests per summer in the United Kingdom in 20 years' time, but I fear that the other countries will just play what they have to, as dictated by the World Test Championship. Here, it is still a good day out, and although I know that this could fluctuate quickly, Test cricket is better to watch now than probably it has ever been. Not just Brendon McCullum, Ben Stokes and 'Bazball', but batsmen all over are more attacking. What we do need is richer nations helping the poorer ones like Sri Lanka out. Readers of the *Telegraph* I am sure are similar to readers of *The Cricketer* – they are worried about this.

A lot can change in 20 years, of course. Twenty years ago we did not have T20. The game has changed more in those years than it did in 50. But I still suspect that it will not change all that much – as long as India want to play Test cricket, it will carry on. I would also like to see women play more Tests. Greg Barclay [the chair of the ICC] ruling that out is a little short-sighted, I think. Youngsters will not differentiate that much – it should be like Wimbledon – men's Test cricket, and women's.

Hoult is right: women's Test cricket is still being seen as an afterthought. It is a shame. The 2023 Ashes Test at Trent Bridge was great to watch. England opener Tammy Beaumont showed tremendous discipline and strength in her innings of 208, and slow left-armer Sophie Ecclestone's bowling is always a delight to watch.

Neil Manthorp, prominent South Africa-based cricket writer and talkSPORT commentator:

The financial reality is that it costs South Africa money to stage Test cricket. The crowds are rubbish apart from the New Year Test at Newlands. If you apply strict business principles then you can understand why they would concentrate their resources on white-ball cricket. I mean two-Test series ... they are not series for a start ... but financially they make sense. It costs the Wanderers in Johannesburg 100,000 rand a day [about £4000] to run the stadium. That is not to say Test cricket is not popular in South Africa ... it is ... but people watch on television or follow it in other ways. Hits on websites and so on suggests that millions are interested. I think that might also be the case in several countries. They did try letting people in for free in South Africa, but there is that old adage: 'If you give somebody something for free then they realise it's worthless.' Crowds went down from 200 to 20. It is amazing to think how popular the Currie Cup [South Africa's old domestic red-ball competition] was, although that was because there was no international cricket... The New Year match between Western Province and Transvaal at Newlands was packed.

In 20 years? I think South Africa will play Test matches as exhibitions, one a year – 'this is what they did in the old days' – with any number of T20s. I don't think the Ashes will change that much. I do think Australia, England and India need to address whether they can play Test cricket without any other countries, though. A decade ago the ICC set up the Test fund. It is now gone. It needs to come back. New Zealand's are the most forward-thinking administrators in world cricket by a country mile, playing at Hamilton with its grass banks and so on. Kane Williamson and co. said it was disappointing; they wanted to play longer series, but the NZCB said, 'Well, you want to play in the IPL, CPL etc., so there is no choice. You give us an alternative plan...' And they went, 'Oh, yes, you may be right.' South Africa could do the same as New Zealand – just play it on a field. Treat it like snooker, which is brilliant for TV, in boutique stadiums, with reduced overheads ... and things like Hawk-Eye should be subsidised.

John Etheridge, the *Sun's* long-standing cricket correspondent:

I would be staggered if Test cricket was not here in 20 years' time. Five-day matches. There might be fewer matches around the world, but not in England. It will look the same here. There is a downward trend around the world, but England have always played more. The Ashes is the skeleton around which everything is built. And the biggest names in world cricket – Ben Stokes, Virat Kohli – they all say Test cricket is the ultimate format and it should be protected. T20 leagues have already reached saturation point. T20 will eat itself. People will get fed up with the same recycled players turning up all around the world. The same old faces. There's no loyalty among the T20 players. Huw, you will be here at The Oval Test in 20 years...

(Ed: Let us hope so. Kohli does indeed say that by the way: 'Test cricket is real cricket. I want it to stay alive. It is the most valued format of the game, the absolute pinnacle. It improves you as a person. For me this is the absolute pinnacle of the game. I will give everything to Test cricket for the time I play.')

Simon Wilde, *The Sunday Times'* cricket correspondent:

If you look at the history of Test cricket, there have always been peaks and troughs. England will always want to play a lot, and other teams will want to keep playing England – for cultural and commercial reasons. England tend to play the teams who are playing well. So, when West Indies were dominant in the 1960s and 1980s, England played them a lot because they were box office. Now we want to play India for that reason. If you go through a period of not playing much Test cricket, it does not mean it is going to die. The top players know it is the ultimate test. T20 is not difficult at all. There are not enough quality players to sustain eight top leagues a year. And some like Ben Stokes do not want to be part of it all. He has had a couple of IPL pay-outs. It is not like he does not want to be involved; it is just that he does not want it all the time. And the people who are involved all the time – Kieron Pollard, Dwayne Bravo and Andre Russell – they are either physically incapable of playing Test cricket or they are not good enough. We have hit peak T20 and maybe in 10 years' time there will be less of it.

George Dobell, chief correspondent of *The Cricketer* magazine:

In one way or another, Tests definitely will survive. There is no room for complacency, though. I fear that there will not be as much Test cricket, or as many teams. On the bright side, it is as entertaining as it has ever been. And I do not want it to survive just because of some sort of Arts Council funding – like opera has. It has to stand on its own two feet. But look around: we have seen full houses every day here at The Oval. Broadcast rights in this country still sell. Unfortunately, I'm not sure five-Test series are the way to go any longer.

Rob Bagchi, sportswriter for the *Telegraph* and novelist:

As far as broadcasters are concerned, it is such a good product. Five days of guaranteed eight hours of television – that is why Sky pay for it. It is a key driver for them. It will continue to flourish in England as long as crowds keep turning up. There are no signs that enthusiasm is waning here. There may be fewer bilateral series between, say, West Indies and Sri Lanka, or Pakistan and Zimbabwe … but I still think marquee series will stay at a good length as they are such profit drivers.

Elizabeth Ammon, cricket writer of *The Times*:

> The British public do not want change. T20 leagues cannot
> dominate forever. The IPL will stay huge, but not the other ones.
> The Big Bash seems to go on for three years. England might not
> have anyone to play against in Tests, mind you... There may be
> fewer countries playing Test cricket in 20 years but it will still
> be there and still involve England. The British cricketing public
> still hold it dearly and that is across the age spectrum and there
> is a next generation who are already in love with Test cricket.
> Franchise T20 leagues are here to stay but not all of them will
> survive long term as the market becomes too saturated.

Melinda Farrell, Anglo–Australian writer/broadcaster:

> I am worried about Sri Lanka, South Africa, New Zealand,
> West Indies and other countries. It is cricket's biggest existential
> question, and what I want to see is somebody in a position of
> leadership in the sport, who has a vision. I do not see anybody
> who can tell me what the plan is – in five years, 10, 15, whatever.

Dean Elgar was the South Africa Test captain during the series in
England. Asked if the South Africans should have played a match in
between the second Test at Old Trafford and the third at The Oval,
he said:

> I reckoned we could have cracked on with the third Test and
> been home already. Every Test match you have to live and die for,
> every game is huge. We have been playing good cricket and pretty
> average cricket. Play every Test as if it is your last – I want the guys
> to have that mentality.

Steve Elworthy, former South Africa seam bowler, now the chief
executive of Surrey CCC, who was responsible for staging this Test
match:

> I think we are going in the right direction with Test cricket. I
> think the World Test Championship is a step forward. Australia and

India, and you think IPL and India, they are still playing seriously good Test cricket. We have to make sure that it does stay. I love Test cricket. I love the County Championship – it is the pipeline to Test cricket. From a playing perspective, you need that base. I certainly hope it doesn't become Wimbledon-esque [as Manoj Badale suggested] … I think that as long as you have your iconic five-Test series, the Ashes, England v India, the big countries are playing Test cricket, they will take Test cricket with us. We need to use our influence with the ICC to make sure Test cricket stays front and centre.

Kumar Sangakkara, former Sri Lanka wicket-keeper/batsman, now commentator and director of cricket of Rajasthan Royals in the IPL, and commentator:

Bazball has been fantastic for English cricket. It has rejuvenated Test cricket in England. It has been as entertaining as any format. Ben Stokes and Brendon McCullum are leaving a legacy and they should be proud of that. It has shown Test cricket in a new light. But we have to ask, 'How much further is Test cricket going to stay relevant as it is? Is it financially viable for some countries? How do we keep something for everyone? How do we attract new fans and new markets?' Countries like Sri Lanka need more support across the board to allow boards to host the cricket that they want to. We talk about Test cricket being the prime format, but do we have equal pay for the greats of the game? Are they available all the time? Is a central fund a possibility? There are lots of questions to answer.

Barry Richards, legendary South Africa batsman:

I am not super-confident about the future of Test cricket because the IPL is taking over the world. It is expanding, so it is a question of how the authorities are going to manage Test cricket. On the whole, the lower sides are not providing the entertainment that we see in the Ashes, where everyone is rapt in their attention towards Test cricket. With T20 getting so much traction, it is going to be difficult in the years ahead to sell Test cricket to the kids. Ten- to 15-year-olds are not interested. The Test format is under threat; it is a hard-sell in some countries and the 50-over game is on life support. The IPL is amazing, but I don't particularly like the concept because it is not a contest between bat and ball. I like to see the bowler get a fair chance. In the IPL, bats are big, fields are small, pitches are flat, so it is just a six-hitting battle. That, to me, is boring. I mean, how many people know the result when they go home?

I certainly would have liked to play it, though, because at the end of the month you are getting a big salary cheque. It would be fantastic and rightly so, because the players generate a lot of television revenue. It would have been nice to play. You adapt, and you can be expansive with the size of today's bats, and because of the size of the boundaries now, you've got a good chance of clearing them. In South Africa, spectators are embracing the T20 franchises, which are IPL-owned. I can see a worldwide IPL franchise and they may try to buy one or two teams in England. I think the whole game has changed. It all depends on what your ambition is. Do you want to play Test cricket or T20? There's a different technique to all of them. Young kids these days are taught to swing that bat hard, so I think the *MCC Cricket Coaching Book* is fairly redundant now.

Ken McEwan, former Essex batsman, would have had a long career with South Africa, were it not for international isolation:

Other than England, Australia and India, Test cricket is being sidelined … all the money is in the short version. That's sad because I believe we have so many good, young players here who should be playing Tests. But life has changed. Everything is instant now. You are never again going to get a Geoffrey Boycott who can bat for days. Tests will become baseball cricket because of the way they bat. Games are not going to last five days because they move on so quickly.

Mark Taylor, former Australia batsman and captain:

I try to stay positive. I, and people in general, still love the longer form. The Ashes is very special. South Africa are not the side they were, though, and I do worry about countries who don't have the history of Tests like Australia and England. If things turn south for them I fear that they will just stick to short-form cricket.

Ricky Ponting, another former Australia batsman and captain:

I'm probably more worried about Test cricket now than I have ever been. I've always been quite a strong advocate of Test cricket, and it being strong around the world. More and more of these domestic T20 competitions are popping up – in the United States, the UAE, and South Africa are off the mark now. The smaller Test nations are going to find it harder and harder to promote Test cricket when there is so much money in the other formats. The ICC has to have a big role here when it comes to equalisation, to make the realisation that payments/contracts are needed across the Test game. If they don't, it is going to be hard for some players to focus on Test cricket.

It was also interesting to read what Ponting wrote about T20 in his *Ashes Diary 2005*:

I am not sure international cricket is the right place for it. The need to score quickly can easily produce slogging – not ideal when you have the best players in the world on view – and I think the lower level it is played at, the more entertaining it will be because that way there is less riding on the result. I think too much T20 could destroy the other forms of the game rather than promote them.

People say journalists are cynical, but actually Messrs Etheridge, Hoult and Wilde came across as rather optimistic – the former's promise that I will be there in 20 years' time felt comforting. The sagacious Scyld Berry is always worth listening to, however, and his thoughts on narrow-minded administrators straitjacketing Test series felt spot on; likewise Neil Manthorp's realism cannot be ignored. 'Don't write Test cricket off yet,' said Nasser Hussain. Let us hope that he is right...

3

DAVID GOWER AND MY GOLDEN YEARS

'If you ignore the situation, one day we will wake up and there will be no Test cricket, and we will wonder how that happened.'

David Gower tells me a story that should be taken on board by England's modern batsmen:

I made my Test debut in 1978, against Pakistan, at Edgbaston, and I made 58 before miscuing one and hitting the ball straight up into the air. My next Test innings was against them at Lord's, and I was really flying that time, on my way to 56, before I played a horrible sweep to Iqbal Qasim. I was out before lunch on the first day, but nevertheless I was pretty happy with the way things were going. Then the England captain, Mike Brearley, took me to one side.

'I don't know if anyone has mentioned this to you,' he said, 'but Test matches actually last for five days, and there is a long time to bat. We are enjoying watching you bat, and it would be quite nice to make some even bigger scores.' I had been used to playing three-day cricket with false declarations and the like. It was a gentle yet firm message that Test cricket is a bit different.

Although Gower fell for 39 in his next knock, against Pakistan, at Headingley, the message had broken through. He made 111 against New Zealand at The Oval, and he was away... Seventeen more Test centuries followed, two of them doubles. He may now be only fifth in the list of England's highest Test run-scorers, but in many people's eyes he is the most elegant that there has been. I watched a lot of him in the 1980s, and I do not recall him being troubled by the extreme pace that he faced, especially from West Indies (although I am sure he must have been at times). With the aesthetic advantage of being a left-hander, he was upright, marvellously top-handed as the coaches say you should be, and there was no hint of a crouch... It all seemed to come rather effortlessly to him – in slight contrast to Graham Gooch, who looked to be concentrating and fighting with every inch of his being. Gower seemed just to caress, clip and flick the ball away with the most exquisite timing, before we all waved it goodbye to the boundary. Some describe him as languid, and they do not always mean that as a compliment; others say that he was exasperating, caught in the slips flashing too often – but that was inevitable if, for the rest of the match, his timing was so perfect.

Gower continues:

Despite Mike's kind and well-meant admonishment, it was a great moment for me to be part of the Test game ... and I am still convinced that Test cricket is the greatest format. My first Test match as a spectator was in 1965 at Trent Bridge, the second Test between England and South Africa. My dad took me along to that. It was the day Graeme Pollock, who I became a great admirer of, made 125. Admittedly I was behind the stand playing with a tennis ball half the day, so I did not watch it all, but nevertheless it was a spectacular day. Every time I watched him he made a hundred, actually. There was that Test match. Then I toured South

Africa with the schoolboy team, The Crocodiles, in 1974/75, and I watched him make one in inestimable style at St George's Park at Port Elizabeth. Then I batted with him in one of those international games at Jesmond near Newcastle in the late 1980s, and Graeme being Graeme as he was so competitive, he made one there too. I scored 60 or 70 at the other end as I did not want to steal his thunder ... but I digress.

As a youngster we lived in Loughborough, so we went to a lot of cricket at Grace Road and Trent Bridge, and watched football at Leicester City, and rugby at Leicester Tigers. High-quality sport ... but cricket soon became my favourite. The great Garry Sobers was wonderful to watch at Trent Bridge, especially when he was in full flight... Some of those shots that he played off the back foot especially ... the speed of the bat, the ball off the bat ... they are memories from way, way back that are still lodged in my brain. Pollock, Sobers and John Edrich, who was the England left-hander of that era and made an unforgettable 310 not out against New Zealand at Headingley in 1965, inspired me to play to an extent, but for me the most important motive-force was just the fun I got from playing sport. I had lots of encouragement from my father and mother, and as an only child I relied on them both to throw balls at me in the back garden.

The premise of this book is the dialectic between Test cricket and T20: how the former is trying to stay upright amid the avalanche of the latter. In Gower's playing days it was Tests v ODIs. 'My first game for England was an ODI, that same summer, 1978, against Pakistan. Even though I made 114 not out in the second one, at The Oval, the ODIs were seen as a leg-up into the Test side: a bit of a warm-up that often preceded Test series,' Gower said. 'Test cricket was a constant learning curve for me, but my stats held up on the whole. There were obviously a few peaks and troughs, but I generally averaged in the mid-40s [finishing with 8231 at an average of 44.25 in 117 Tests]. In ODIs I started very well with 50s and 100s, but I tailed off.' By the end of 1983, in 58 ODIs he had made 1995 runs at 41.56, with six centuries. In the next 56, until his ODI career ended in 1991, he made 1175 at 21.36, with only one more hundred. 'It might well have been that that tailing off was a subconscious reaction to playing in what seemed like a lot of less-meaningful matches than Test cricket. Obviously we wanted to win, but they did not carry the same weight, and that is reflected in my figures [ending with an ODI average of 30.77].'

I have happy memories of Gower in the duck egg blue gear, batting merrily and snaffling catches at short-midwicket in the one-dayers in Australia in 1986/87. My defining memories of him playing are from Test cricket, however. His *annus mirabilis* in 1985, when he scored 732 runs at 81.33, and led England to a memorable Ashes. His hundred at Perth 18 months later on that incredible tour. His 157 not out against India at The Oval in 1990 that resuscitated his Test career. And his centuries at Melbourne and Sydney on the 1990/91 tour to Australia in the twilight of his playing days, even if his relationship with Gooch had entered the Captain Mainwaring/ Sergeant Wilson phase.

So is he worried about the future of Test cricket?

I think that we are all worried, yes, anyone with a love of the longer form – Test cricket and four-day/first-class cricket – is entitled to be very worried indeed. The number of tournaments that have popped up in the last two years, in Nepal and so on, not just the Test nations, is incredible. Now the Saudis are wanting to host matches as well. Manoj Badale, the owner of the Rajasthan Royals in the IPL, has suggested a window for Test cricket… Twelve months before that, administrators were trying to work out how to create a window for franchise cricket. That is how quickly things can change. If you ignore the situation, one day we will wake up and there will be no Test cricket, and we will wonder how that happened. So the battle is definitely on…

I was in the Caribbean in December 2023 for the ODIs and T20s between West Indies and England. I was talking to Johnny Grave, the chief executive of West Indies cricket, and he said it was a straightforward situation: they can make more money from eight limited-overs games over 18 days than three Test matches in three weeks. The former makes money; the latter loses it. That is their conundrum. The emergence of Shamar Joseph, West Indies' match-winner against Australia at the Gabba [Brisbane Cricket Ground] in January 2024, has been one of cricket's great stories recently. Now the general trend, though, is that if someone makes a name for themselves, the next step for them is franchise cricket. Rovman Powell, Jason Holder and Nicholas Pooran came from the pressing business of the T10 in Abu Dhabi to play the T20s for West Indies after missing the ODIs. If that does not highlight the problem, I am not sure what else will.

Not for the first time, I find myself clapping Mr Gower. I do believe that there is a prescient lesson there, from the comments concerning Test cricket and ODIs. About 35 years ago, there was a real fear that ODIs would stampede over Test cricket. Now it is the 50-over game that is fighting for its life. T20 could well be similar: fun, exciting, but ephemeral. Unlike Test cricket, which can be epic, rich and nation-uniting.

4

THE SKY EFFECT

'The England men's team are playing the most exciting cricket that they have ever played – but it seems futile. Kids are not engaged with it because they do not see it.'

In September 2005, cricket was cool again. England had won an Ashes series for the first time since 1987. Michael Vaughan's men had played in swashbuckling style, long before the term 'Bazball' had been invented. They totalled 407 in 79.2 overs on the first day at Edgbaston. Their batsmen had scored rapidly, with Kevin Pietersen providing the genius and dare that had been lacking. They had an all-rounder, Andrew 'Freddie' Flintoff, who men wanted to be, and women wanted to be with. They had the 'Fab Four' seam bowlers: the rapid Steve Harmison and Simon Jones, along with Flintoff, brilliant to the left-handers, backed up the redoubtable swing bowler Matthew Hoggard. They took screaming catches (I sat behind the one by Andrew Strauss at Trent Bridge and it was the best I have ever seen in the flesh). The fans in the grounds were thrilled, and people at home were watching spellbound on Channel 4. This was the chance for the game to rise again: a renaissance, 24 years after cricket had last captivated the nation with Botham's Ashes. So what did cricket do? Thanks to the England and Wales Cricket Board, chaired at the time by David Morgan, it hid its prime product behind a paywall…

All because in 1998 the Labour government's culture secretary, Chris Smith, had been persuaded to take Test cricket off the list of 'crown jewels', those sporting events 'protected', to be shown on terrestrial television. It was designed to give the ECB more leverage in negotiations with terrestrial and satellite companies, but when new chiefs at the ECB came in, the tectonic plates shifted. From 1999 to 2005, Sky had shown one Test match a summer (and all England's white-ball matches). Now they scooped the lot. It was a classic 'sliding doors' moment – a missed opportunity of epic proportions. As the populist columnist Richard Littlejohn writes so often in the *Daily Mail*, 'You couldn't make it up…' England v Sri Lanka at Lord's in 2006 was the next Test match to be shown live on British television, but on satellite: Sky TV, not terrestrial. By the next home Ashes series in 2009, the audience had been quartered from 2005.

One of my friends, Tom Maslona, was a teacher working at Oriel High School in Crawley, West Sussex. 'Cricket was not really played at my school, so I set up a club. I had so many youngsters join on the back of the 2005 Ashes series that I couldn't really cope with the numbers, but I tried,' he said to me. 'Now I am at Mossbourne Community Academy in Hackney. People don't want to play cricket. It is argued that the England men's team are playing the most exciting cricket that they have ever played – but it seems futile. Kids are not engaged with it because they do not see it.'

We are not saying it is all bad news when it comes to Sky. They have put a lot of money into the game. Some of that manifests itself in projects like NatWest CricketForce. Maybe your club has been one of the lucky ones to have benefitted. Sky's production standards are high. Innovation and technology have been at the heart of their cricket coverage over three decades. Hawk-Eye, the ball-tracking brainchild of Paul Hawkins, is now a staple of their coverage, as is Hot Spot and Spidercam. And they are genuinely committed to Test cricket, because the seven/eight-hour blocks that a day's play entails are great for filling up their dedicated channel (there is no cutting to the 3.40 at Haydock, as the BBC and Channel 4 used to do, which was maddening, for cricket fans at least). I will always be grateful to Sky for showing England Tests overseas from 1989/90 (before that you would only get snippets from the BBC, usually only Ashes tours). On balance, however, it is a crying shame that there is not at least a shared deal anymore. Not one of Sir Alastair Cook's 12,472 Test runs was seen live on terrestrial TV in the UK. Former England fast bowler Alex Tudor is a teacher now. He invited Cook to his school, and most of the pupils did not know who he was. Ben Stokes should be an even bigger household name, following in the footsteps of Ian Botham and Freddie Flintoff. Sky do not seem to appreciate county cricket either. Its bullish producer is a big fan of having an eight-team 'T20'-style tournament, The Hundred, which does not involve the counties.

The BBC are not blameless. They had become complacent up until 1999 and their coverage was staid. They had paid peanuts for the rights and were shown up for their lack of innovation and dedication by Channel 4. They then seemed to go on a 20-year sulk. You never heard that they were interested in showing cricket on their television channels again, despite it being the national summer sport. They have four channels now. When they returned to the negotiating table at last in 2020, they agreed to show The Hundred – new and funky, just what their commissioners adore – and the odd T20 international, but no Test cricket. It sounds as if the 2025–28 deal will not even include the live T20Is.

To be fair, league football has not suffered the same fate by being siloed on satellite stations. The game has taken off to become a national obsession, a behemoth that dominates media coverage, marginalising everything else. It needed a deep cleansing after the hooliganism scandals of the 1980s, the shoddily substandard stadiums that led to disasters, and the trains that were stripped of furniture and used to herd fans around like cattle.

The difference is that Sky's football chiefs have not insisted on having an eight-team league, however. The Premier League still has 20 teams. There is no criteria to have super stadiums only. So Sky are happy to show Luton Town against Liverpool, Manchester United's visit to Bournemouth, and Burnley's hosting of Arsenal. Of course it is not all sweet. The hyperbole is off the scale. The Premier League is dominated by six sides or so. There are aberrations like Leicester City winning the League in 2016, but it seems far less likely that teams like Ipswich Town (runners-up in 1981 and 1982), Watford (runners-up in 1983) and Southampton (runners-up in 1983) could finish in the top two again in the foreseeable future. I and many others miss the purity of the 1980s – Brian Clough's Nottingham Forest winning the European Cup twice (1979 and 1980) and Bob Paisley's Liverpool winning it three times (1977, 1978 and 1981), playing in those luscious plain blood-red kits – in the days when the European Cup would have been far more validly called the Champions League than it is now. But it would be difficult to argue that Sky has ruined football, which you *could* say it has potentially done to English cricket...

As he was leaving after his reign as ECB chief executive, Tom Harrison slipped a cheeky extension through for Sky, meaning that they will have home Tests until 2028. This seemed a tad restrictive for Richard Gould, who was replacing him. The spinmeisters said that the new ECB chair Richard Thompson had been party to these discussions, though. Which seems odd, as he later hinted that he was rather hamstrung by the deal, speaking on Sky in Pakistan in 2022... After all, it did not factor in the spiralling inflation that hit the UK in 2023.

Maybe a return to terrestrial television is now fantasy. Maybe Sky's opposition will continue to come from TNT Sport (formerly BT), which has been scooping up overseas rights – they struck an 11th-hour deal for the India v England series in 2024. Whatever happens, it seems unlikely that Test cricket in the UK will ever recapture those massive, engaged, unified audiences that sat enthralled through the 1981, 1985 and 2005 Ashes.

5

GRAHAM GOOCH AND *GRANDSTAND*

*'People do not just come to watch the cricket. They
come for the day, for the experience. They come
for the social day out − it is more than just a sport.'*

As youngsters in the 1980s my friend Neil Cutts and I would break
off from our garden 'Test' matches and come in for a cuppa and to
watch 15 minutes of *Grandstand*, which would put up the cricket scores
from around the shires. In my mind I still marvel that it seemed to be
'Graham Gooch 113 not out' every time. He was driven by an insatiable
hunger for runs and would do everything that he possibly could to
equip himself for that challenge. He was ahead of his time. To describe
him as the roundhead to David Gower's cavalier is a cliché, but it is

true. I try to write an article with him every year. He asks me what I think about batting. *Me,* who was selected twice for two Suffolk 2nd XI matches. He calls me 'maestro'. Can you imagine how that feels?

I will always cherish memories of watching the England Test team of the mid-1980s, often with my wonderful mother, and bask in the recollections of their exploits (on and off the field). From 1986, Mum and I would go to a Test match every year, nearly always at The Oval. We would invest emotionally in these characters. We watched grainy television pictures of Gooch sweep, sweep, sweeping the Indian hosts to distraction as he made 115 in the semi-final of the World Cup at Bombay's Wankhede Stadium in 1987. We were at the Test at Lord's in 1990, again against India, when Gooch made 333 and 123. We watched the 1991 Test against West Indies at Headingley, when he made a superb, unbeaten 154 against an attack of Curtly Ambrose, Patrick Patterson (the one bowler Gooch said he felt physically threatened by), Malcolm Marshall and Courtney Walsh. The next highest score was 27, made by both Mark Ramprakash and Derek Pringle. The weather was also dank, the light gloomy. 'All I could do,' Gooch said to me, 'was to fight every ball and hope that runs would come from somewhere.' Many feel that that innings was the greatest ever. It was the difference between defeat and the victory that England claimed (by 115 runs).

When, near the end of my mother's life, we bumped into Gooch on the beach in Southwold near her Suffolk home, it was an unbelievable thrill, and he was kind to her. He has been delightful each time I have met him. The latest occasion was when he invited me to dinner on HMS *Victory* in Portsmouth. He does some work with the British Navy. The Gooch I know is a sharp contrast from the dour, lugubrious character that he sometimes appeared to be in his playing days … although it was obvious a dry sense of humour lurked underneath. He has a holiday home in Southwold, and my team plays at the cricket club once a year. I dream that even though he is now over 70, one day we will open the batting together. This is what he said when I talked to him about Test cricket and its battle to survive in the face of T20:

I fell in love with Test cricket the moment that I first saw it on Mum and Dad's black-and-white telly. It would have been the England v West Indies series here in 1963. They had a fantastic side. I can name most of them, I think: Conrad Hunte, an opener called Easton

McMorris, Rohan Kanhai, Basil Butcher, Seymour Nurse, Garry Sobers, Wes Hall, Charlie Griffith, Lance Gibbs and Deryck Murray (who I played against 20 years later). And England also had all the great names: Ted Dexter, Ken Barrington, Colin Cowdrey, John Edrich, FS (Fred) Trueman, Brian Statham, Fred Titmus and Tony Lock. Sobers was my hero. He was a superstar. He could bat, bowl, spin and pace, and was a great catcher. He was compelling to watch. His style was fantastic on the eye: the back-foot drives, which was a shot we struggled to do regularly in this country as we're all brought up on slow pitches. In the West Indies you had true, fast and firm surfaces, and you did not have to move your feet so much – you just drove the ball off the back foot. Looking back now, the run-rates in the Tests were a bit tepid at times, but no one ever talked about it. That was just the game. You had attacking players, and you had grafters. Like everything in the world, it got faster.

Then you had the fast bowling of the 1970s. The first time I saw Dennis Lillee was in 1972, when the Australia touring side played Essex at Valentines Park, Ilford. I have never seen such a long run-up. Richard Hadlee was the same – a long, ungainly run-up, until they both refined them. That led to the West Indies pace batteries of the 1980s. The 50-over World Cup was introduced in 1975, and by 1992 when it was in Australasia, the 50-over format had become incredibly popular. When we played the Test series in New Zealand in 1991/92, the crowds were not great, but they were in the World Cup matches there that followed on.

Back then it was all about 50-over cricket taking over from Tests. Then the T20 domestic league started in 2003, and it spread around the world. And it surprises me, but it seems to have lost none of its gloss. It appeals to youngsters, and they watch it, and the clips, on their iPhones and iPads. Every country wants their own league. Fans can dip in and out of it. It is a short game. We fill Chelmsford out with 6,000 people. And it does not seem to really matter to people whether Essex are winning – they still come for the night out. They come for the beer, burgers and Balti. It is a night out for the boys, girls and families. There are not many weeks of the year where there is not a T20 tournament taking place. We are at saturation point. Test cricket in the United Kingdom is always well-supported. People do not just come to watch the cricket. They come for the day, for the experience. They come for the social day out – it is more than just a sport. But that doesn't happen all over the world. I don't think that social scene happens in India, Pakistan or Sri Lanka. It might happen a little bit at Adelaide, Cape Town or places like that.

In terms of some of the skills, you would have to say T20 has been good for Test cricket, like the fielding. Fifty-over cricket started that. Fielding has now been taken to a different level. When they throw themselves over the line and claw the ball back into the air to another fielder… I never saw anything like that when I was a player. When we played Test cricket in Australia there was a storm gulley before the fence, and that was the boundary. You could effectively lean on it and take a catch. So that has changed.

I don't want to do T20 down, because there is a lot of skill with the batting, with the ramp shots and all these things, and that is exciting to watch. But somebody who just clears their front leg and slogs it over midwicket every ball … that is boring. And they have brought the boundaries in, and that is meant to make it more exciting, as it is higher-scoring, and there are more balls flying over the boundary. I think for me personally, though, the most interesting part of T20 is the skill of the bowler who can bowl in the blockhole, who can bowl slow bouncers, and several types of slower ball. That is why they are the most valuable, and they are signed up for the most money by IPL teams. Somebody like Sam Curran. He is a decent bowler, a left-armer who looks to take wickets with good variation, and he is also a handy batsman. Bowlers like him can change the game … you have to take wickets, as the batters all come out playing the same away. When we played the 40-over league it was more about a good line and length bowler exerting a lot of pressure. Somebody like Barry Wood, who bowled similar-paced stuff to me, would open the bowling for Lancashire and Derbyshire and bowl his eight overs straight through for less than 20. You do not see that sort of thing any more. The batters all come out ultra-positive now; they play one way. So you cannot pressurise those players in the same way; the only way to control the scoring rate is to take wickets.

The belligerent approach to batting has transferred to Test cricket, with England pioneering Bazball. I do not think this England side is comfortable playing a more traditional style of run-making: play the conditions, make sure you get a good score to help your bowlers and put your side in a good position. They have been brought up on T20 cricket. Sir Alastair Cook was probably the last one who had played before that came in. So they need to go on the attack, play aggressively. The Ben Duckett stat is still amazing. He left only seven balls in the channel in his first 1000 Test runs. When I was coaching, we told players that leaving the ball was a shot in their arsenal, like the cover drive, pull or cut. It shows the bowler that you know what you are doing. They have exploded that myth a little bit, haven't they?

That is because they are used to putting bat to ball, guiding the ball to third man even if they are not trying to hit a four... Joe Root and Kane Williamson do it well. They play the ball late, let it come on and then angle the bat. In Test cricket that is quite dangerous. In one-day cricket it is safer as the white ball does not do as much, there are no slips probably, and it is probably a fair shot to keep the ball moving. Root is particularly good at it, but when you are playing with half a bat against three slips and a gully ... you should be adapting your game for the different formats, but it is bound to creep in.

Has T20 banished the genuine spinner to the grave? It has in this country. Not just because they bowl darts, but because they have to bat to get in the team. Jack Leach and Shoaib Bashir are exceptions, I suppose. Genuine spinners are not getting the conditions. Essex have only one specialist spinner on their staff [Simon Harmer]. Facing a good spinner was a battle of skill and technique. I would hate to see all that drop off.

How confident am I about Test cricket's future? It depends how much money and resources each country pumps into it to maintain it. I am not confident, no. I am not confident because of the amount of T20 that is being played. The extra remuneration from that format will mean that players will opt out of the longer form. I would hate to see it go, because the world would miss the drama, the skill, the tension. I do not remember many T20 games, by comparison. I concede a high-scoring Test where one side scores 600 and the other 500 is maybe not that exciting, but a lowish-scoring game still has the most tension and the most excitement: to see all the skills of the batsmen, and all the extra skills bowlers now have, but bowling with a red ball that moves more than the white ball, that is brilliant to watch.

6

OPEN A WINDOW FOR TEST CRICKET

*'A three-month dedicated window for Test cricket
every year for both the men's and women's teams is
the only way to protect the greatest format.'*

Sunday 28 January 2024 was the date when two cricketing miracles happened on the same day.

The record under Ben Stokes and Brendon McCullum had been relatively strong, so some would say that England winning a Test should not have been seen as a seismic event. It was in India, however, with England deploying the rawest spin-bowling attack that had ever been deployed in a Test, with the exception of nations' inaugural matches. And it was after India had dominated the first half of the match at Hyderabad. England trailed by 190 runs after the first innings, but Ollie Pope played one of the finest innings by an overseas batsman in a Test in India, his 196 helping set the hosts a target of 231. They fell 29 runs short thanks to the bowling of Tom Hartley, who two months earlier had been working in his family's garden centre in Lydiate, a village in Merseyside. On his Test debut he took 7 for 62, eclipsing his modest record for Lancashire (40 first-class wickets at 36.57 apiece). It was another triumph for Stokes, McCullum and their boss Rob Key, who identified Hartley's style of bowling – his height and subsequent trajectory, and pace – as perfect for the subcontinent. The view of umpires has often been sought by selectors over the years, but this was a new type of view from them – cameras had been attached to their coats in county cricket the previous summer.

Then, nearly 6000 miles away, another result occurred that no one saw coming. This Test was even closer, with West Indies winning by only eight runs. They had sent a squad to Australia with seven uncapped players. They had been comprehensively beaten in the first Test at the Adelaide Oval. Now they were playing the second and final Test at the Gabba in Brisbane, Australia's fortress. Remarkably, however, they won, for their first Test victory in Australia since 1997. Until January 2021, the last time an overseas side had won at the ground was in November 1988. Did former captain Tim Paine jinx Australia, though? 'Can't wait to take you to the Gabba' was his taunt to India, inspiring the tourists to win there in 2021.

West Indies then inflicted only a 10th defeat on Australia at the venue, in the 66th match (there had also been 13 draws). One of the seven uncapped players in the tourists' squad was a fast bowler called Shamar Joseph. The 24-year-old had only played five first-class matches when he made his debut at Adelaide, but he started well, taking five wickets for 101 in the match and scoring a half-century. He surpassed that at Brisbane, however, recording match figures of 8 for 124. Not long ago he had taken a job as a security guard to look after his young family. Now, riches beyond his wildest dreams were at his fingertips. His muscular, bustling action and strong, broad shoulders allowed him to propel the pink ball at 146km/h (91mph) – a speed that was too much for Travis Head, who was yorked for his second first-ball dismissal of the match, and Alex Carey, who had his stumps castled. Steve Smith singlehandedly defied the West Indians, his crisp strokes echoing around a ground that was, alas, far from full. At nine wickets down, with last man Josh Hazlewood in, he produced an incredible, audacious ramp shot that went for six over fine-leg off the bowling of Alzarri Joseph. The final strike was launched by Shamar Joseph, however, Hazlewood's off stump being uprooted, to inspire his side to sprint around the Gabba turf in scenes of unbridled joy.

To make the achievement all the more remarkable, in that second-innings seven-wicket haul, the Guyanese had been encumbered by a sore foot after being struck by a crunching Mitchell Starc yorker the day before. It was stunning and incredible. Brian Lara, West Indies' former captain, and one of their finest batsmen of all time, was moved to tears in the commentary box: 'Unbelievable … young, inexperienced, written off … this West Indies can stand tall today.' Captain Kraigg Brathwaite said that the words of Rodney Hogg, the former Australia fast bowler, who called his side 'pathetic and hopeless', had spurred them on. Once again we were reminded what a fertile breeding ground the Caribbean is for thrillingly gifted and athletic cricketers. It was truly a Super Sunday for Test cricket. Afterwards Shamar Joseph made all the right noises. 'I will always be available to play Test cricket, no matter how much money is out there,' he said. The moneymen were soon putting that to the test.

Of course, the longer game did not have long to bask in the sunlight, however, for there were soon reminders of how T20 and franchise cricket was really starting to call the shots. South Africa had made the hugely controversial decision to send what was not even a second-string side (a third-string?) to complete a two-Test series – the standard, minimum fare – in New Zealand, to fulfil their obligations (lip service) as part of the World Test Championship. Their best cricketers, certainly with the white ball, had stayed behind to play in the second edition of the SA20, their T20 tournament. The South Africa side was predictably dismantled, at Mount Maunganui and Hamilton. (There was a quantum of solace about it all: at least people like Kagiso Rabada had not permanently turned their backs on Test cricket, unlike so many West Indian T20 specialists.) Despite trying to defend the outrageous decision while attempting to reaffirm their commitment to the longer game, the South African Cricket Board appeared to have nailed their colours well and truly to the mast.

That day of shocks at Hyderabad and Brisbane should be used as a beacon to save the Test game and reaffirm its primacy, though.

There has been a lot of talk about creating a window for Test cricket, to cloister it from the franchise flood. So far, however, that is all it has been: talk. A few days after that 'Super Sunday', former England captain Michael Vaughan suggested a window for the longest game: 'A three-month dedicated window for Test cricket every year for both the men's and women's teams is the only way to protect the greatest format... No other cricket but Test around those 3 months,' he wrote on X. The initial inclination was to say, 'No way!' Why should the best form of the game (Vaughan agrees with that) be restricted to a quarter of the year? I wanted to scream, 'It should be at least six months!' Is that a realistic ambition, however? I suppose it is more generous than Rajasthan Royals' owner Manoj Badale's suggestion of a 'Wimbledon-style' two-week window in the English summer.

Which three months did Vaughan have in mind, one wonders? Christmas in Australia and South Africa – the MCG Boxing Day Test, the Sydney Cricket Ground (SCG) match soon after (it used to be over New Year) and festive fun at Newlands surely has to be sacred. March is generally the favoured month of Test cricket for Sri Lanka and West Indies. Then there is the English summer. At the moment we have Test cricket in four or five months. Concluding the men's Ashes before the August summer holidays in 2023 was deeply unpopular with so many cricket fans. ECB chair Richard Thompson initially spoke out against that, then seemed to acknowledge that it had its merits, shielding it from the start of the football season.

Vaughan is a successful broadcaster with the BBC here, and he is also tearing it up in Australia with Fox Sports. It is frustrating that certain former players feel the need to be so uber-modernist/progressive when it comes to these matters, though. Former stars like Graham Gooch, Mike Gatting and David Gower, no longer affiliated to a single broadcaster, are far more sceptical about the wonders of franchise cricket, albeit they are from an earlier era. Compare Gatting's comments in *The Cricketer* in August 2023:

I would have maybe three two-month slots for premier leagues – 180 days of franchise cricket, 180 for international. Maybe we have a two-tier Test system as it would be a shame to lose Ireland, Afghanistan and Bangladesh as Test nations. Maybe the Test nations give us 15 or 16 players each. Pay them £100,000 each to play in the three slots. It is only a template but we need to start somewhere. We would love to keep our great game going and there is enough money to do that. It is down to people's consciences.

Rob Key, the managing director of England men's cricket, agreed that such a change was needed: 'Test cricket needs to have windows. There was a two-month window for the Ashes last summer [2023] – that could be one. There could be one at Christmas. There are all of these franchise competitions, like the IPL, and there is a global white-ball competition every year,' he said. 'Test cricket needs a window where you can't play anything else. The rest of us – England, Australia, India and the International Cricket Council in particular – need to look after the other countries.'

Jason Holder, the former West Indies captain, was another proponent. Speaking to the *Hindustan Times*, he said:

If we continue in this manner, Test cricket will die. It is sad, but it is true, based on the current structure. You have the 'Big Three' who practically command all the revenue regarding the disbursement of ICC funds. And it is difficult for smaller territories such as West Indies to compete. We just do not have the financial resources that they do. We are struggling to even stay afloat in terms of cash flow. And it is hard to develop our facilities and structures the way they are meant to be. And with the little finances that we have, pretty much all the money we get goes straight back up into covering expenses and debt. The only way you can honestly see Test cricket being saved is if you have a window for it in a year so that you can have your best players available to play there. And on top of that, you need to compensate players fairly. It cannot be a situation where Australia and India are up there, and all the other teams are way, way down below. So, when you have a situation – a dilemma – similar to mine, where you can play a Test series for x amount and a franchise for three times the amount, you will constantly have players going toward more money. If we could come up with a model where you can have a minimum wage where you cannot fall below a particular threshold, it would actually incentivise players to say, 'Well, look, this is the benefit of me playing Test cricket.' I think, maybe, cricket may go in the football model where you have an international window, and you have the franchise window. Maybe that might be a model going forwards, but who knows?

Vaughan was particularly vocal early in 2023. He also said he would switch to four-day Tests only. Excluding England's match that was scheduled for four days against Ireland at Lord's in early summer 2023, 10 out of 17 Tests up to the start of 2024 since Stokes became captain and McCullum coach went to the fifth day. There were some absolute thrillers in there.

Would Vaughan just cut off those remarkable Tests at home to New Zealand in the summer of 2022, when England pulled off stunning run-chases in scintillating fashion? What about the Test at the Basin Reserve in Wellington in February 2023, when hosts New Zealand defeated England by one run? Three of the 2023 summer's five Ashes Tests went to the last day – the matches at Edgbaston, Lord's and The Oval. And two of the three did too, in the remarkable 3–0 series whitewash in Pakistan in 2022/23. If it ain't broke, surely... Just leave it alone.

At the height of his fame – wonderful batsman, fine captain, one of England's greatest – Vaughan was involved in selling some paintings created when he smacked a paint-smeared ball against a canvas. Was this the equivalent? See what sticks? (For further reading, we could add Kevin Pietersen's brainwave in early 2024, to award 12 runs for a 'six' hit that travels more than 100 metres.)

For the record, England's heroics at Hyderabad were soon forgotten. India won the next four Tests. The tourists' at times reckless strokeplay played into their hosts' hands. That was not the point, though. Miracles can still happen. Test cricket is the format that gets the whole cricketing world talking together.

7

WHY CAN'T I BE MORE LIKE JARROD?

'Test cricket is my favourite sport. T20 is my second favourite.
Basketball is my third. ODIs are not far behind.'

It is painfully obvious that I am in danger of becoming irrelevant, a dinosaur, left behind in a land that time forgot. I wonder if I have time to recalibrate, to be given an 'attitude adjustment', as the alien leader Diana gave to resistance chief Juliet Parrish in the 1980s sci-fi classic *V*. Maybe I could take a leaf out of the book of one of my journo colleagues who seem so wildly enthused by T20. So, I turn to Jarrod Kimber, always a friendly face in the press box. A 44-year-old Melburnian who has lived in London for 17 years, he is anything but a fogey. As a journalist – whether it be with his writing, audio or video work, on talkSPORT, and in features, blogs, podcasts and even feature films – he is imaginative, inventive, supremely knowledgeable and unorthodox. He strikes me as a bit Hunter S. Thompson and his 'Gonzo' journalism, mixed with 'The Analyst' (Simon 'Yozzer' Hughes), mixed with a graphic designer. He speaks like a machine gun, rat-a-tat-tatting ideas at us, and subsequently was hard work to transcribe for this. So, I ask him, why do you appear to like T20 so much… Does it not worry you that it is seemingly consuming the longer form?

He tells me:

Test cricket is my favourite sport. T20 is my second favourite. Basketball is my third. ODIs are not far behind. For me they are all different sports, and they all offer different experiences. I got into the game because my family played club cricket. Then I found out that there were grounds, where professionals play, and you can go and watch them. I followed Victoria in 50-over cricket. Then I got into Test cricket. So T20 can be a similar gateway, as it is a more accessible version of the game, as I am sure limited-overs cricket was a gateway to the Test game over the last 30 years. I have trouble with people saying that T20 is not cricket, when it is bringing in more cricket fans, more people who care about the game, who want to play.

I made a film in 2015 about why Test cricket might die [*Death of a Gentleman*], and we interviewed [former Australia captain then selector] John Inverarity, and he said, 'Well, we don't have gladiators anymore.' Some things just die; some things just stop. We have a very narrow understanding of what history is. Before Test matches, cricket was a street game, a one-on-one game, then three v three, five v five, then 15 v 26… Before that it was played by women and probably evolved from stoolball; before that it was played by shepherds on the wealds of Sussex and Kent. Test cricket came way later. We have convinced ourselves that Test cricket is the only game that matters. I do not think it is true, and I do not think that it was ever true. That does not mean it is not the best, or most challenging, or most interesting… I still think it is, compared to T20 … but T20 is still interesting, and developing. We have just had an IPL where the par total was 240, and now we have a T20 World Cup (2024) where the par score is 90-odd. Even within T20 there is black, there is white, there is grey… different shades of everything … but there is still genius within that.

If Test cricket is going to survive, part of it needs to be administered a lot better. Which is why I think it should be separated as a sport. Would that mean Test cricket would not be so good in the short term? Probably, because 75 per cent of cricketers would go to T20, and 25 per cent will go to Tests. And you would probably be saying, 'Well, it is not as good as it used to be…' But it would still exist. I was not around when rugby league and rugby union split [in 1895] but I am pretty sure that at that point it meant that rugby union was not quite as strong. When it first happened, that would have been massive. Over time, though, who gives a damn? It is like motor sport. Drivers switch cars and competitions all the time. We eventually just accept that as the new norm.

Regardless of that, though, people have to keep wanting to go and watch Test cricket… And if that doesn't happen, then fine. You and I will be very, very sad, but that is what society has decided. I love the way action movies were made in the late 1980s and early 1990s. They were a lot more brutal. Take *RoboCop 2* [1990] … Look at how they remade the original [in 2014] … they could not make it like the original, because it was so sick, and wrong, and twisted, and weird. You could not make a Hollywood mainstream movie like that any more. The movies that I grew up with are no longer going to exist.

We live in Presbyterian, more morally prudish times, for sure, and the liberal consensus has ensured on-screen violence has been toned down. I think *Top Gun: Maverick* (2022) was quite like *Top Gun* (1986), if not as good, but I do take his point about *Prometheus* (2012), which did not much resemble its incredible, feral progenitor, *Alien* (1979). I do not disturb his chain of thought, however.

They are going to be different by design, but that does not mean that there will not be great movies, different genres, and different directors that will come through and move forward. That is a perfectly acceptable thing that society does. We cannot just hold on to things from the old days. And cricket's biggest issue really is holding on to things that sometimes are not even true, like the 'Spirit of Cricket', and amateurism… The notion that we have to get these things back … both of them are basically nonsense when you drill down on them even a millimetre. The truth is that the world will move on, and cricket will move on.

So, this is my problem, I tell him: administrators, broadcasters, do not seem to be considering the facts. Test cricket is still popular in England. Matches sell out. It still makes up the lion's share of the television deal. These movers and shakers might think that they are Mystic Meg and prophesise a future where that is not the case. They are foolish, though. They are like the owners of the goose that laid the golden egg. They are taking a knife and opening the bird up, and killing it, because they want all the eggs now. It does not work like that, though. What they should be doing is preserving Test cricket, and not over-farming T20. For when the 1992 ODI World Cup happened, a lot of people thought that the 50-over game would kill Test cricket; but now that format is the one fighting for its life even more than the longest form.

Kimber replies:

If cricket didn't exist in 40 years, I'd be heartbroken because it has changed my life. But if there are forms of cricket, and people are playing a different version of it, and it is still helping people, and bringing people together, and still doing wonderful things, who am I to say, 'My favourite part of cricket doesn't exist any more, so therefore it is dead'?. I just do not think that is fair. I grew up in a particular era when Test cricket was king. My kids are not going to grow up in that era, however, and in two or three generations' time, who knows if Test cricket will be around... But that is how the world works.

The way Test cricket has been written up, especially in England, has been over-romantic ... that people played for the love of it. Well, W.G. Grace, a so-called amateur, was paid more than the professionals ... and the pros have always been paid. The minute they put a fence up at The Oval, the first major ground where that happened, and it was decided that cricket was about people paying to watch it... It has always been that way, and it is disingenuous to suggest otherwise. And now for the first time since the 1870s we have opened cricket up to private investment. That means it is hurtling towards this new direction... That you do not want, because it is not the cricket that you grew up with. We can all look back and say this period is great... It is like that running joke about music. Ask 100 people what the best era of music is, and 95 per cent will say it was the era when they were aged between 13 and 25.

Well, I recall when I was that age: 1985 to 1997. Is Jarrod correct? I was addicted to listening to Simple Minds' album *Once Upon a Time* (1985), Madonna's *True Blue* (1986) and U2's *The Joshua Tree* (1987) on my Sony Walkman, but then I still would never say that was the greatest era of music – it wasn't as amazing as the 1960s, and the Beatles, Rolling Stones, The Who and the Kinks, or even the 1970s with David Bowie, Steve Harley, Lou Reed and T. Rex. But I suppose that I take his point.

At this point Jarrod seems to switch lanes slightly, maybe to make me feel better:

It would be very silly of cricket administrators to let Test cricket die, because it still makes money. What if T20 is not as popular in 20 years? I know that Test cricket is profitable; I was told this by TV executives years ago when cable TV was around. They said, 'Do you know how good it is to have a sport that goes on for five days, and you know the customers are going to come back to it every single day because of the way the narrative unfolds?' You do not get that in many other sports, and that was before streaming. Test cricket is made for streaming. It is exactly what streaming platforms want. You are going to be watching it for seven hours. And then tomorrow you will watch it for seven hours again. And then there were two more days, and maybe a fifth day if there has been some rain... So it actually fits into the modern world. And letting it die would be silly. But equally it is silly when people say that because it is the best format and we should love it forever. Tom Waits is a better singer than Justin Bieber, but who sells more albums? At a certain point, money actually matters.

At this point, not for the first time in his life I daresay when it comes to this argument, Jarrod hears the name of a certain fast-food restaurant. 'McDonald's sells more than Marks and Spencer, but it doesn't make it better food,' I say to him. To which he replies:

McDonald's got famous on the back of the Big Mac. But then sales went down. The Quarter Pounder came in and proved popular. Then the McChicken Sandwich. Then the Filet-O-Fish. McDonald's didn't dump the Big Mac, though; they realised that it meant something to their core customers, and their brand identity. And I hope that cricket does not dump Test cricket. Because people playing in whites, with a red ball, at Lord's, stands for something. It looks like something that does not look like other things. It is why Wimbledon have kept going with their traditions.

It is actually making money, anyway. I think it is getting more interest than ever before, with highlights, and people looking at scorecards. Part of that is the way the internet has changed. The thing that has happened is that another format, T20, has got bigger, and more popular, and is easier to sell to casual fans... But why would you get rid of your hardcore fans? Because you can never trust casual fans ... whereas hardcore fans are always going to be there. So, it would be silly for red-ball cricket to go from a business point of view. You do not need to be romantic. It is about brands, business and customer loyalty. That is why it is frustrating that cricket is making short-term decisions at the moment – like certain political parties ... well, all of them actually – and it is silly, and what they should be doing is asking, 'Where will Test cricket be in 20 years' time?' For Test cricket can help nation-building, it helps individuals. It is a great sport to learn because it is a sport that cannot be conquered. And the Test game is the version of cricket that is the most extreme and most dramatic. So that is what they should be doing, but what they are doing is concentrating on T20, and then they will come back to Test cricket and see if it is still alive. Which is foolish.

He is right, of course. If I were the chief executive of the ECB, and I had a blank piece of paper for the summer, I would plot out the five- or six-men's Tests first, then go from there. Make England the home of Test cricket. Like this country is the home of lawn tennis. The battle seems lost, however. And in the new landscape, some, like Jarrod, will adapt, and others will not.

8

VIV RICHARDS: THE KING AND I

*'We have to do whatever it takes it to
keep Test cricket alive, and attractive.'*

West Indies are the miracle of cricket. An alliance of 13 independent island countries and 19 dependencies in three archipelagos, picking a cricket XI from there requires money, means of travel, diplomacy, a concession to politics, tact, patience and skill. That they dominated cricket from about 1975 until the 1990s thanks to dynamic and powerful batting, fearsome fast bowling and electrifying fielding was the equivalent of alchemy, even if there is no denying the abundance of good athletes from the area.

Viv Richards was the king of West Indies cricket from 1974 to 1991. He appeared to middle everything; his ability to clip good balls on the stumps through the leg side seemed to defy physics. He reserved most of his destructive performances for England, against whom he struck eight of his 24 Test centuries. All with swagger and style. The modern Richards conveys a mixture of power, passion and politeness, and he remains a champion of the Test game. He told me:

> Test cricket was not on the telly, so I became aware of it as a little boy listening on the radio. I loved the commentary – John Arlott, Brian Johnston and later, Tony Cozier – I have memories of when I was seven, listening to that great Australia v West Indies Test series in 1960/61, when we were led by Sir Frank Worrell, and that tied Test at Brisbane. They were exciting times for West Indies cricket and the team enjoyed a triumphant homecoming to the Caribbean.
>
> Although I'll get a few knocks from the T20 players, Test cricket is the ultimate... It is the format for you if you want to understand the game on a proper basis. I would have played T20, and had some fun and excitement, but only after I had been through the mill, and gone to war, in the Test game. Folk are leaving in the direction of T20 for monetary returns, but I maintain both can be in bed together. I want administrators to be firmer about how many Test matches are played, how many T20s. Tests came before T20. Just because something is new, do you eradicate the thing that came before? No. The ball is in our court. All the best T20 players have good, basic techniques from Test cricket. The ones who struggle are the ones who do not have their base. I watch a lot of basketball in the United States; players start off in the colleges before going on to become NBA stars. In T20 it is becoming too easy; players are being given a quick route to the top. The establishment needs to make them work harder if they want to match the great players of the past, like Sir Garry Sobers and Sunny Gavaskar. T20 players need to play Test cricket too, to attain that same status.

Richards now works for the Antigua and Barbuda Tourism Authority, travelling the world to encourage visits to those splendid islands with his other fellow knights from there, Sir Curtly Ambrose, Sir Richie Richardson and Sir Andy Roberts. They all, you will not be surprised to know, desperately want Test cricket to survive.

Ambrose was the purest of bowlers. Persistently pacy and accurate, sending down thudding deliveries from about 10ft (3m), giving batsmen precious little to score from. Ambrose tells me:

Cricket was not my first love, funnily enough. It was behind football and basketball. My mother was a cricket fanatic, though, and forced me into playing. I watched my first Test live in [March] 1978 when I was 14; West Indies played Australia, at Antigua. It was Desmond Haynes' debut [he made 61] and West Indies won by an innings. Gradually, my reluctance to become a cricket fanatic started disappearing. I realised that it was the game for me. I have always preferred Test cricket. The word 'Test' says it all. At the end of a career, cricketers will be judged on how many Tests they have played, how many runs they have scored and wickets they have taken, to become legends. T20 is exciting, and there is room for both. You have one-day specialists, T20 specialists, but to be a true legend, you need to crack Test cricket. Hearing Shamar Joseph commit to Test cricket was interesting to hear. Like 'the skipper' [Richards] said, the financial T20 rewards are huge, but I believe that it will not take over. Test cricket, the purest form, will remain.

There is no discord from the other Antiguan stars. 'Test cricket is the ultimate,' said Richardson in *The Cricketer* (April 2022), who thrilled us all with his cover drive, launching himself at the ball, his speed of hand compensating for occasionally minimal feet movement. He was also a tremendous puller and hooker, which partially explains why nine of his 16 Test centuries came against Australia. He continued:

When I was about eight I went to my first Test match in Antigua, and every adult on the village was there. Garry Sobers, Frank Griffith, Wes Hall and Rohan Kanhai were playing and there was huge excitement. That was when I vowed to follow in their footsteps. I started taking our games with tennis balls and cans as stumps a bit more seriously. We moved to a hard ball when I started secondary school. I started rolling my own pitch back in my village and organising sessions with my friends. We played for many hours at a time, and my hands sometimes were sore, but we had a purpose. I was selected for Combined Schools, Antigua, the Leeward Islands, West Indies, and the rest is history.

I did love the pitches in Australia, but actually something from my childhood inspired me. As a young teenager I watched West Indies' 5–1 defeat in Australia in 1975/76. There weren't many TVs in the village, so I went to a particular house every night to watch that series. I saw our team being brutalised: Dennis Lillee running in from the boundary, the crowd shouting 'Kill! Kill! Kill!' Batsmen were being hit in the face. I thought then I would love to play against Jeff Thomson and Lillee: whenever I would come up against them, I wanted to avenge that '74/75 side. Lillee retired the season before I arrived [1984/85]. Rod Marsh made the statement that 'the only way to beat West Indies is to knock their so and so heads off', which motivated me even more. Thomson was playing for Queensland. I scored 65 [Thomson's figures were 5.1–0–48–1]. I remember that after the match the headlines were 'Young Richardson kills chances of Thomson making a comeback'. He was not as fast as he had been, but I had my degree of revenge.

We have to do whatever it takes it to keep Test cricket alive, and attractive. All the great players in the world play all formats, because if you can play Test cricket you can play it all. Of course, T20 is here to stay – it is exciting and attractive – but we have to find the right balance. It's difficult to be a well-rounded cricketer just playing T20. I would be devastated if Test cricket dies but maybe it is just me [Ed: It is not just you, Richie.] I too have been impressed by Shamar Joseph's enthusiasm and approach. He clearly has heart.

Roberts, a cunning and at times spiteful fast bowler, says the first Test that he saw with his eyes was his own debut, against England at Bridgetown, Barbados, in March 1974. 'It is true, as the first Test was not played in Antigua until 1981 against England.' He too is desperate for Test cricket to fight back.

In an earlier interview, I had to face legendary opening batsmen Gordon Greenidge and Desmond Haynes together. They were quite intimidating, until I bowled them over with my enthusiasm and a barrage of statistics. The Bajan duo fronted up 148 times in Tests, scoring a record 6482 runs together at an average of 43.80.

They shared 16 century stands and four doubles. In their own way, they were as formidable as West Indies' four-pronged pace battery. Greenidge, who had one of the most fearsome cut shots cricket has ever seen, conceded that he would have enjoyed T20:

> Definitely – I would have been able to buy a new house! Viv and the guys were playing shots like that back then – hitting the ball inside out, and reverse-sweeping. It is nothing new. Cricket needed a lift, an injection, though. I have to say I began to really love T20 when it started when Stanford came along. Unfortunately, he did not go on! But it started to give me a different perspective on the game because I'd finished playing. It was beautiful seeing the territories representing themselves: Antigua, Jamaica…

Haynes, who had been powerful and with an excellent all-round game, was not so keen on players transferring allegiances between islands, however. Note that this was before he became chair of selectors. In fact, he made me a promise that I would help him land the job with a positive story. It worked.

> It is different in the Caribbean now, with franchises. I do not like seeing Barbados players playing for Trinidad, and so on. I don't agree with that at all. Why do you have to take somebody from Guyana to play for Barbados? We are islands, with different governments; players have to leave their families, it is disruptive… It will be different in England: you just drive up the motorway, up to Yorkshire. The impact may not be so great.

On the subject of Test cricket's survival, he said:

> We are fearful of Test cricket dying because every day we see the writing on the wall. It would be sad to see players like Joe Root only playing T20; you would not realise the ability that the young guy has. In Tests he is getting short balls; you can judge his character. That is why it's important to preserve it – the true test.

Johnny Grave, the West Indies' CEO whom David Gower referred to earlier, has explained to me how tricky it is to keep West Indies on the road. I told him, I understand why the West Indies had cut from 10 for five first-class rounds of matches: sheer economic necessity. He said that Covid was a big factor, and that they are doing their best to keep red-ball cricket alive. Two-day matches are played at under-17 level, and three-day cricket at under-19. There is a home and away academy tour each year with four-day cricket, two A-team tours a year (playing purely four-day cricket...) and their four-day championship has now gone to eight teams with the addition of academy and Combined Campuses & College teams. So there are a minimum of seven matches per side now, plus local three- or four-day trial matches beforehand in January. 'We spend more in percentage terms on red-ball cricket than any other board in the world!' Grave said. 'Think how expensive it is to fly 90 under-17s to an island and keep them there to play two-day cricket and 50-over cricket.'

I can only applaud his/their efforts, and just wish the Board of Control for Cricket in India would help more. Only 4.58 per cent of the ICC's redistribution funds go to the West Indies, whereas the Indians get 38.5 per cent. I do not doubt those figures reflect market forces, but surely India do not want to just play Test cricket against just Australia and England, do they? 'A cosmos without the Doctor scarcely bears thinking about,' said the Master in the feature-length episode of *Doctor Who*, *The Five Doctors* (1983). Well, Test cricket without West Indies would be equally bereft.

9

TEST CRICKET BEFORE 1980

'Bradman, though. He had a shot for every ball, and a brain like a computer when it came to piercing gaps in the field.'

Bazball, with its high-octane approach to run-making, precarious declaring, rejection of draws and seemingly-at-times carefree preparation (Blasé-ball), is undoubtedly entertaining. It is also a little insulting to what has gone on before, however. Now you could argue that Test cricket in recent years has had to evolve to combat the multitude of rival activities that are on offer, whether that is physical, on television, or on electronic devices. Whichever era you look at, though, there has been thrilling Test cricket, whatever the run-rate.

In what is now regarded as the first ever Test match, in March 1877, the innings of Charles Bannerman set the bar for everything to follow when it comes to feats of fortitude. He made 165 at Melbourne, which was 69.6 per cent of Australia's runs from the bat in that first innings of the match, the total 245. That percentage is still a record in Test matches. He would surely have scored more, but had to retire after his hand was cut by a delivery from George Ulyett. No one else in the home side managed 20, and they defeated England by 45 runs.

Then, at The Oval in South London in 1882, the tension was palpable, and it had nothing to do with run-rate. England needed only 85 to win, but Australian pace bowler Fred Spofforth, known as 'The Demon', was determined to thwart them. With a quote that should inspire us all when we are facing adversity, he declared 'this thing can be done', and took 7 for 44 as England came up eight runs short. The anxiety was too much for one spectator, who died of a heart attack, while another is famously said to have gnawed his umbrella as a coping mechanism. Thankfully, English cricket did not really die, as *The Sporting Times* newspaper famously declared afterwards.

The Victorian era saw great entertainment from England Test players like W.G. Grace, Gilbert Jessop and Ranjitsinhji, the latter without an India team he could grace with his presence. Grace dominated the scene in the latter quarter of the 19th century and beyond; Ranjitsinhji's bold, long innings were remarkable when you factor in the pitches, for he was a master of digging out the pea-rollers that were consistently such a menace on them. He also relished taking on fast bowling.

Jessop's century for England against Australia in the fifth Test at The Oval in 1902 retains the record for its rapidity – 76 balls in 77 minutes – even if some dispute the accuracy of the timekeeping and Harry Brook and co. are closing in on it each time they receive a bag of ever-meatier blades. Jessop's knock was so riveting that buses pulled up on the side of the road so passengers could watch, and it led England to a one-wicket win. It was a bright time to be living in London. The expensive and disastrous Second Boer War had just come to an end, and with Edward VII being crowned, the population was quite emotional for the time.

England arriving in India three days before the Test series started, as they did in 2024, would have horrified Ranji. His preparation was immaculate. He hired professional bowlers from Surrey to come to Cambridge, where he was at university, and bowl to him so he could become accustomed to English conditions after a childhood in India. His batting is said to have had a peerless charm, but he was also a master on wet wickets.

Victor Trumper of Australia would have easily slipped into a Bazball team, not thinking twice about the advisability of trying to hit the first ball of the match to the boundary. Jack Hobbs, whose England career stretched from 1908–1930, was able to score at a cracking pace, as was his successor as the king of English batting, Walter Hammond.

Everybody lived in the shade of Don Bradman, though. He had a shot for every ball, and a brain like a computer when it came to piercing gaps in the field. A new strategy was devised to restrain him. The 1932/33 Ashes series in Australia, dubbed 'Bodyline', was exciting and tense, but violence played a key role in that. Harold Larwood's fearsome bowling at Australian batsmen in an era when helmets were a long way off caused ructions on a diplomatic scale between the two countries and led to a Law change, preventing three fielders from being deployed behind square on the leg side. In similar fashion, it was felt that West Indies' minacious quicks with their barrage of bouncers needed neutralising in 1991, when they were only allowed to bowl one bumper an over. For a while it had been four or five an over, of which there were only about 12 an hour, so only about 20 balls to hit if the batsmen were lucky.

You could imagine Denis Compton slipping into a Brendon McCullum-coached England side. 'Been at the casino until the early hours, and you haven't slept, you say? Here, let me hold your dinner jacket; you go out there and get us some quick runs, pal.'

Len Hutton will rightly go down in history as one of the greatest batsmen. His batting could be graceful and he had all the shots but telling him there was only one way to play – all-out attack – would have been anathema to him. Likewise, there would not have been the nonsense of declaring when his batsmen were in full swing on the first night of a Test match, as Ben Stokes did to Joe Root against Australia at Edgbaston in 2023. Hutton suffered years of humiliation against the Australians. Winning back the Ashes in 1953 after 19 years meant a huge amount to him, and the nation.

Keith Miller, Australia's greatest all-rounder, did play in a cavalier manner in this era, though. Nothing was going to faze him as much as 'having a Messerschmitt up your arse', as he had no doubt numerous times while serving in the Royal Australian Air Force in World War Two. On the England side was Miller's antithesis, though: the 'Barnacle', Trevor Bailey. Another fine all-round cricketer, I wonder what he would have made of Bazball. At times, he was the opposite of it. Bailball, maybe. He is most famous for his heroics in that 1953 Ashes rubber at Lord's. In the second innings of the second Test, he made 71 in 257 minutes – that is four hours, 17 minutes. England ended on 282 for 7, forsaking the chance to go the whole hog in chasing 343 to win. Then, in the final Test of that series at Headingley, he bowled down the leg side to deny the tourists the victory. Pragmatism ahead of entertainment. In the following Ashes, Down Under in 1954/55, he did his best to repeat those batting heroics in the series opener at the Gabba, making 88 in 261 minutes – four hours, 21 minutes. 'Trevor was such a pain if you were playing against him – a damned nuisance in fact,' said Miller. 'You knew that if you could get this bloke out of the way, the chances were that you would win. All too frequently Ray Lindwall and I would find the task beyond us and it got under our skin.' The fast bowling of Frank 'Typhoon' Tyson in 1954/55, giving him 28 wickets in five Tests, was distinctly entertaining, however.

There was one additional famous 'Barnacle' effort. Bailey nearly rescued England in the opening Test of the 1958/59 series, again at the Gabba, when he made 68, from 427 balls, in 458 minutes – that is seven hours, 48 minutes. A seriously impressive display of obduracy and defiance. It was the first Test match to be televised in Australia and was probably not the best advertisement for the longer game, for anyone who had never been to a live game. 'Bloody Bailey, stop crawling, let's see some cricket,' infuriated Australia fans howled.

West Indies had thrilling Test sides after the Second World War. In 1950, Alf Valentine and Sonny Ramadhin took 59 of the 77 wickets that saw England beaten – a shock result on their home patch. The bespectacled Valentine's slow left-armers fizzed through the air with lashings of spin on them, while nobody knew which way the ball would turn from by Ramadhin. It must have been captivating. Then, in the 1960s, the three Ws – Frank Worrell, Everton Weekes and Clyde Walcott – entertained spectators with their contrasting styles. Worrell batted with unhurried style; Weekes was fleet-footed and attacking; and Walcott was powerful: strong off the back foot, and a savage cutter, driver and puller. Garry Sobers delighted everyone who watched him with his wealth of skills. That decade probably did need an injection of pizzazz if any did, though. Geoff Boycott and Ken Barrington were guilty of flattening the mood somewhat with some of their Test knocks, especially against the so-called weaker nations. One-day cricket came along thankfully to offer more entertainment and variety (yes, I am not saying that *only* Test cricket is a good thing!).

In the 1970s, Viv Richards arrived and soon established himself as the epicentre of entertainment. His West Indies teammates Gordon Greenidge and Clive Lloyd were also exciting batsmen, while Australia's Dennis Lillee and Jeff Thomson fought fire with fire with their sizzling thunderbolts. It is a relief that no one died, and inevitable that helmets had come on the scene by the end of the decade. The West Indians encountered racism in Australia and England in those years. Thankfully, their victorious and entertaining cricket shut the morons up.

The point is: for every cavalier there was a roundhead. Bradman might have been the maestro, but somebody like Bill Woodfull and his more adhesive style played a crucial role too. Miller might have played with flair and abandon, but he respected Bailey's cussedness and determination. There is more than one way to skin a cat ... and is that not what makes Test cricket so great? The contrasting styles — ying v yang? Sweet *and* sour. Bazball and...

10

FAROKH ENGINEER AND INDIA

'The way I played cricket was "Bazball". The ball is meant to be hit, and hit hard; I firmly believe in that. They did not invent it.'

Farokh Engineer knows that Bazball is not a new invention. The wicket-keeper/batsman was playing his own version of it long before Ben Stokes and Brendon McCullum took charge of the England Test team. Now 86, the Indian–turned–Lancastrian was one of the game's great entertainers and he still speaks well. He was always dashing, with a mop of dark black hair and thick caterpillar eyebrows; he remains as hirsute, and although the hair is now white, the eyes shine bright.

Although he says that Test cricket is the best, he is no idealogue. 'Test cricket is the pinnacle of all cricket without any doubt, but T20 is very entertaining and has spread the game globally in a wonderful way,' he said to me. 'It has brought lots of money for the boys, and the associations. Playing both in conjunction with each other cannot be a bad thing. The game is progressing; that is the main thing.'

So, I ask him, what does he think of Bazball? 'The way I played cricket was "Bazball",' he said. 'The ball is meant to be hit, and hit hard; I firmly believe in that. They did not invent it.'

Engineer made his Test debut against Ted Dexter's England at Kanpur in December 1961. The first Test at Brabourne had been drawn. 'I was facing [Surrey left-arm spinner] Tony Lock,' he told me. 'The evening before he had been very friendly at a cocktail party, wishing me good luck. When I strode out to bat I got an absolute mouthful from him to distract me. The first three balls I received went for three fours. I had fielders all around me, the ball was turning sharply. I put my front foot forward and swept him … step out, front dog out, and swipe it … it was done out of sheer nervousness. Luckily, I middled them all. That is how I started, and it gave me a lot of confidence.'

Although that Test and the next was drawn, India took the last two for a famous series victory. Like Baz and Ben, Engineer was no fan of draws, although he said he did not go quite as far as the cavalier duo:

The draw is the last possible thing we want, although I agree it is better than losing; but you should never play for a draw from the start, for goodness' sake. I never played for a draw. Play for the win!

I used to play for Lancashire in the John Player League in the same way. Except the reverse sweep, which was not really a thing back then… But I did play the odd scoop over the head. The Lancashire lads were bemused. 'Farokh, you are [the] most inventive player we have ever seen,' they would say. But to me it made sense to hit the ball where there were no fielders. Why not try to loft the ball there?

Engineer was born in 1938. India had been playing Test cricket for six years. They had no Tests between 1936 and 1946, however, and he took up playing late.

I went to a Jesuit school, Don Bosco High School in Bombay. There was no cricket, but athletics, soccer and hockey instead.

I represented the school in those sports. I still grew up aspiring to play Test cricket, and to play for India, though. Fortunately, I had parents who were exceedingly supportive. My older brother Darius was also a very good cricketer. He played in the Ranji Trophy, and he should have played for India... He was good enough. He took his studies seriously, though. He went to London to study at the Imperial College of Technology and was later partly responsible for the building of Heathrow and Gatwick airports. He was my inspiration.

Darius took Farokh to the Brabourne Stadium in Bombay, where they saw Denis Compton fielding. Compton, another cavalier of course, gave Farokh a piece of chewing gum, which he kept as a prized possession for years. He also recalls India's first Test series victory, at home to Pakistan in 1952/53, and the series in England, in 1952 (3–0 in a four-Test rubber) and 1959 (a 5–0 whitewash). 'India had no answer to Fred Trueman and Brian Statham.'

Engineer's own opportunity came that winter. 'I was a reserve for the last two Tests against Australia, at Madras and Calcutta. Ray Lindwall, Neil Harvey and co. That gave me a springboard. Then came that series against England. Ted Dexter was an entertainer, and a great man. Test cricket in the 1960s could be a bit dour, however; there were a lot of draws.'

Engineer played 46 Tests, scoring two centuries: 109 against West Indies at Madras in 1966/67, and 121 against England at Brabourne in 1972/73. I interviewed him for *The Cricketer* in 2018 about India's first series win in England, in 1971. Its architects were the three spinners Bhagwath Chandrasekhar, Bishan Bedi and Srinivasaraghavan Venkataraghavan. Defeat came as a surprise to England captain Ray Illingworth. 'It was a hot summer,' recalled Engineer. 'India tended to do much better in those.' Lord's staged an exciting draw in the series opener, India taking a first-innings lead of nine and finishing on 145 for 8, just short of their target of 183 (Engineer making 35), in a rain-affected match. The Test will be recalled for John Snow colliding with Sunil Gavaskar. The fast bowler was ordered to apologise by MCC secretary Billy Griffith but he refused and was dropped for the next Test at Old Trafford, another draw – the incident even cost him a place on the next Ashes tour in 1974/75. 'A good deal of over-reaction by everyone except Gavaskar,' said Illingworth. 'We should have won,' remembered Engineer.

India's win came at The Oval. England looked handily placed when they bowled India out for 284, Illingworth taking 5 for 70, to establish a first-innings lead of 71. Engineer scored 59 with (strangely for him) no fours. England then crumpled to 101 all out, with leg-spinner Chandrasekhar taking 6 for 38, before knocking off the runs for the loss of six wickets, albeit slowly against the miserly Illingworth and Derek Underwood. Engineer saw them home with an unbeaten 28 (this time with three fours). 'Syed Abid Ali came in at No. 8,' Engineer told me. 'I said to him, "Take it easy as we don't have much batting to come." He charged down the pitch and was nearly stumped. I said, "What are you doing? Don't do anything silly." Next ball he took an enormous swipe and top-edged it... Luckily it went for four. I was carried off in triumph when we squeezed home. People in India to this day talk about that great series win.' Illingworth wrote in *The Cricketer* (August 2018): 'It was a shock. India did it with grim determination ... and a bit of charismatic sparkle from Engineer.'

Hilariously, I recall Illingworth, who spoke to me for two hours for my book, *The Toughest Tour*, about England's win under his captaincy in Australia the winter before, declining the chance to talk about the following summer's defeat in India, courteously but swiftly putting the phone down.

Alas, Engineer never had the chance to lead India.

I wasn't captain for political reasons [he was the last Parsi, an ethnoreligious group that descended from Persia, to play for India]. I used to be the voice in the team, to try to give the boys – MAK Pataudi, Ajit Wadekar and all-confidence. I said, 'Attack, attack, let's go for the win. Attack is the best form of defence. Hold your heads high. Show some confidence when you go out to bat, otherwise you are giving the bowler a lot of confidence.' I'm 86 now, but I still have a positive attitude. It keeps me going.

His positivity made him popular with supporters of Lancashire, for whom he scored nearly 6000 first-class runs, and took 429 catches and 35 stumpings. 'I was a bit of rebel. I scored 96 before lunch in a Roses game, and Cyril Washbrook, who was on the cricket committee, had a quiet word with me. He said, "Listen, Farokh, in Roses games we don't hit a four before lunch." I wondered why not: a half-volley is a half-volley; a long hop is a long hop.'

Engineer had another entertainer, Clive Lloyd, to play in tandem with.

We were going to sign Garry Sobers, but he and the club could not agree terms, so he went to Nottinghamshire instead. I got the first registration, and I recommended Clive to be the second. Cyril said, 'But he wears glasses!' I said, 'Never mind, Mr Washbrook, if you sign him, you won't regret it.' Clive was my room-mate for 10 years.

Our latest discussion took place during the India v England series in 2023/24. He had left his home in Mere, South Cheshire, to return to his motherland. 'I went to the first Test at Hyderabad as I was given a lifetime achievement award by the BCCI [Board of Control for Cricket in India]. It was a good series, fortunately not one-sided.' He was pleased to see his fellow Red Rose legend James Anderson back in the England side. 'I've known Jimmy all his life; he is going very well. When he was dropped by England, I was sitting next to him at the christening of Freddie Flintoff's son. I said to him, "Jimmy, you are a great swing bowler, you will always come back with a bang." Whenever I see him he always recalls those words, saying, "Thank you Farokh, I needed that."' Positivity of the sort that Baz and Ben would be proud of.

11

TEST CRICKET IN THE 1980S

*'I loved everything about Test cricket, I decided. The whites
were perfect … The sweaters especially were beautiful:
the three lions woven into the front – one of the most
striking and iconic sporting designs of all time.'*

My love of Test cricket was born in the 1980s, and the strength of
my memories ensures that the flames will never be extinguished
in my head. 'When you come back to England from any foreign
country, you have immediately the sensation of breathing a different
air,' wrote George Orwell in *England Your England*. 'Even in the first
few minutes dozens of small things conspire to give you this feeling.
The beer is bitterer, the coins are heavier, the grass is greener, the
advertisements are more blatant. The crowds in the big towns, with
their mild knobby faces, their bad teeth and gentle manners, are
different from a European crowd.' I recall this quote when I think of
my love for cricket in the 1980s.

All decades are distinctive, of course; in fact, all summers are. The 1980s just seems so special to me, though. The England team was laden with talented, idiosyncratic, and yes, flawed, characters. It felt like a Shakespearean cast. Throw in vast quantities of sex, alcohol, drugs and controversy, and the plot had everything.

The Falstaffian Ian Botham was at the epicentre of it all: a hyperactive, hypnotic colossus of strength and skill, benevolence and generosity, and occasional ill-advised oafishness. His sidekick was Allan Lamb, a diminutive and brave warrior, who refused to flinch against the fiercest of fast bowlers. They reminded me of Asterix and Obelix, the cartoon book characters I loved reading about at the time. To stretch the metaphor further, the head of their tribe of Gauls fighting their Roman invaders was Vitalstatistix – the portly Mike Gatting, remembered for his pugnacious batting and love of long lunches, and an embarrassing entanglement with a barmaid in 1988 that, while he maintains nothing happened, cost him the England captaincy. 'In the 1980s if having a woman in your room was enough to get you dropped, then we wouldn't have had a team at all,' joked David Gower to *The Cricketer* in August 2023, 35 years after the event. Gatting told Gower and me over a particularly long and enjoyable lunch that culminated in jam roly-poly and brandies at his favourite restaurant, Oslo House near Lord's, how he felt the selectors had messed him about, offering then retracting the captaincy for the Ashes in 1989. And then to extend the Asterix metaphor further, for the druid with magical powers, Getafix, it has to be Gower himself, the golden-haired left-hander with timing that would transfix the gods. My introduction to Graham Gooch came later, but he soon made up for lost time in my affections.

You need heroes in life. After watching Oliver Stone's 1991 film *JFK*, I became transfixed with President John F. Kennedy. When somebody tried to persuade me to read Seymour Hersh's *The Dark Side of Camelot*, listing all his imperfections, I refused. I did not want to think less of him. I have subsequently read it. I still admire JFK. The same goes for my 1980s heroes.

I came to work with Gower at *The Cricketer* and we built up a bit of a rapport. I enjoyed his laconic sense of humour. He is languid and needs somebody to organise and cajole him, but his brilliance has earned him that right. He has a certain style reminiscent of another of my heroes, Roger Moore. When I said to him, tongue in cheek, 'You must follow me back on Twitter [now X],' an eyebrow raised slightly, he replied, 'Must I?' I was starstruck when he hosted me at his Hampshire home, especially when I came out of the loo and encountered his wife, Thorunn. These were characters I had seen on television, and read about it in books, none more vivid than Frances Edmonds' indiscrete *Another Bloody Tour* and *Cricket XXXX Cricket,* about the 1985/86 and 1986/87 tours to the West Indies and Australia respectively. We took Lamb for lunch. When I arrived the cheeky duo had predictably already ordered champagne – knowing that I was paying. Lamb's stories were incorrigibly naughty and entertaining, even if we could not print a fair few of them. And he really did not like... Oh, I cannot say!

I went to interview Ian Botham in Newcastle and in those 40 minutes he was perfectly obliging; I did not want to spoil that memory, my memories of him as a player, and I cannot help but turn a deaf ear when he puts his foot in it. For me he will always be the man who enthralled us with his six-hitting, swivel-hipped swing bowling and stunning slip catching; and who raised more than £20m for youngsters with leukaemia. And as the chair of the ECB Richard Thompson said when asked about Botham criticising the Independent Commission for Equity in Cricket (ICEC) report into the state of equity in cricket (2023): 'We live in a democracy, and he is allowed to say those things.'

I am grateful to my friend Neil for introducing me to cricket, with one caveat. It was a year too late. His father was into all sports, and they were obviously enthused by Botham's Ashes in 1981. I was into *Doctor Who* and *Blake's 7.* So I missed that most extraordinary, beefiest of summers. Neil had the bug, though, so come the start of 1982, we would be playing in his perfectly sized garden. It had a long strip, with a wall on one side and a hedge on the other to act as fielders. Hit the caravan that was stationed at midwicket, and you were out ... or *in*, actually, as his dad would call stumps on the session after inspecting the damage. As an only child I also learned to play on my own in my garden, throwing the tennis ball against the wall, acting out imaginary Tests and one-day internationals. I would play the shot, then award myself what I felt were the requisite number of runs. Bear in mind there was no internet then, and my

father was not a fan of the game, so there were no *Wisden Cricketers'
Almanacks* in the house. Some of the teams in my notebook appear
odd, looking back.

When I was not playing, I started to watch. I vividly recall the
first day of Test cricket I sat and enjoyed in full. It is a wonder it did
not put me off. It was the second Test of the later three-match series
of the 1982 summer, England v Pakistan at Lord's. The tourists piled
up 295 for 3 on that first day. As a partisan youth, I was frustrated
watching Mohsin Khan eventually compile 200, the highest of his
seven Test centuries. England went on to lose by 10 wickets. Looking
back at that scorecard, it is surprising to see Derek Randall opening.
Asking middle-order bats to do that rarely works. His partner Chris
Tavaré tried his best to defy Pakistan, with a trademark, anti-Bazball
82 from 277 balls, but Mudassar Nazar took six second-innings
wickets with his gentle nibblers including – yes – Gower, his bunny.

I loved everything about Test cricket, I decided. The whites were
perfect, not cluttered with sponsors' names as they were soon to be.
The sweaters especially were beautiful: the three lions woven into
the front – one of the most striking and iconic sporting designs
of all time.

There were the characters I talked about earlier – and let us not
pay mere lip service to the quirky Randall, patrolling the covers with
his slouching gait that would spring into action when an ill-advised
single was taken to him like a cat tricking a mouse; Derek Pringle, a
giant who held his bat like a toothpick and made up for his lack of
pace with guile and craft; and the rotund Eddie Hemmings, likened
by fans to a beached whale. Cricket in the 1980s was wonderful for
accommodating such characters of all shapes and sizes.

Many of Pakistan's players were equally entrancing. Imran Khan
played for my mother's beloved Sussex; she would purr about his
dishiness as she took time out from her busy schedule to sit and
watch with me; Abdul Qadir … political correctness dictates that we
are not allowed to describe the leg-spinner as exotic and a sorcerer
any more, so let us just say his skill was beguiling, and of a like that
we were simply not used to seeing in England at that time; and Javed
Miandad, such a skilful manipulator of the ball, and the owner of an
impudent grin – somebody who knew how to get right under the
skin of opponents.

The grounds were a delicious, eclectic mix – the stands, the scoreboards, the pavilions. Even the umpires seemed eccentric and quintessentially English. Dickie Bird, a bundle of gnomish eccentricity, subject to affectionate teasing by the players; David Shepherd, ruddy-faced and stout, he would hop up and down when the score was on the unlucky 111 (or multiples of) in homage to Lord Nelson (for reasons that have never quite been proved); even Mervyn Kitchen, who sounded like a character from *The Archers*. He also looked a bit like Postman Pat.

Then there was the BBC television coverage. Teeing off with the unique, iconic theme tune, 'Soul Limbo', by Booker T. and The M.G.'s, who originated from Memphis, Tennessee (cricket had not taken off there at that stage). That they did not originate from the Caribbean came as a surprise, but actually the song stems from a Trinidadian dance called The Limbo. It certainly seems tailored for cricket, as if the instruments are bails banging against stumps, and leather balls bouncing off bats.

The BBC commentators included Jim Laker, shrewd and modest, and Richie Benaud, Australian but non-partisan, like a wise old owl, with a twinkle in his eye, reeking of understated authority. Little did I know then about his golden career, of his inspired bowling and captaincy at Old Trafford in 1961, and of his role in the Kerry Packer crisis.

Even the scorecards were a thing of beauty. Generated by Honeywell computers, they were imposed over the cricket scene; neat, custard-coloured capital letters in a blocky sans-serif, with faint black shadows. Never beaten in my view.

England actually won the first and third Tests of the 1982 series and must have felt reasonably confident that winter as they ventured to Australia to defend the Ashes that they had improbably taken the summer before. In those days Sky was only a gleam in Rupert Murdoch's eye, so we had to wait until early evening for the highlights from Australia on BBC2. I watched them on a little telly in my parents' bedroom as Dad was reluctant to miss any of the three major TV news bulletins of an evening, and the latest Cold War news that I believed ardently would plunge us into thermonuclear annihilation at any moment. And what a revelation those highlights were. The theme tune, 'New Horizons', made the hairs stand up on the back of the neck. The Channel 9 commentary team had Benaud as its skipper, of course, but everyone else was the antithesis of Laker. Tony Greig bold and brazen, like a lion, squabbling with the easily riled Bill Lawry, whose long nose and wiry frame made him look like a bookkeeper from a Dickens novel. Ian Chappell was authoritative, with a steely streak. When a wicket fell, they shouted. They seemed intent on winding each other up. Crowds seemed two or three times bigger than those in England. The spectators held up banners. Daddles the Duck waddled across the screen when a player fell without scoring; he was the cutest, most adorable feature to my 10-year-old eyes. And then there were the one-dayers. The pyjamas, the black sightscreens and white balls, the floodlights. It was the same game that had attracted me in England, yet it wasn't. It was incredible.

I still did not fully understand what was going on. I was elated when Tavaré and Geoff Miller's juggling act in the slips resulted in the dramatic three-run win at Melbourne, and was full of admiration for Hemmings' knock of 95 at the sumptuous Sydney Cricket Ground, with its elegant green ladies' pavilion, even if I did not know what a nightwatchman was yet. Mum had to explain to me why England's efforts were ultimately in vain, however, and how Australia had regained the Ashes.

The first half of the following summer was dominated by the 1983 World Cup, which was a revelation, but I will talk about limited-overs cricket later. A four-Test series with New Zealand followed. The first thing that struck me about them was their endearingly naff sweaters, like something rustled up by your Auntie Pat, who had been told by her sister that you liked cricket. The Kiwis were carried by two brilliant cricketers, Richard Hadlee and Martin Crowe, with a support staff of triers and grafters. Bruce Edgar, the opener, was fascinating. He made Tavaré look flamboyant. (Incidentally, Tavaré became so fed up with hearing jokes about his obdurate batting that when he granted me an interview for *The Cricketer* because he was head of cricket at Sevenoaks School, he said it would be the last that he would ever give – which was a shame, as he did a fine job on many occasions for England. Botham was a fan.) It is no surprise to read that after cricket, Edgar became a chartered accountant. John Wright could be dour too, so must have loved batting with Edgar, as it made his batting look sexier. A Gower century at Lord's and a run-a-ball 103 at Trent Bridge from Botham ensured a 3–1 series win for England, and, all in all, it was a pleasing summer. I had started playing cricket at school by now, too, combining – in my mind – the gritty opening batting of Gooch with unorthodox seam bowling that owed something to Pringle, and something else to Lance Cairns, whose bustling shuffle and drag amused us schoolboys. We had a teacher, Mr Riley, who did not like hanging out with the other members of staff and instead played cricket with us in the breaks. It was us against him; he would score about 70 with his single wicket, then bowl us all out for 40. We thought he was Botham. I captained him later in adult cricket, which was fun.

I cannot say I recall a heck of a lot of England's winter adventures in Pakistan and New Zealand. Considering that it has gone down in the chronicles as the 'sex, drugs and rock 'n' roll tour', it is probably just as well. I vaguely recall some telly highlights from New Zealand, which bore as much relation to Channel 9's scintillating packages as *One Man and His Dog* did to *The Old Grey Whistle Test*.

Up until now, England had been involved in some fairly even contests since I had started watching… And then West Indies arrived in the summer of 1984. It was too much to bear. In the first Test at Edgbaston, poor Andy Lloyd was skulled by Malcolm Marshall, who looked fearsomely skiddy. Joel Garner resembled a gigantic wrecking-ball machine. Michael Holding glided in smoothly and then unleashed hell. It was a blessed relief for England when Eldine Baptiste and Roger Harper came on, but even they did their bit, and England failed to reach 200. West Indies then made 606. Viv Richards was the king of course, but Larry Gomes looked special too. What on earth was going on? How could one side have such dominance over another? My hero at the time, Pringle, did pretty well to take 5 for 108, all things considered.

The second Test at Lord's was even more confidence-shattering. I recall being quite excited when the teacher told us that Gower had actually declared, setting Clive Lloyd's West Indies 344 to win. They romped home, losing only one wicket, scoring at 5.2 runs an over. Gordon Greenidge cut with a savagery I did not know a player could be capable of. The misery continued, the 'blackwash' as it became known, inevitable. I recall being riled as an 11-year-old upon hearing the team's own signature calypso, 'West Indies Touring

Team – West Indians Are Back in Town', which they rendered to the melody of 'Jamaica Farewell', on *BBC Breakfast*:

We've arrived under Captain Clive
The cricket team Englishmen fear and dread
But we're glad to say we're in the UK
West Indian batsmen can bat all day

What a po-faced prat I was for taking umbrage at it. Looking back, I should have rejoiced at the glory of the lion king Richards and co., and the joy that his side gave to those fans dancing and blowing into their conch shells in the open stands of The Oval, many of whom had made the short bus ride or walk from Brixton. Cricket was a source of gleeful pride for the Caribbean community there, at a time of high unemployment and financial strife. An embarrassing draw against Sri Lanka in the one-off Test at Lord's should not have come as a surprise, such was the duffing-up England had received in the summer's main event.

Gower did incredibly well to resuscitate his side and claim a hugely laudable win in India that winter. Hearing about the assassinations of Prime Minister Mrs Indira Gandhi and British Deputy High Commissioner Percy Norris at lunch with Gower and Lamb in 2022, it was a wonder that England stayed the course. They actually lost the first Test, but fought back to win the second and fourth, with the third and fifth drawn. I do recall the highlights of Graeme Fowler and Gatting's mighty stand of 231 in the fourth Test at Madras (now Chennai) on Saturday afternoon *Grandstand* on BBC1. That seemed a superhuman feat of stamina and endurance at the time.

My first home Ashes followed, in 1985. It was a wonderful summer. Gooch had served his ban and was back, and although he took a little time to be at his best, his 196 at The Oval proved his class. Gower looked in control as captain, and made two big, stylish centuries. For Australia, I was full of admiration for Allan Border, the man I would choose to bat for my life. The summer was full of scintillating vignettes, like Richard Ellison's spells of swing bowling in the fifth Test at Edgbaston – 6 for 77 in the first innings. I had never seen anybody move a ball like that. It was hugely frustrating when the cricket cut to the news on the BBC, and I had to make do with my grandmother's crackly radio before catching up with the late-night highlights. The world seemed Ellison's oyster, but his light shone all too briefly, alas.

And then there was Botham's belligerence. England, batting second, were 237 runs ahead. They needed quick runs to give themselves enough time to bowl Australia out a second time. Enter Ian Terence Botham on day four. No helmet. Craig McDermott steaming in. The BBC highlights on YouTube show that the director cut to a banner in the crowd: 'Hit 'em for 6, Botham!' He obliges. Over long-on. 'What about that?' chuckles Laker. 'Quite incredible, first ball plonked for six.' The third ball leaves the middle of Botham's Duncan Fearnley Attack with even greater elevation. 'And there's another one. Six more to follow.' Summariser Ray Illingworth says this one goes about 10–15 yards (9–14m) further than the first. Botham made 18 off seven balls as England raced to a declaration. My appreciation of the man could not have been higher. When my father woke me up with a cup of tea and told me that he had heard on Radio 4 that my hero had been a 'naughty boy' and admitted taking drugs the following year, it made no difference. Everybody loves a bad lad, eh? England won that Edgbaston Test, thanks to a heroic mop-up, and umpires Shepherd and David Constant taking the England fielders' word for it that Wayne Phillips had been caught; it was hugely unlucky for him, the ball popping up off Lamb's boot into Gower's grateful paws. England made sure of regaining the Ashes by also winning at The Oval.

For England a tour to the West Indies followed, and this time they were ready, right? Gower's sarcastic 'I'm sure they will be quaking in their boots' remark to the BBC's Peter West hinted that the belief was not there, though, and England were hammered again. Gatting's broken nose inflicted by Marshall may as well serve as the central image of that campaign. West Indies now had Patrick Patterson, which must have prompted England's batsmen to check their life insurance before they went out to face him on pitches that were rock hard after baking in the Caribbean sun.

The summer of 1986 was pretty depressing for this England fan, with defeats to India and New Zealand. Gatting became captain after the first Test loss to the former and batted well for 183 not out against the Indians in Birmingham, but there was little to hint at the amazing winter to come. Hadlee had mastery over Gooch in New Zealand's shock series victory. One particular passage of play stands out in my memory. Gooch was a magnificent player, but if he had one weakness, it was against bowlers like Hadlee. Medium-fast, does a lot with it, both ways. Nip back into the pads, nip away. Of course, 1989 against Australia's Terry Alderman was a more extended period of torture. In 1986 Hadlee had troubled Gooch at Lord's, dismissing him for 18 in the first innings (although he had made 183 in the second innings). I distinctly remember thinking that Hadlee's supremacy was playing on his mind, however. And the second Test was at Trent Bridge, Hadlee's adopted home. Ron Allsopp seemed to forget that he was English, instead tailoring a surface perfect for Nottinghamshire's adopted Kiwi. There has been a lot of talk about English openers struggling in English conditions against the Dukes ball in the last decade or so, and the huge struggle to find a reliable opening partner for Sir Alastair Cook. McCullum and Stokes have settled on Ben Duckett, who thinks leaves are only something that grows on trees, and Zak Crawley. Gooch v Hadlee was like Zak Crawley that day. 'I'm not going to let him dictate to me,' he might have said to himself. 'He is on his home ground, the Allsoppian pitch is as green as the elms around the ground. The ball is going to do all sorts.' So Gooch, under his trademark white lid, tried to hit him out of the attack, just as Crawley does now. Aggressive strokeplay. Driving pacemen on the up. For a time it worked. Gooch raced to 18 off only 17 balls. And then the heart sank again. Gooch, bolt upright, desperate to play down the line, tried to whip a ramrod-straight delivery through mid-on and he was gone, leg before wicket (lbw) again. 'Gooch didn't even turn to look at the umpire,' said Benaud. He knew.

Hadlee took 10 wickets for 140 in the match. New Zealand won the Test, and the series 1–0 – the first time they had taken a series in England. There was one bright spot for England in that series: Botham returning from his ban for smoking marijuana, and taking wickets with his first and 12th balls against the Kiwis in the final Test of the summer at The Oval. The latter made him the greatest Test wicket-taker of all time, surpassing Lillee. My schoolboy pals and I were all thrilled.

Our hero was back, ready to play a key role against his old frenemies that winter. England in Australia in 1986/87 cannot ever be beaten for me. There were highlights again on TV, but this time there was some live coverage on BBC1. It was seemingly broadcast on a whim, probably by some cricket-mad producer (it certainly cannot be found on the schedules at www.genome.ch.bbc.co.uk). I know that was not the best Australian side that winter. The deadly duos, the Chappell brothers and Dennis Lillee and Jeff Thomson, had gone, but, with the exception of Gooch, all of England's big guns were present and correct. Gatt, Beefy, Lubo (Gower), the spin twins John Emburey and Philippe Edmonds, Graham Dilley with his best series, Chris Broad immortalising himself with three Test centuries, and cameos from Bill Athey, Jack Richards and Gladstone Small. It has to be the definitive England series abroad of the modern era, although India (1984/85), Pakistan/Sri Lanka (2000/01), South Africa (2004/05), Australia (2010/11) and India (2012/13) were also memorable winters/triumphs, of course. That trip had more thrilling set-tos than a James Bond film. Botham filleting Merv Hughes for 22 off one over in the Brisbane series opener. 'I should be telling you to calm down,' Gower said to his partner, 'but I'm having too much fun.' Bob Willis, commentating on Channel 9, purring, 'People should savour every moment they can to watch this player; they only come once in a lifetime.' Broad, Gower and Richards all making centuries at Perth, thwarting any hopes of an immediate home fightback. Broad again and Gatting making three figures on another belter at Adelaide. Then England's killer blow at Melbourne. Small and Botham taking five-fors in a truly abject, gung-ho batting display by Australia. Steve Waugh called it an 'abysmal showing', adding: 'The worst part of our display was that Botham took five wickets on his reputation alone... Long hops were nicked to the keeper or chopped on to the stumps; it was the presence and aura of a great cricketer that had us spellbound.' The Ashes were secured, and it was time for England to party again: the worlds of cricket and pop intertwining, Elton John, Phil Collins and George Michael all making appearances.

People say that the Australia team was not great, but they had the makings of the fantastic side that would emerge: the dynamic, swashbuckling Dean Jones; redoubtable top-order stalwarts David

Boon and Geoff Marsh, and Steve Waugh was also emerging. And it is worth noting that Australia at least gave West Indies a contest for most of the decade. Jones had made a name for himself a few months earlier in India. Vomiting and suffering from diarrhoea at Madras, he pleaded to retire hurt. Border goaded him that the situation 'needed a tough Queenslander' not a city slicker Melburnian. Jones fought on for one of the bravest centuries of all time.

The summer of 1987 should have seen that side that Gatting constructed consolidate their success, but the wily Pakistanis did not play ball. England were the better team in the rain-hit first Test, the second was again ruined by the weather, but a careless display by the hosts saw the tourists triumph at Headingley. Things became heated there, with wicket-keeper Saleem Yousuf claiming that he had caught Botham, sparking an angry response from the all-rounder. England made a mess of a T20-style chase at Edgbaston, and then Pakistan batted England out of the series in the drawn final Test at The Oval. We saw a different side of Botham there: he faced 209 balls to make 51 not out, ensuring the draw.

What followed for England that decade was mostly terrible. Biased home umpiring tipped Gatting over the edge in Pakistan, and he famously clashed with Shakoor Rana. Mudassar Nazar said that he was embarrassed by the standard of officiating when I interviewed him in 2023. Imran had been calling for neutral umpires, to be fair, but it was a shame that extreme events like that had to happen before the change was made. And before anyone thinks that is racist, or micro-racist – as theorised by The Independent Commission for Equity in Cricket (2023) – it was not just Pakistani umpires who tended to favour their own side: New Zealand's did not excel themselves either against West Indies. Holding became so frustrated that he kicked the stumps over, and Colin Croft deliberately crashed into the back of umpire Fred Goodall in 1979/80. Going further back, Australian umpires failed to give Ray Illingworth's bowlers a single favourable lbw verdict in the triumphant 1970/71 series.

Then there was the summer of 1988, when England had so many captains it was a wonder Messrs Nemo, Kirk and Birdseye did not turn up. It was no surprise when West Indies administered another battering. After the last two series had resulted in 5–0 defeats, however, England drawing the first Test felt like an excuse for a national holiday; but then Gatting had that alleged dalliance with a barmaid in the Rothley Court Hotel during the Trent Bridge Test, and that gave the establishment the excuse they needed for regicide. Step forward Emburey, who was struggling for wickets and was then dropped; followed by Chris Cowdrey, a redoubtable county all-rounder and leader but who had not yet proved himself as an international player, and – at last! – Gooch (with a splattering of Derek Pringle thrown in when Gooch had to leave the field with an injury). The *Sydney Morning Herald*'s Mike Coward said Gooch was 'undeserving' after 'thumbing his nose at the establishment' six years before and captaining an England rebel team in South Africa in 1981/82, but he went on to prove an effective skipper, and should probably have been chosen to replace Gatting first up. There were 23 players used by England over the five Tests against West Indies, then another five, including four debutants, in the subsequent Sri Lanka Test (England actually won that one). Then India cancelled the tour that winter, as Gooch the captain was *persona non grata* for his South Africa links.

The summer of 1989 stays in my memory for the extraordinarily compelling character that was/is Merv Hughes, and Terry Alderman's cruel hold over Gooch. Mark Taylor, Border, Boon, Marsh, Steve Waugh, Jones and even Ian Healy just batted, and batted … and batted. Border adopted a single-minded, uncompromising approach, barely exchanging a word with Gower, who he had previously been chummy with. Australia stormed to a 4–0 victory (with only the weather saving England in the other two Tests) and Border became the first captain since Bill Woodfull in 1934 to regain the Ashes in England that he had lost. England had no answers, as the selectors, headed by the newly appointed Ted Dexter, scoured the county averages, calling up 29 players for the six Tests (Australia used 12, with the nondescript Greg Campbell playing once).

Injuries and defections to that winter's 'England' rebel tour of South Africa – the news broke during the fourth Test – took their toll. Once it was mission accomplished, Border told his bemused counterpart: 'David, the last time we came here I was a nice guy who came last.' Ian Chappell had set Border straight about that. Alderman's swing-bowling sorcery brought him a staggering 41 wickets. He had my hero Gooch on toast, trapping him lbw five times, and dismissing him on seven occasions in the series overall, and it was painful to watch. The doubt and indecision must have seeped into his every pore.

It signalled the end of a decade that had enthralled me, but looking back, that talented England side underachieved badly. The wins in India (1984/85) and Australia (1986/87), and the home Ashes victories of 1981 and 1985, were superb, but there should have been so many more. That Gatting only won two Tests out of his 23 in charge speaks volumes, although those triumphs at Brisbane and Melbourne were unforgettable. With Botham, a once-in a–lifetime talent, at the core, as well as the gifted Gower, and Gooch, Lamb, Gatting and even the unlucky Broad; and the spin twins Emburey and Edmonds… Yes, it's true that there was not a truly great paceman like Fred Trueman, especially with Willis bowing out in 1984, but that side in my view still badly underachieved.

12

MY LOVE OF COUNTY CRICKET

*'As T20 dominates, the one thing that county cricket
possesses, to enable it to fight back against the
franchise hordes, is beauty, charm and tradition.'*

There is something unique and lovely about the county game. I think
I can pinpoint when I fell under its spell. It was 1983. I thought I
had already said goodbye to my best friend, Nick Pagan, when we
jumped off the train at Halesworth station at the end of a school day,
but there he was again, outside the town newsagents. That is strange, I
thought. And what is that he is holding up? Oh! That is exactly what
I had just bought: a *World of Cricket 83* Panini/TCCB sticker annual.
Of course, in the ensuing weeks we swapped Geoffrey Boycott for
Geoff Miller, and Paul Parker for Paul Pridgeon. We completed it,
but sadly, they did not make it every year, like the football version.

My parents never chucked anything away, but I cannot find it anywhere. But I do have fond memories of it. A Google search confirms that there was a double-page spread of all 17 first-class counties (before the breakthrough of Durham in 1992) and foil stickers of the badges. I also loved reading the county scores in my father's *Daily Telegraph* and seeing counties play on the BBC the day after the Test (Tuesday or Wednesday depending on whether there was a rest day).

Every county had great players who I am fond of: Derbyshire had Phil DeFreitas and Devon Malcolm, for instance; Durham (a bit later on) had David Boon and Steve Harmison; Essex had too many to mention (but mainly Goochie and Pring, although I am now fond of Toppers and JK Lever) ... and so on.

County grounds are special places. Hampshire, of course, played a blinder by leaving their dilapidated, hemmed-in ground in Southampton for the elegant Rose Bowl. It has not been plain sailing, however. The pitches took a while – 10 to 15 years? – to settle down, and visitors still find it hard to access it – well, *leave* it! – on busy matchdays. The old ground was far easier to get to by train. But Hampshire will finally host a men's Ashes Test for the first time, in 2027. It is mission accomplished for businessman Rod Bransgrove, who pumped money in to save the club.

There is a lot to be said for other county clubs like Essex and Sussex, both close to my heart, to follow. Increasing capacity from about 6000 to double that would put them in the frame when it comes to hosting franchise teams and international matches. Essex had the chance to move to Braintree in the past, and their ground at Chelmsford receives a lot of flak for being down in the dumps. Yet spectators, including my son, love it for being so close to the action. If Sussex left their grassy banks and deckchairs and beautiful wooden pavilion for a concrete bowl out of town, perhaps next to Brighton & Hove Albion FC's ground down the train line at Falmer towards Eastbourne, something unique and historical and special would be lost. I have been going to Hove since the 1980s. I spent a fortnight with my beloved grandfather in Haywards Heath every summer and he took me on the train. I found Imran Khan, Paul Parker and the Wells brothers et al. compelling characters. I recall the thrill of being given a Polaroid camera for a Christmas present and taking pictures at the ground. There were only 10 photos in a pack, and each was quite expensive, so I had to be careful not to waste them. I still have the shots of Garth Le Roux, the fearsome South African fast bowler who posed obligingly for my camera; and his compatriot, Ian Greig, switching from third man to fine-leg. Another is of the scoreboard at Hove. Next to it is one of the famous – or infamous – eggs. They were put there by sponsors Stonegate. If a player hit one with a six, he won £1000. Parker managed it, I believe... I still love the sea air, and the seagulls on the outfield, and sitting in the deckchairs, and the Harvey's beer. In Jon Filby they have a true fan as chairman, somebody who is taking pride in lovingly tweaking the ground, rather than butchering it. We all feared the worst when The Sussex Cricketer pub inside the venue was knocked down, but the new, more modern bar with the same name is perfectly agreeable.

Kent's Canterbury is another beauty, with the characterful Woolley Stand and 1930s scoreboard, although the Sainsbury's and flats, bringing in vital money, have spoilt it for those who fell in love with it before. I am sure Somerset fans feel the same love for their Taunton home, their classically English ground perched near the beautiful Quantock Hills, with the churches of St James and St Mary Magdalene also in view.

As I was writing this it was announced that Worcestershire were considering a new home, out of necessity, it seems. The irritatingly regular flooding at New Road is threatening to make the pitches unusable. This would be upsetting. It is the quintessential county cricket venue. A ground rather than a stadium. With peerless views and quirky charm. The stunning cathedral looks wonderful in the near-distance, and the grounds-man's house and the ladies' pavilion with delicious homemade cakes for sale also inspire much affection. Worcestershire without their home is like battered cod without the chips; cheese crisps without the onion; stumps without the bails. As T20 dominates, the one thing that county cricket possesses, to enable it to fight back against the franchise hordes, is beauty, charm and tradition. New Zealand has concentrated its Test game on boutique grounds like Mount Maunganui, Seddon Park in Hamilton, the Hagley Oval in Christchurch, and Queenstown these days. Can a purpose-built new facility elsewhere serve much purpose for a non-Test county in the T20-saturated decades to come? Northamptonshire are edging closer to what they are describing as a 'second home' on farmland at New Manor Farm at Moulton, near Northampton. They will use it for academy, women's and disabled matches. They say Wantage Road will remain a cricket ground, and their home; the sceptics have their doubts.

Northants' County Ground is no New Road, but it has its charms. I spent many a Saturday afternoon there reporting for the *Sunday Telegraph*. The facilities need updating, but it has traditionally been a good track. Nasser Hussain used to say when he was England captain that it was the closest this country has to an overseas Test surface, playing a valuable role in the development of spinners Graeme Swann and Monty Panesar. It was sweet when Jason Brown, the junior partner of that twirling triumvirate, was also operating there, watched by his parents in their caravanette parked on their boundary. I just worry that if all the non-Test counties abandon their historical homes, they will lose their USPs.

I have been to the HQs of all 18 first-class counties, and I would have to say Trent Bridge is the perfect cricket ground – an excellent place for Test cricket *and* the county game. Attractively designed on all sides, and with a couple of good pubs close at hand. The Larwood & Voce actually has a staircase that leads to a function room *in* the ground. The Trent Bridge inn is a 'Spoons'. They are not for everyone, but you can buy a good pint and the chicken wings are competitively priced. Nottinghamshire are renovating the pavilion to make it fit for purpose for the women's game, so we shall have to see how that takes shape. Hopefully traditionalists' fears will be allayed.

I have had many happy days at Surrey's home The Oval to watch county cricket, despite its vastness. In the summer of 1999 I moved from Suffolk to try my luck in the capital. I spent a year at the *Evening Standard* newspaper. Sometimes the shift started at 6 a.m. The good thing about that was that they ended at 1 p.m. I could then head over to The Oval to watch the afternoon session from 2 p.m. onwards. All for a ridiculously low price as a Surrey member. I sat there, one of a few thousand, often in disbelief that more people were not there, to watch Graham Thorpe, Mark Butcher, the Hollioake brothers, Alex Tudor, Ian Salisbury, Saqlain Mushtaq and Martin Bicknell in action. In a way it felt like having a magical secret; in another it felt so sad. At various stages Surrey have invited youngsters in for a pound. I know the Championship is played when most people work, but still. The pavilion is a labyrinthine edifice jammed with treasures including books, bats and a pinacotheca of team photographs. It also has great views overlooking the Houses of Parliament and central London, depending on which of the five storeys you decide to sit in.

Now counties are seemingly under threat like never before. Rumours abound that certain people at the ECB think that there are too many. They will not mind seeing the back of a few (perhaps even Somerset, who came to out-of-form Andrew Strauss's rescue in 2011 by allowing him to play for them in a tour game against India, do not forget). I read in disbelief when I see players who have had long and distinguished careers with a county call for a franchise to replace them. I have a surplus of sentimentality I concede, but sometimes I wonder if these people must be devoid of it. Michael Vaughan told *Wisden* journalist Melinda Farrell: 'I want to make very clear that I love county support-ers. Absolutely adore them. I had 20 years playing county cricket and I loved every one of them, but we have to move with the times. I know I'll get caned by some county members, but why can't you have 10 prominent franchise teams? Why can't women's teams take over the rest of the counties and other grounds and bring them through?' Stories about culling counties have existed for years. They will not go away. It is tragic. I have just returned from Portsmouth, where I attended a cricket dinner. I have no affiliation for Hampshire, but I realised what a vast county it is, ram-packed with cricketers and cricket clubs. Special play-ers have appeared for the county over the years – Gordon Greenidge, Malcolm Marshall, Barry Richards and Shane Warne to name just a few of the overseas stars. Hampshire cricket should be proud of what they are and what they can be. They do not need Southern Brave, or whatever nonsense some marketing guru has decided to call it.

That is not to say that the counties can do no wrong, of course. There is a perception in the media clique that they can be their own worst enemies. 'Counties couldn't organise a p★★★-up in a brewery,' I was told by an influential figure. Worcestershire confiscating a girl's chocolate muffin at a Blast match in June 2022 was cited as an example. Yes. Grim. Mounting energy bills add to their woes. Sussex denied that their decision not to use their floodlights in County Championship matches in 2024 was a factor in that (and I believed them – the difference that they made was negligible). If counties are to survive, they must shape up for the battle of their lives. Kent's chair Simon Philip was leading the fight for a while: 'We'll not allow our club to be rendered irrelevant,' he told *KentOnline*. You tell 'em!

Strauss said that there will be more Championship matches in high summer. With none in August, that is pure snake oil, right? There were five rounds in June and July in 2023. All a reduction from 14 rounds to 10 would really do is shave off the games played in early April and late September. Beware prospectors hiding behind the excuse that 'it's what the kids want' in cricket's version of the culture wars.

ECB chair Richard Thompson told Surrey fans at the end of the 2023 season that they will learn to love The Hundred (despite saying he objected to it when he was Surrey chair in 2018). Tony Blair told Labour members the same about Peter Mandelson. They never did…

A couple of prominent figures from overseas have championed the county game, and it was good to hear. Jamie Cox, the former Tasmania opener, is now chief executive of Somerset. 'Counties don't just exist to make an England team. Playing for Middlesex or Somerset or Leicestershire is a great achievement. There are actually fantastic first-class careers and playing for Middlesex or Somerset or Leicestershire is a great achievement, and for someone to actually get to that level is really quite substantial,' he told me for *The Cricketer*. 'And to actually play in Leicestershire v Somerset is an event in itself. A lot of people care about that. There are some who can watch it at the ground, but there are a whole heap of others who care about the result on the internet.'

The South African coach Mickey Arthur, who took charge of Derbyshire from 2022 to 2024, is another. 'County cricket is the showpiece for the counties and to be given so much disrespect is, for me, not great and I am quite strong on that,' he told *The Cricketer* in February 2023.

> I do genuinely believe that the game does itself a disservice in this country. County cricket is revered all over the world. There are players all over the world who want to come and play county cricket and it is only in England that county cricket is disliked a little bit. I was really excited about last year [2022] with Derbyshire. I loved everything it stood for. It is something that I find really special. It is up to us as leaders and coaches in our counties to keep pushing and making those players better because then it becomes exciting. I've seen first-hand the alternative domestic structures in place around the world. County cricket is right up there with the best. It is certainly better than a lot of other countries, for sure. So county cricket should be celebrated, not smashed, in my opinion. It is something very special to England. Yes, there is a lot of cricket in the schedule, and it could be structured a little bit differently, but overall it is a very healthy system.

13

THE HUNDRED, DECISIVELY DIVISIVE

*'The Hundred had one of the most disastrous births
of any professional sports competition… It has had
trouble clawing credibility back since.'*

The Hundred is an effective litmus test when it comes to assessing where you stand on the progressive v reactionary chart in cricket. So English cricket unleashed 20-over cricket as a professional format in 2003. India picked up the baton in 2008 and created their Indian Premier League. It went supernova, making our T20 Cup look a little nanoscopic by comparison. Certainly, when it was said English cricket needed its own version, with eight teams rather than 18 (counties) to produce concentrated talent, I did not dissent. The Hundred had one of the most disastrous births of any professional sports competition, however. It has had trouble clawing credibility back since.

The counties gave the green light for an eight-team tournament in 2016. Then the concept of it being 100 balls per innings (15 six-ball 'sets' – not overs, please note – in addition to a final one of 10) rather than 120 in 20 overs was nervously slipped out in a tentative press release two years later. The BBC reported that 'some fans described the concept as "needless", "a gimmick" and "simply ridiculous". Others thought it was so madcap that "players should wear clown outfits" and "the stumps should be made out of jelly".' We were told that modernisers do not want clubs to be named after counties. That concept is deemed old-fashioned by them. 'Middlesex as a county does not even exist,' they trot out. Instead, we have London Spirit, and Manchester Originals, Oval Invincibles, Northern Superchargers...

The Hundred continues to divide opinion. That more women, children, families and non-white fans who do not follow the county game attend matches is laudable, even if TV audiences dipped in the second, third and fourth years (probably because the novelty had worn off). Everyone is seemingly in agreement that it has boosted women's cricket, its double-headers giving them a shared platform with men. I am still sad, and always will be, at the collateral damage it has done to men's county competitions, however. For every new fan it seems to have attracted, two established lovers of the game have been alienated by it. People say that there is room for county cricket, with its T20 Blast, and The Hundred; but the English summer is shorter than Australia and India's.

The creation of the 100-ball-per-innings format was a shock. The ECB at the time, led by chief executive Tom Harrison, let counties have T20 to themselves. The ECB probably wanted something shorter, pre-empting the desire of the BBC, who had finally been coaxed back to show some live coverage of the national summer sport after they had been ousted for Channel 4 and Sky in 1999. The creation of the new format, which hardly anyone of note overseas has embraced, is credited to the competition's managing director, Sanjay Patel. It smacks of Mr. Silly's car in 'Nonsenseland' in Richard Hargreaves' Mr. Men book series for children of all ages. They have a cup for the silliest idea of the year. The winner one year, Mr. Foolish, invented a car with square wheels. The 100-ball format is the brainchild of someone who wants to be chronicled in history as an inventor. It is a vanity project. Let tennis have its sets and let us revert to overs, the universal currency of cricket.

You may have gathered that I am not a fan. An alliance of Mumsnet, metropolitan progressives and avaricious administrators continues to scrap like ferrets in a bag for its survival. We were being told by a number of journalists that the third year was the best so far, even though it received precious little coverage of the actual matches in the newspapers. 'It's here to stay!', 'It can't possibly be scrapped because of the damage it will do to women's cricket!', 'The new fans will leave!' The fourth year was eclipsed by the Olympics. Players like Shaheen Shah Afridi (Pakistan) and Pat Cummins (the Australian Test captain) opted instead for stints in the T20 competitions in Canada and the United States respectively.

The bewildering thing is why it is *so* popular with some people. I met an old acquaintance in the pub. He told me that he loved taking his daughters to The Hundred games at the Kia Oval. They had never shown any inclination to go to cricket before.

'Why?' I asked.

'The fireworks and the music,' he replied.

'But you have that at Surrey's Blast games. Would they go to them?'

'No.'

'OK, is it the dual platform for men and women?'

'No, we mainly watch the men's games although sometimes we catch a bit of the women's.'

'OK, is it that your kids like to be at the vanguard of something new? To be there at a team's genesis?'

'No, that's never been mentioned…'

He never did tell me *why* they like it. They just do.

Some counties like Surrey, with their leviathan conferencing and banqueting empire to supplement the success that they have on the field (they also make about £50m for hosting a Test), never needed it. Some counties clearly do need/like the money, however, even if it imperils their long-term futures. It is the devil's dilemma – take £1.3m per year from the ECB, or actually be allowed to host some proper matches in the summer holidays. Glamorgan seemed to be the classic example of the latter, at the end of the 2023 season. Sophia Gardens hosted seven Glamorgan men's T20 matches, attracting 33,000 spectators. Then in the school holidays, when the county side played in the second-rate 50-over competition ('now contested by has-beens and wannabees,' according to former Somerset and

England all-rounder Vic Marks in *The Cricketer* (October 2023), 38,000 came to four Hundred evenings (a women's match for Welsh Fire, then the men's). To explain it another way: 'Dear County, here is a load of money to *not* stage cricket.' Glamorgan are particularly keen on The Hundred, and keeping it at eight teams, seemingly failing to acknowledge how lucky they are to be at the top table, considering the cricket that they have played in the last 20 years and the lack of England players that they have produced in that time. It has opened up the differences between the haves and have-nots, the counties with Test grounds and those without, into a schism. Lancashire chief executive Daniel Gidney was heard to liken some of the non-Test counties to 'heroin addicts' for not investing sufficiently in 2nd XI cricket and player pathways.

Surrey is actually a curious case. By late 2023, chair Oli Slipper was seemingly a fan of The Hundred (and presumably the team that play at his county's ground, Oval Invincibles). For the life of me I cannot understand why – as I said, Surrey do not need it, and never needed it. Speaking about the ECB's possible plan to expand to 10 Hundred sides, with new ones based at Taunton and Chester-le-Street, and to give counties 50 per cent ownership so they can sell and bring in private money, Slipper seemed pleased. He said in *The Standard* he wanted the Oval Invincibles to be called the Surrey Invincibles. What will Kent, who they are in bed with for The Hundred, say about that? Now I see why Slipper would prefer this new set-up to the one that has been in existence since 2021. But why/how could it be better than a Surrey T20 side, one that they own completely, and not one that they share with Kent, and that is half-shared by the ECB? Perhaps he is being pragmatic. Sky are really keen on The Hundred – no, I mean *really* keen – as are the BBC (or they certainly were at the start). Because a match is played in two and a half hours. You could do that with T20, if you played a block of overs without switching ends – five or 10. In an emphatic case of the tail wagging the dog, Sky, it is believed, would accept an increase to 10 teams, but they say one involving all 18 county clubs is 'mediocre'. Suddenly the man in charge of Sky cricket, Bryan Henderson, had become the most powerful person in English cricket. When *The Cricketer* magazine compiled a Power List of the main people in English cricket from one to 50, he was said to have been disappointed at his lowly placing of 45th. He could be No. 1 now ... certainly in the top five. (Incidentally, Henderson, Harrison, Patel and Sky Sports' managing director, Barney Francis, all at one point played university or club cricket together. Small world.)

Football fans who do not have cricket in their DNA are unable to see why traditional fans are becoming so riled. They think that both the Blast and The Hundred should be retained, as – quote – 'they make all the money' – unquote. It is a false economy. One such foolish friend of mine even sent me 'evidence' to back this assertion up. 'Four-day cricket as a business is completely bankrupt. It makes no money and costs a hell of a lot to put on. Compared to other formats. It simply makes no sense.' Now if my friend was saying that, he could be forgiven, but he was actually quoting Rob Key, who wrote a lively and candid autobiography, *'Oi, Key' Tales of a Journeyman Cricketer*, before he surprisingly landed the job of managing director of England men's cricket (appointed by Andrew Strauss ... fancy that). Surely Key knew that the County Championship develops and produces players for Test cricket – and Test cricket is still the big earner, representing the lion's share of the television agreement with Sky (the latest of which stretched to 2028).

'What about women's cricket?' people say. 'You must keep the men's Hundred for that reason alone.' But would, for example, having Oval Invincibles v Southern Brave women then Surrey v Yorkshire men (the latter in the top flight of a two-division county T20 competition) in a double-header at The Oval be so terrible? The women's 2024 eliminator semi-final there attracted a crowd of 15,823 anyway – without a man's game before or after.

Near the start of my journalism career I was at the *Evening Standard*, and often found myself in the graveyard shift working on a series about the London Underground. I rather enjoyed it. Reading those articles, it was easy to think that in many ways it would be better if the Tube was torn up and a new railway was laid in its place. As charming and incredible as it is, it is frustrating and antiquated. But that is not going to happen. *You have to work with what you have.* In many parts, lines are shared. Circle Line trains must wait for District Line ones to trundle through, the Hammersmith and City Line has to share with the Metropolitan Line, and so on.

English cricket is like this. You should not just create new teams, occupy the counties' grounds like cuckoos, cherry-pick all the best players who have been developed by years-old pathways that run for 52 weeks of the year, and then not pay a hefty price. That price is £23.4m per year (£1.3m per county). In its first two years (2021–2023), The Hundred lost about £58m. Its supporters rage against the dying of the light (the real ones, as well as those who feel that they need to be supportive because it makes them look progressive), but that is unsustainable. Yes, if the £23.4m payments stopped then it might work, but like the abolition of the Circle Line, that is not going to happen. (As I was sending this book to the publishers by the way, I was delighted to hear Richard Gould, the chief executive of the ECB, talk about unwanted 'cuckoos' who do not contribute to 52-weeks-a-year player pathways when it came to The Hundred – I like to think he has been reading my words.) As the independent-minded Mike Atherton wrote in *The Times* newspaper – despite also working for the tournament's most ardent supporter, Sky: 'The Hundred adds a headache-inducing layer of complexity to the fixture list and the advantages it has been given (ticket prices, timing, marketing budget and so on) will have negative consequences for the existing structure of the game and other formats.'

Private money is coming into English cricket via The Hundred: 49 per cent stakes in the teams were sold off. Todd Boehly, co-owner of Chelsea FC, bought 49 per cent of Trent Rockets. The American made the Blues comedic fodder by signing too many players, some on ludicrously long-term deals. Durham, Hampshire and Northamptonshire are already privately owned. Chair/owner Rod Bransgrove completed the sale of Hampshire to Delhi Capitals' co-owners, the GMR Group. 'This is the fulfilment of a dream for me and, I hope, for all Hampshire supporters,' he said. A dream? Really? Sorry, I'm not seeing it. If he has his money back, he deserves it; he helped the club hugely. I guess Hampshire fans hope Delhi's Virat Kohli turns up. But you must worry about what this means for red-ball cricket. Yorkshire's demutualisation is expected. Colin Graves is back as chair after a stint as ECB chair, helping devise The Hundred: he can now reclaim the £15m–22m or so that his family trust is owed by Yorkshire. The privatisation system has been hailed by those who benefit from it, including Durham chief executive Tim Bostock. Talking to journalist Ben Bloom for his book, *Batting for Time: The Fight to Keep English Cricket Alive*, Bostock said:

> Members don't realise that what they are trying to say [Ed: should that be 'save'?] will kill the game. We're running a multi-million-pound professional sport and yet the long-term, big decisions are made by a handful of … I don't want to call them activists because they will get on their high horse [Ed: But you are going to do it, anyway, aren't you?] but they are effectively activists. Of all the millions of people who watch cricket in an English summer, the whole structure is being dictated to by what might only be about 10,000 people. You have chairmen threatened with removal if they do not do what a small handful of Luddites say – and they are Luddites. They are passionate Luddites, but they are Luddites. I just do not know how they think it will survive without radical change. We've ended up with the lowest common denominator ruling the day.

(As one chair of a rival county told me, arguably Bostock is the Luddite for destroying the machinery – the county game – that delivers him his livelihood.)

India businessmen like Mukesh Ambani and Shah Rukh Khan have been mentioned as possible investors. Did we really want to sell off English cricket to the highest bidder again? There is a report that London Spirit might become Mumbai Indians London (MI London for short). Did we not have enough of that when Giles Clarke arranged the tie-in with the now disgraced and incarcerated Sir Allen Stanford – which led to the creation of the embarrassingly crass Stanford Super Series in Antigua in 2008?

I hate using football analogies when it comes to cricket, but … the England Test team and Liverpool FC are my two sporting loves, and when it comes to private ownerships, I cannot help but think of Messrs Tom Hicks and George Gillett. David Moores, who died in 2022, was the Liverpool chairman and felt that his money had taken the club as far as it could go, so he allowed the American duo to take over in 2007. How naive we all were. We thought that the good times would roll. But it was a leveraged buy-out – Hicks had used the same tactics to buy out Weetabix ... he was a cereal offender. They borrowed the money, and Liverpool paid back the loan – about £40m a year. No more big transfers, no more Fernando Torres. In my opinion they did nothing that Moores could not have done himself (except perhaps I will begrudgingly concede that the Americans knew how to 'maximise their asset' more effectively). Ultimately, they were flushed out of Anfield by their own greed, and the campaigning power of the fans, thank goodness.

Another set of Americans, the Glazer family, were still getting away with it at Manchester United at the time of writing, however – they have taken £1bn-plus out of Old Trafford. United co-chairman Avram Glazer has bought a franchise in the T20 league in the UAE. Lucky them...

The latest example of what private money can do in football is at Reading, where the owner Dai Yongge tried to sell the club's training ground to Wycombe Wanderers (he was thwarted). Liverpool now have different American owners – the Fenway Sports Group – who have invested their own money but hope to make a killing one day. In 2022 it became clear that they were seemingly starting to think about selling up.

Overseas owners in cricket can no doubt provide clubs with commercial nous. They can put money up that might allow better players to be recruited on more enticing wages. They might lend clubs cash to improve infrastructure – both stadiums and training facilities – but ultimately they may want to use cricket to 'sportswash' their reputations or to leech money out, either sooner or later. Cricket can walk alone.

George Orwell's two most famous books never lose their relevance. In *Animal Farm*, the pigs Snowball and Napoleon lead the animals on a revolution against the farmers, only to end up being the rich rulers instead. Take the story about The Hundred being partially sold off. On 10-year deals, I believe. It would make some people very rich indeed, and those administrators are telling the counties that they too will benefit. I am not convinced. I fear that some of them will end up like Boxer the carthorse, dragged off to the knacker's yard. There are so many questions about any potential deal – not least for me, is there a guarantee that The Hundred will remain at 28 days' duration, rather than ending up being two months long, like the IPL is now?

Richard Thompson, a keen amateur cricketer who founded M&C Saatchi Talent, gave impressively balanced interviews on Sky when England were playing a Test series in Pakistan in the winter of 2022/23. 'Richard Gould and I recognised that three domestic competitions and an increased international schedule was already causing problems and bringing in a fourth [The Hundred] will only make things worse,' he said. 'The game needs a debate … selling a tournament means selling a part of the English summer. If we are going to sell four or five weeks of the English summer we have really got to understand the unintended consequences… The next few years will decide if The Hundred lands.' In another interview he said that he will support The Hundred if it did not cannibalise county competitions. Which it clearly does. Which is odd. He said accommodating the County Championship, a 50-over competition, the T20 Blast and The Hundred into the men's calendar is like playing the most complicated game of Jenga ever.

Alas, Strauss is not the only one who seems to think county cricket is not cool enough. Gary Lineker, for instance, told *The Cricketer* that he did not think county cricket would cut it in the 21st century when we had a lunchtime chat for the magazine with David Gower (although he also said 'T20 is good for the game overall, but Tests feel proper.') 'Do you think county cricket can crawl on?' Mark Nicholas asked Gower in another lunch in the autumn of 2023. This from a man who lists 'captaining Hampshire' as one of his proudest achievements. How sad is that?

When the county fixtures for 2023 were announced, our worst fears were averted. There were still 14 rounds of four-day matches, and for a change some of them were even being played in mid-summer. Alas, those out to compress the Championship are unlikely to give up. The insults have started again, too. 'It's not the tail wagging the dog but the fleas on the tail wagging the dog,' an 'exasperated source' told the *Telegraph*. We paid to watch these people play, and now they call us 'fleas'. At least we are not parasites.

The last few years have felt like a putsch by white-ball enthusiasts ousting red-ballers. Scheduling decisions have been made on the basis of personal predilection, the whims of biased administrators and television producers: done in the name of youngsters, but also sating the cravings of data-devourers, new journos who love being at the start of something, and gamblers. I have nothing against T20, I stress, but there is a balance. You do not want it to be all T20 ... like Basil Fawlty's gourmet night: 'If you don't like duck, you're rather stuck!'

Ageism is a factor in all this, of course. Anybody older than 65 is told to shut up. 'You have had your time.' Because I opposed The Hundred, one of its most passionate champions contacted me on WhatsApp. 'Your views are shameful. You are living in the past. I don't want to read you anymore. A middle-class, middle-aged guy lecturing younger generations on what they should watch, fuelled by your own tunnel vision.' For goodness' sake, say what you really think!

Player power also has a lot to do with it. They have never had it so good, to paraphrase Harold Macmillan. They now have about 15 T20 tournaments to aim for (as well as the T10s – Scotland have one now). Players even seem to dictate who coaches them these days, as McGrath lamented: he was upset to see his former teammate Justin Langer, admittedly authoritarian and intense in style, replaced by Andrew McDonald, even though Langer had helped Australia retain the Ashes, taken them to the T20 World Cup in 2020, and helped them to No. 1 in the world Test rankings.

At the forefront of this T20 hegemony is the IPL, which started in 2008 at 40 days' long, and in 2023 stretched to 60. India are the biggest of the 'big three' countries (the other two are Australia and England), their share of the wealth increasing with each four-year sale of media rights. The Board of Control for Cricket in India is expected to earn about US$230m per year between 2024 and 2027 – or 38.5 per cent of the ICC's annual earnings of $600m. The ECB is next, but miles behind, at $41.33m, or 6.89 per cent. That to me would put cricket on a par with baseball – India playing the America role, with a few satellites playing the game as offshoots. In cricket, England and Australia. In baseball, Mexico and Japan. Strauss may think that T20 has expanded cricket's frontiers, but in many ways it is narrower – and more India-centric – than ever before.

14

MUDASSAR NAZAR AND PAKISTAN

'Test cricket is the ultimate. Being tested in all kinds of conditions, against top-class bowlers, including pacemen who are allowed to bowl more than one bouncer an over.'

Mudassar Nazar was a resourceful, determined opening batsman and a handy medium-pace bowler for Pakistan in 76 Test matches – with his gentle, nagging wobblers, he was David Gower's unlikely nemesis. The son of a Pakistani cricketer, he was born in 1956, only four years after their entrance into the Test game, so he seemed a perfect person for me to talk about his country's relationship with the longest game.

Since retiring as a player, he has had a long coaching career, and even dabbled in the frozen food business in the North West of England for a decade. He lives – for most of the year anyway – just outside Manchester, and he is a passionate United fan, going to matches with his adored and adoring grandson.

He told me:

Right from day one of playing, and accompanying my father to coaching, I cared about one thing and one thing only – playing Test cricket for Pakistan. And that never changed throughout my cricket career. Test cricket was the ultimate. Cricketers earn a lot of money for these shortform tournaments these days, but we lost contracts missing out on things when schedules clashed so that we could play Test cricket for Pakistan. Money in those days was secondary. It was important, but if it got in the way of our ambition to play Test cricket, it was disregarded.

Test cricket is the ultimate. Being tested in all kinds of conditions, against top-class bowlers, including pacemen who are allowed to bowl more than one bouncer an over. In the past 10 to 20 years, bats have been getting heavier, though, and boundaries have become smaller. It is all about T20 now, and bowlers getting bashed about the park. I see the trend. I coach a lot of under-16s and under-19s, and they know exactly where all the T20 and T10 tournaments are going on around the globe. I don't have a clue where they all are. It is a dangerous pattern, and it is catching.

For Shaheen Shah Afridi to miss the third Test in Australia [in the winter of 2023/24] – I would have been devastated if I had been made to miss a Test like that. Workload issues were cited. Yet he spent 16 hours on a plane and then played the next day. Money is the factor. We are also getting some very poor cricketers, thanks to all this T20. Solid batting techniques are becoming rarer. I concede that players' fitness has improved, thanks to T20, but even then, flying from Australia and playing in Bangladesh or the UAE straightaway cannot be good for a player's health. A decade or so ago there were people like Ian Chappell warning about this situation, but now more and more people realise that this is a real threat. I really fear for Test cricket now.

Pakistan gained official Test status in the English winter of 1952/53. Mudassar's father, Nazar Mohammad, played in all five Tests of that debut series, in India. 'He made a century in the second Test at Lucknow and came back to Pakistan a hero,' said Mudassar.

He had a very good name in Pakistan. They didn't come into international cricket until that series, but they had played a few unofficial 'Tests', against West Indies and Ceylon, and MCC toured a few times. He scored a century against them, their attack including a young Brian Statham. Dad was very helpful to me. He gave me good coaching, sent me to a cricketing school, and I wanted to emulate him. Growing up in Lahore was fantastic. Everybody loved the cricket grounds; the set-up was excellent. We had three-day games, and I came through the ranks. It was a wonderful upbringing.

I started watching Test cricket when I was about four. My father took my older brother to the Test against England at Lahore in 1961/62. They left me at home, and I played havoc in the house. I never forgave them [laughs]. I missed out on Javed Burki's innings of 138. The atmosphere at these matches used to be absolutely brilliant. The stadiums used to be full, with as many people again standing outside. The whole city would be buzzing. Everyone was up for it. There were flags and banners. Food was served inside and outside the ground. There were no restaurants outside back then, now there are 10; but you could buy chicken curries, chickpeas, samosas and kebabs from the carts. The spectators would be very vocal about Pakistan, but they were very knowledgeable about the game of cricket.

Hanif Mohammad was my hero. I couldn't sleep at night if I knew that he was in Lahore… I *had* to go and shake hands with him. He must have got fed up shaking hands with me. Mushtaq Mohammad was my role model, and it was a privilege to play under his captaincy. I played my maiden first-class match in 1971 when I was 15, and while I did not do much, my eyes were already open … my ambition was to score enough runs so I could play for Pakistan. They had a top side, but I broke in because I was an opener, bowled a bit, and I was a reasonably good fielder. Majid Khan and Sadiq Mohammad were high-class players, then there was Hanif and Mushtaq, so it was pretty settled. Javed Miandad emerged, and he became Pakistan's greatest batsman of all. Then we had Imran Khan at No. 7. He put so much work into his game. Wasim Raja [leg-spinning all-rounder] was actually more talented than him, but it was the amount of hard work and thought that Imran put in. He had such burning ambition. Then there was Abdul Qadir. We would never play a one-day game without him. He was a magician, a fantastic bowler.

Mudassar himself made 10 Test centuries, including four in an incredible sequence against India in 1982/83 — 119 at Karachi, 231 at Hyderabad, 152 not out at Lahore, and 152 back at Karachi... Pakistan won the six-Test series 3–0, and he made 761 runs in the rubber. 'Every dog has his day. I was seeing it quite well at that stage. Sunil Gavaskar says everybody has a golden period in their career, and that was mine. Once you get one hundred it can quickly lead to another as you start to believe.'

Pakistan had a strong side in the 1980s, with a key component being the gifted, whippy left-arm quick Wasim Akram. 'I had the fortune to play with Wasim, but just missed out on Waqar Younis, alas.' Mudassar had success against England in 1987, making 124 at Edgbaston, then 120 at Lahore two Tests later. 'The ton in my home city was a good one on a turning track against John Emburey and Nick Cook. It was a terrible series.' This was to do with the umpiring controversies that came to a head before neutral umpires were introduced into Test cricket, when Shakoor Rana clashed with England captain Mike Gatting at Faisalabad. 'I got on well with the England players, and it was not enjoyable,' said Mudassar. 'I had enormous sympathy for Mike. Too many umpiring decisions went against England. It was a shame. After that my form fell away. I didn't like the way things were being run in Pakistan cricket.'

He also dismissed Gower four times in Tests, and seven times in ODIs. 'I don't know how it happened. I swung it across him a bit, and a couple of times brought it back in. He was caught behind and clean-bowled. People remember it, and they used to show me dismissing him on that BBC show [They Think It's All Over] but people forget the times when David was in and he took a lot of runs off me,' he continues. 'I also got Viv [Richards] a few times. The hardest to dislodge was Sunil Gavaskar. I got him in the one-dayers but never in a Test; he was unbelievably solid.'

He says Pakistan had their strongest ever Test side in the 1990s.

It was as talented as Australia, but the Australians conquered everything – goodness knows why. I think Pakistan were so scared of losing. Match-fixing had surfaced, and every time Pakistan lost, people would say, 'Oh, they threw it.' Inzamam-ul-Haq emerged, and he was fantastic. I picked him for Pakistan Under-25s in 1991 to face England A, led by Nasser Hussain. The tour did not take place in the end, but we did have a month-long training camp, and I could see how special Inzamam was.

While we swore by Abdul Qadir, the players of the 1990s hailed [off-spinner] Saqlain Mushtaq. I got to umpire him in the mid-90s. Bowling from my end, I thought he must have had a caught behind, but he just made the ball drift away so much. I didn't know he had bowled that ball – the doosra. It was the start of something totally different in world cricket: Saqqy, Harbhajan Singh [India], and Muttiah Muralitharan [Sri Lanka]. They dominated. Murali said Saqlain taught him how to bowl the doosra.

Pakistan were then lucky enough to have Younis Khan, Mohammad Yousuf and Misbah-ul-Haq. Misbah would have played another 30–40 Tests (as opposed to the 75 that he did play) in another era; but for the first seven or eight years of his life he just could not get in the side.

After all that amazing history, Mudassar now worries for the Pakistan Test team.

I attended the first IPL meeting in Singapore in early 2008. It prompted me to meet the chair of the Pakistan Cricket Board, and I told him and the International Cricket Council, 'You need to think really hard about T20. It will take over Test cricket. You need to find a balance.' Even now they do not really listen, though. Most of the office holders are non-cricketers. I travel to coach cricketers in a lot of Associate nations, like Kenya, Uganda and Nepal, and, even there, all the talk is of T20 and T10. This thing is speeding fast. I fear for Test cricket.

15

TEST CRICKET IN THE 1990S

*'Australia were probably the greatest all-round side Test cricket
has seen. There will be advocates of West Indies in the 1980s,
with their pace and power, but the Australians had Warne,
and even MacGill ... wristspin wizardry.'*

The 1990s began with what seemed to me a near-miracle: England
giving West Indies a good contest. The first Test victory in Jamaica in
the 1989/90 series was one of the most memorable in my lifetime. Such
was the professionalism that they showed in the Caribbean, without
the 'rested' Ian Botham and David Gower, it begged the question:
why had it taken so long to install Graham Gooch as captain? He got
them all fit, and the bowlers were encouraged to be disciplined with
their line (this is when we heard about the 'corridor of uncertainty'),
with Angus Fraser proving to be England's best bowler in the decade,
even if he struggled with injuries. One thing the Gooch captaincy

94

lacked was luck, however. Ezra Moseley broke his hand in the drawn second Test, and Allan Lamb stepped up. And he was not quite such a good leader – although England would have won the third Test if it were not for rain, and the time-wasting of West Indies, led also by a stand-in skipper, Desmond Haynes. The hosts reimposed themselves in the last two Tests with Gooch sidelined, still exerting his influence in the dressing-room (but not on the field), but a 2–1 defeat was miles better than what had happened in the 1980s.

England started to look consistent under Gooch, defeating New Zealand at home 1–0, thanks to his 154 in the third Test at Edgbaston. By now he had a promising opening partner in Mike Atherton, who started the series with 151 at Trent Bridge. India were next up and the series began with an extraordinary Test at Lord's that I was lucky enough to witness in the flesh. Gooch making 333 and 123 in the same match was an incredible feat, even if India's attack was a bit popgun. Robin Smith, who looked as if he would become one of the greats, thanks to his courage against the quicks; Lamb and Mohammad Azharuddin all made hundreds; Kapil Dev hit Eddie Hemmings for four successive sixes over long-on to avoid the follow-on; Sachin Tendulkar was emerging as a future star and took a stunning one-handed catch, and England won. It was all anyone could want from a Test match. I have vivid memories of it, sitting next to a professor of English literature from India on one side, and Mum on the other. What was Kapil Dev's spectacular display of hitting, if not Bazball? Tendulkar showed what a talent he was at 17 with a century in the draw at Old Trafford, and Gower justified his recall at The Oval with an unbeaten 157. He and Gooch were reluctant bedfellows, and trouble between them would soon flare up again.

That winter saw the emergence of Brian Lara for West Indies, the loveliest player to watch in the decade, his high backlift allowing for a range of crisp strokeplay that seemed to owe something to guillotining. England were in Australia, however. They felt that they had a chance if they played like they had in the West Indies, but Gooch's luck ran out again. This time he was bitten by a spider (yes, really); alas, it did not give him even greater powers of adhesiveness, and the infection forced him to miss the first Test. The Australians had a decent attack, with Terry Alderman taking the new ball alongside impressive left-armer Bruce Reid. They also unearthed another

Waugh, Steve's twin Mark, who made an elegant century on debut at Adelaide. Gower scored two hundreds in the series, but still his casual style grated with Gooch. He hired a Tiger Moth to 'buzz' England's batsmen in a tour game, something that was only going to irritate the intensely focused captain. As well as Fraser, England in this era had four West Indian-born quicks who, on their day, were extremely effective. Devon Malcolm was really fast but inconsistent, and the coaches later tried to tinker with his action to dire effect. Chris Lewis sadly underachieved for somebody with his immense talent. Gladstone Small and Phil DeFreitas were pretty decent Test bowlers on the whole (although the latter had the talent to have scored more runs). Nevertheless, this Australia tour was a bitterly disappointing campaign, with home captain Allan Border really coming full circle, which just goes to illustrate that no situation in life is irredeemable.

England showed in the 1991 summer that their improved display against West Indies last time was no fluke. They won the first Test at Headingley, thanks to 154 from Gooch, an innings that was rightly lauded as one of the finest in Tests of all time. West Indies still had a fearsome foursome: Curtly Ambrose, Patrick Patterson, Courtney Walsh and Malcolm Marshall. Gooch found an able assistant in his Essex teammate Derek Pringle, who stuck around with the bat, and exerted control with the ball. DeFreitas also had one of his best Tests, with four wickets in each innings. Thanks in part to a dazzling spell of spin from Phil Tufnell at The Oval, England drew the series 2–2. What a turnaround this was for England against West Indies, thanks to Gooch's disciplined captaincy.

Tufnell's bowling was a key component of a Test victory in New Zealand in the winter of 1991/92. There was an unfortunate incident in the final drawn Test at Wellington when David Lawrence collapsed with a shattered knee. Lawrence had more to do in the match, thanks to an injury to DeFreitas. The matches were poorly attended, however, and some suggested that this showed that Test cricket was dying, with most of the attention on the forthcoming World Cup in Australasia. At this time Twenty20 was a thing only talked about in opticians. The 50-over game was the threat. The one that everybody said was going to consume Test cricket. Which goes to show that fashions change, and cricket would be wrong to put all its eggs in one basket with T20.

Australia's 4–0 Test series win in India, meanwhile, showed how good they were becoming, and how weak the hosts were at that time.

A new phenomenon put paid to England in the summer of 1992: reverse-swing. Well, it was new to most of us, anyway. Wasim Akram and Waqar Younis were wonderful to watch. Quite often England would make a steady start, with Alec Stewart emerging as a superb player of pace, only for the ball to start going around corners when the fielders went to work on it. There was all sorts of talk of one side of the ball being scuffed up by bottle tops and the like, but nothing was proved, and one just had to marvel at Wasim and Waqar's skill. It illustrated how conspiracy theories develop out of incomprehensibility when new phenomena emerge.

I do recall buying *The Times* on holiday in France and being thrilled to read about the Test debut at Lord's of Sussex's Ian Salisbury, the first specialist leg-spinner I had seen bowl for England. Sadly, he never enjoyed an extended run in the side. Gooch led from the front again in Leeds, with 135, but Wasim and Waqar were too good at The Oval in the series decider.

Soon after this, Australia had found their own leggie, who endured for rather longer. After an inauspicious start to his Test career, Border threw the ball to Shane Warne at Colombo in 1992/93 as a last resort, and a dramatic three-wicket burst against Sri Lanka kick-started a stellar career that saw Warne become the bane of England's batsmen. That winter also saw the return of South Africa after their enforced exile because of apartheid. It gave the Test game a fillip, especially seeing quick bowlers like Allan Donald and Fanie de Villiers. West Indies won a thrilling series in Australia in 1992/93, with Lara achieving superstar status at Sydney by scoring 277, and Curtly Ambrose delivering one of the greatest spells of all time, 7 for 1 at Perth. Desmond Haynes said: 'Watching a guy bowling at that level where it looked like he was going to get a wicket with every ball – that is not normal.'

Alas, that winter saw the beginning of the end for Gooch's captaincy. England were hammered 3–0 in India in a ramshackle campaign that was captured on Dermot Reeve's cine camera and lost a one-off Test in Sri Lanka (with Stewart in charge) – their first defeat to them. The following season they were then destroyed by Warne. The ball of the century at Old Trafford to clip Mike Gatting's off stump, after pitching outside leg, has been chronicled in enormous detail. So let us talk about his consistency: Warne's wicket returns per innings were four, four, four and four as Australia went 2–0 up. Tim May was an accomplished partner – I had never seen an off-spinner turn the ball so much, pitching it outside off stump rather than spearing it into the pads as English counterparts did/do. Atherton was in charge by the time of the fifth Test at Trent Bridge, which he lost, but he did lead England to a consolation win at The Oval which at least hinted at brighter times. Gooch graciously rallied the troops when Atherton was out of the room. England also blooded Graham Thorpe during that series, and he made a hundred on debut at Trent Bridge. He became a fine player, held back by personal problems at times.

Atherton is a bright man with qualities – determination and resilience – that have served him well in cricket and journalism. He was a sweet clipper of the ball, especially off his legs, and was courageous against fast bowling. His batting stats held up well as captain. He can come across as a hard-nosed fellow, who does not suffer fools – or those he perceives as fools anyway – gladly. Sometimes he did not appear to have faith in a bowler who had been picked for him. The English system did not help him. There was too much cricket – it was ever thus – and there were still no central contracts. Seam bowlers were required to deliver over after over for their counties, as opposed to the Aussies, who were wrapped in cotton wool by the national side. Compare poor old Fraser, a superb bowler who looked so tired – running in 'like a man who has his braces caught on the sight screen' wrote Martin Johnson so memorably – to Glenn McGrath, who seemed as fresh as a daisy.

Results were generally disappointing in the years ahead. In the West Indies in 1993/94 England lost 3–1. Lara had taken Richards' throne, and Ambrose and Walsh were potent match-winners. I was at university when this series was on. I watched the first Test in a grimy West London pub, on a cold night, wishing I was in the Caribbean. But not in the middle at Sabina Park, for Atherton faced one of the most ferocious spells I have ever seen, from Walsh. My word, the England captain was brave. England quite often took a consolation victory in the 1990s, and this time it came at Barbados. It was Stewart the batsman's finest hour. He had been disappointed to be overlooked for the captaincy, with many whispering that Atherton's Cambridge background had swung things in his favour. The duo were certainly chalk and cheese in many ways (and yet there are similarities). Stewart was regimented in his behaviour, immaculately attired, a graduate of the Gooch school of fitness. Atherton appeared more cerebral, and casually dressed. Neither, frankly, have the affability and flamboyance of some of the 1980s crew. They were never soulmates but there was mutual respect. Nevertheless, they combined well at the Kensington Oval. Atherton made 85 alongside Stewart's 118 in the first innings, then the latter followed up with 143. It was a performance that ensured that if and when Atherton handed over the baton, it would be to Stewart.

Lara's 375 ensured that the last Test at Antigua was a draw, although Atherton and Smith also struck centuries. How did Lara play such epic innings? As a youngster he practised hitting a marble with a broomstick, a novel twist on a stump and a golf ball that worked so well for Don Bradman. Garry Sobers said that one-day cricket was diminishing players' ability to bat a long time. Lara was an exception. His powers of concentration were phenomenal.

One puzzling aspect of that England campaign was the treatment of Matthew Maynard. I had watched him slay county attacks for Glamorgan, and he did seem to think that he could take the same approach, slashing at wide, quick balls with minimal foot movement. He also looked nervous. Maybe the selectors had seen enough after four Test caps. This struck me as unfair, however. He had been identified as good enough to play Test cricket: so give him an extended chance to show it, as they do now. Hugh Morris and Steve Watkin (three caps each) received similarly harsh treatment. Maynard could well have flourished in the Bazball era.

For the summer of 1994, England turned to one of their finest former captains to be chair of selectors: Ray Illingworth. The architect of the brilliant 1970/71 Ashes campaign, great things were expected. He was too old by then at 62, though, and should have stayed in the commentary box. The thing that struck me most about his reign was that while he was still capable of identifying diamonds like Darren Gough and Craig White (both Yorkies, please note … well, in the latter case an adopted one), he had strange blind spots about others, never seeming to have much confidence in Fraser and

Jack Russell, for instance. The latter weirdly missed out to Steve Rhodes in the series against New Zealand – although his Bradford roots might explain it. Yorkshiremen have the utmost confidence in Yorkshiremen.

England won the opening Test at Trent Bridge, thanks to Gooch's 210, still going strong at 40, although this was the last of his 20 Test tons. South Africa proved tougher opponents in the second half of the summer, though. Up to now Illingworth and Atherton had been having a bit of a benign power struggle: Yorkshireman v Lancastrian, state-school boy made good, somebody who had fought the establishment to earn everything he had ever achieved, v the public schoolboy who had received the captaincy by anointment. Wonderful stuff… Shakespeare wrote plays about less. When the captain was fined £2000 by the England management for allegedly using dirt in his pocket to tamper with the ball for encouraging reverse-swing and not disclosing the true facts to the match referee, the tectonic plates shifted in Illingworth's favour, however. Atherton's captaincy was on the line, but, luckily, he had an ace up his sleeve. Malcolm had one of those days when everything clicked into place: rhythm, direction, and pace allowed him to bowl like the wind. He had been hit on the head by Fanie de Villiers while batting, and only he could tell you whether the identity of the opposition – apartheid and all that – also put fire in his belly. He took 9 for 57, record figures at The Oval. England drew the series.

Alas, Malcolm could not replicate this form in Australia that winter. England were pitiful, which was pretty annoying considering the thousands of pounds I had earned pulling pints to go out and watch them. Gooch and Gatting were too old, and Warne was too good. In fact, it was a fine Aussie side, led by the upstanding Mark Taylor, who opened the batting with the talented Michael Slater. Boon was still around, along with the Waugh brothers. McGrath made an inauspicious debut, but they had the pace of Craig McDermott, and the swing of Damien Fleming.

I saw a classic drawn Test at the Sydney Cricket Ground, a match in which Fraser showed his character and proved Illingworth wholly wrong. It was here that Atherton made one of his most controversial decisions, declaring with Graeme Hick on 98. I do recall being puzzled that Hick patted back an over of back-of-a-length deliveries from Fleming just before the call was made, but Atherton now regrets the decision, and Hick still resents him for it, apparently. The mood in the dressing-room was grisly afterwards, by all accounts. It is such bold, stubborn calls that have allowed Atherton to go seamlessly from gamekeeper to poacher in the press box, and to be such an unyielding interrogator in post-match conferences. The irony is that when he was captain, he notoriously refused to play ball with journalists, even calling one a buffoon in Pakistan in 1996. 'Quite right!' said my mum, 'Why should he give them anything?' 'Well, that's part of the job of being England captain,' I replied.

Here is a tale that illustrates the them-and-us make-up of the England dressing-room. In Australia, the senior players had been given cars by sponsors Toyota. One of them did not know how to get to a ground, so a younger player with local knowledge volunteered to show him. After the match, when the youngster made to hop into the car again, his elder said that his services would not be needed that time, and he had to go on the team coach.

In the summer of 1995, England fought well for another 2–2 draw at home to West Indies, despite the brilliance of Lara, Ambrose and Walsh. They discovered a new bowling weapon in Dominic Cork who, when the ball was swinging, could be a match-winner. His return of 7 for 43 at Lord's was the best by a debutant, and he went on to take a hat-trick at Old Trafford.

A frustrating campaign followed in South Africa. Illingworth had insisted on becoming 'supremo', the equivalent of an England football manager, and his age and methods were exposed. Malcolm, on a high after meeting Nelson Mandela, who called him 'the destroyer', reacted badly to attempts to tinker with his action and run in straighter rather than falling to the side, and it all got a bit grisly. Malcolm hinted at racism, but the bowler soon retracted this claim. Illingworth and bowling coach Peter Lever's treatment of him was certainly heavy-handed, though. Malcolm was 32; he was the man who South Africa feared, and the coaches really should have let him be. The first four Tests of the rubber were drawn, with Atherton enjoying his finest hour at The Wanderers, dredging up every ounce of cussedness and defiance in his 185 not out that spanned 165 overs. Russell gave him admirable support. England tossed the series away with poor batting at Cape Town in the final Test, however, and Malcolm got it in the neck when his waywardness failed to end the 10th-wicket partnership between David Richardson and Paul Adams.

The next summer saw David 'Bumble' Lloyd appointed as coach, and he certainly injected more levity and unpredictability. England beat India but lost to Pakistan; Wasim and Waqar were impressive again, as was Inzamam-ul-Haq, a bearlike batsman with exquisite touch and timing. Two Tests in Zimbabwe then saw Bumble's temper tipple over. The hosts used whatever tactics they could get away with at Bulawayo, bowling wide and slowing things down. The scores finished level, prompting the coach to declare, ludicrously: 'We flippin' murdered them.'

The 2–0 win in New Zealand was much better, though. In fact, it was the best campaign under Atherton, with no series victory coming in the major ones against Australia (1994/95, 1997) and West Indies (1993/94, 1995 and 1997/98). With Stewart, Thorpe, Nasser Hussain and John Crawley in New Zealand, that was a talented batting unit; and then they had a bowling battery of Gough, Cork, Andrew Caddick, Alan Mullally and White, as well as two good spinners in Tufnell and Robert Croft. All in all, that was a strong, balanced side. Something important was happening behind the scenes too, now. Illingworth had moved on and the sensible, diplomatic David Graveney – a prince of protocol – was head of selectors, and Lord MacLaurin had become chair of the England and Wales Cricket Board. With his experience of running Tesco and Vodafone, things would be altogether more professional in the years to come, with the fastidious Tim Lamb, a former Northamptonshire seamer who strangely had the Indian sign on David Gower, as his chief executive.

The following summer's Ashes could not have started more excitingly for England: Hussain, with 207, and Thorpe, who made 138, combined to help England win at Edgbaston. When McGrath bowled the hosts out for 77 at Lord's, it looked a false dawn, but the weather saved them there. Steve Waugh made back-to-back centuries at Old Trafford, and Warne and McGrath took 16 wickets between them. At Leeds, Atherton was handed Mike Smith, Gloucestershire's in-form left-arm swinger, by the selectors. He was denied the new ball. Thorpe at slip dropped opener Matthew Elliott off him on 29, and he went on to make 199. Smith went wicketless, and told a journalist that hardly anyone spoke to him throughout the match.

Which sounds like an incomprehensively shabby way of treating someone. Jason Gillespie was this time the Australian bowler who was too good for England. The hosts were clutching at straws when they picked the Hollioake brothers at Trent Bridge. Adam's main strength was leadership, and Ben had a special all-round talent, but was raw. McGrath and Warne took seven wickets each, and Australia had won the Ashes again.

A consolation victory at The Oval persuaded Atherton to carry on with the job for that winter's tour to the Caribbean, beyond the traditional four-year cycle that had become the norm for England captains. It was not a success. The first Test on a Sabina Park death-trap in Jamaica was swiftly abandoned after 10.1 overs. The teams then played back-to-back Tests at Trinidad and won one each. They were low-scoring thrillers. It was game on. Alas, Shivnarine Chanderpaul's 152 on a poor pitch at Guyana laid the foundations for victory, with Atherton managing only 0 and 1. He battled hard to save the series at Barbados with 64 in the second innings – an innings that must have required every ounce of his famous determination, but West Indies held on. It was a bitter disappointment, and he called time on a captaincy tenure that had promised so much.

Stewart's moment had come. He was well-organised, a fine player of pace, but he was less adept against spin, especially Warne. He kept well, which rightly sees him categorised as one of England's finest all-rounders (if you include wicket-keepers/batsmen in that discussion). At this stage there was no scandal. In 2000 he was accused of receiving £5000 from an Indian bookmaker, after being named in a police report. He denied the charges and to my knowledge never talked about it publicly again. His tenure started well, with a terrific 2–1 series win at home to a strong South Africa side that featured Donald, Shaun Pollock and Jacques Kallis. Atherton made a century in the drawn opener at Edgbaston. Stewart demonstrated his Stakhanovite work ethic by batting at No. 3 and keeping. The tourists' aforementioned trio were instrumental in bowling England out cheaply twice to earn victory at Lord's. Stewart's 164 helped England scrape a draw at Old Trafford. Back-to-back five-wicket hauls from Fraser then saw England level the series at Trent Bridge.

The Test is famous for Donald's wrath at Atherton, after he was not given out for an obvious caught behind by New Zealand umpire

Steve Dunne. Fury and fire were unleashed at him, but he stood firm to make 98 not out. England then took the series at Headingley, with a few questionable decisions by umpire Javed Akhtar upsetting the tourists. This was a fine start for Stewart, although he was livid when England were spun out by Muttiah Muralitharan at The Oval on a 'Bunsen burner' in a one-off Test against Sri Lanka to conclude the summer. Ideal Ashes preparation it was not. Many people branded Murali a chucker, but to me it was clear. Chucking is when you start with a straight arm and it bends, or vice versa. Murali had a bent arm that stayed bent, thanks to a quirk of his anatomy.

Nevertheless, despite that annoyance for England, hopes were high that they could give Australia a better contest than had been the case in recent times. The hosts were the better side at Brisbane, until rain saved England. Fraser dropped Ian Healy at third man on 36 – which probably wakes him up in the night still – and he went on to make 134, with Steve Waugh scoring 112. Mark Butcher struck a classy century in reply. On his day he looked wonderful, but he lacked consistency. Fleming was the spearhead of Australia's attack at Perth as they took the lead in the series, and centuries from Slater and Justin Langer saw Australia go two-up. Even though Warne was injured, Stuart MacGill was an able locum (if only he had been English), and McGrath was in his pomp by now. So, it was commendable that England won at Melbourne. Stewart made a century and a half-century, and Dean Headley's memorable spell of 5 for 26 on the final day sealed things. It was such a shame that he was restricted to 15 Tests through a combination of lazy stereotyping that he was an overseas specialist, and injury.

Warne returned for the final Test – Taylor's 50th and last as captain – and took a wicket in each innings, but it was MacGill who destroyed England, with match figures of 12 for 107. All in all, it was not a bad showing by England, though – probably their best in all the series against Australia from 1989 to when they finally turned the corner, in 2005. Stewart was not a hugely imaginative captain: he tended to share Gooch's view that if the cupboard of English spin bowlers was bare, do not bother with them, but he was at least getting his team to play reasonably consistently. After a dire World Cup campaign at the start of the following summer, which saw Stewart and his side publicly express their displeasure about money, England decided to turn to a new leader, however. It was harsh on Stewart, although his replacement, Hussain, did a superb job.

The spring of 1999 was made considerably more bearable for me from my unadorned flat in South London by watching a gripping contest in the Caribbean. In many ways it was the last time West Indies could claim to be a world force (although they still regularly embarrass England at home). When Australia thumped the hosts at Trinidad, things did not augur well. Lara, by now captain, made 213 in Jamaica to help his side level the scoreline, and then made 153 not out in one of the most gripping Tests of all time, in Barbados. It was a Sunday night, and my housemates and I did not move for hours as McGrath, Gillespie, Warne and MacGill threw everything at it. With Jimmy Adams' help and even Curtly Ambrose chipping in with 12 priceless runs, Lara snuck his side over the line for a one-wicket win. Sport does not get any better. Steve Waugh was skipper by now and led his side to a series-levelling win in Antigua. He dropped Warne for the match, something that their relationship never really recovered from. Warne's injured shoulder was proving bothersome. Could this be the end? Alas for England, the answer was no.

Many had been surprised to see Hussain appointed. As a youngster he was seen as solipsistic and a hothead, the type to bash chairs with his bat when he was out. He channelled that inner aggression and determination for the good of the team to become a shrewd and inspirational leader, however. I ghost-wrote columns of his for several years during this time, and do the job again now for *The Cricketer*. He can be genial and charming, although he is still hugely focused, and if he feels something is not right, he will call you out. As captain he was a shrewd handler of the media, and this gave him an undoubted advantage over Atherton. In my experience, rightly or wrongly, journalists will give players and coaches an easier ride if they are friendly and co-operative with them.

The Hussain era began with a memorable victory over New Zealand at Edgbaston, one that saw the nightwatchman Alex Tudor score 99 not out. The enormity of the task ahead dawned on Hussain as that first summer unfolded, though. The cool and calculating Zimbabwean Duncan Fletcher was to become coach, but not until the winter. He wanted to see out his contract with Glamorgan. New Zealand won at Lord's and The Oval; no England batsman scored above 64 in either match, and in Chris Cairns, the tourists had a champion all-rounder. At the end of the summer, England were ranked bottom of the unofficial world Test standings, which seems odd considering that they had beaten South Africa the year before. Nevertheless, in many ways it made the challenge facing Hussain – and Fletcher – easier. The only way was up.

Fletcher was an interesting, if shy and slightly awkward, man. He helped devise Zimbabwe's vehicle number-plate system. It illustrates his attention to detail, and talent at devising accessible and effective methods and protocols. He was excellent at watching a batsman and assessing what they were doing wrong. Steve James says he had 'the sharpest brain in cricket'. The bowlers were never quite so keen on him, however.

With England 2 for 4 after being put in by South Africa on the first morning of the first Test at The Wanderers, Fletcher must have wondered what he had let himself in for. England had picked some new players. Some immediately belonged, like Michael Vaughan, but others – Chris Adams, Gavin Hamilton and Darren Maddy – did not cut it. Fine county players, not Test cricketers. Was this because they were picked by Graveney, for whom the same description could apply?

So the decade ended on a flat note for England, but statistics show that they were more successful in the 1990s than the 1980s, despite having fewer obvious match-winners. It did not always feel that way. Results had improved against West Indies, but they were much worse against Australia. To be fair, Australia were probably the greatest all-round side Test cricket has seen. There will be advocates of West Indies in the 1980s, with their pace and power, but the Australians had Warne, and even MacGill … wristspin wizardry.

Maybe it was my age, but Atherton and Stewart did not quite seem such characters as Gooch, Gower, Lamb and Gatting; Fraser, Malcolm and Tufnell produced some thrilling moments, but the latter duo certainly lacked consistency. And there was no one like Botham, which I suppose is not all that surprising. He was a one-off.

16

JACK RUSSELL, THE ARTIST

*'The most aggressive players, who could kill you, destroy you
... all had the best defence. You couldn't get them out.'*

Fortunately, Jack Russell is less secretive these days. As the wonderfully
quirky wicket-keeper for Gloucestershire (1981–2004) and England
(1988–1998), he was fiercely protective of his privacy. If anybody
visited his house, then they had to be blindfolded.

Russell, 60 at the time of our interview, has calmed down since
his retirement, his painting giving him serenity. He asks me to meet
him in a tearoom in Bishops Park, Fulham, and when I arrive, he
kindly buys me a cuppa. There is a new teabag in each mug – not
like the same one that he used to recycle through a tour, hanging it
on a clothes peg to dry out.

I have interviewed him a few times, and he is probably the most
amiable former cricketer I have had dealings with (OK, level with
Goochie). A sheer delight. He is in Fulham for a few days, and his

sojourn there will culminate in an intriguing commission sitting in Craven Cottage on the Saturday, painting the hosts' 3–0 win over Tottenham Hotspur. It sounds delightfully old school, fitting for the ultimate boutique London football stadium.

At this stage I have assembled a number of voices I know I can rely on to be as reverential to the Test game as I am... It is still my intention to find a few T20 devotees – after all, we would not want an echo chamber, a modern crime.

He is there when I arrive, of course, and is taking up a small corner of the establishment. An easel, folded up, and several bags of kit are all stashed away neatly. I ask him when he first discovered Test cricket. He tells me enthusiastically:

> My very first memory was being called in from the village green where I was playing cricket by my dad, who said, 'Come and watch the news.' We only had a black-and-white telly, and it was England's 1970/71 Ashes series in Australia, and the jubilant England players were carrying Ray Illingworth off after the final Test victory at Sydney. I continued watching Test matches through the 1970s. I saw Bob Massie's amazing series for Australia in England in 1972: 16 wickets at Lord's... But I recall the 1975 and 1977 Ashes series better. I would get my scorebook out – I still have it. I kept a scorebook for John Edrich's 175 against Australia at Lord's in 1975. That sticks in my head. In 1977, at Headingley, Alan Knott caught Rick McCosker off Tony Greig, diving, one-handed. An amazing catch. That was the moment that I decided that I was going to keep wicket for England. And 1976 ... the drought summer ... watching Viv [Richards] bat for West Indies and Michael Holding bowling. With the cans banging.
>
> The 1970s... that is when my love of Test cricket sank in. Then Kerry Packer came along to upset the applecart, but they eventually sorted it. We lost Knotty to Packer, but Bob Taylor came in. You couldn't copy Knotty, although later I did pick his brain, but I copied Bob. I also have memories of England in Australia, and the Channel 9 theme ['New Horizons'], with Richie [Benaud].

I make a mental note that it was interesting to hear him talk about Edrich, as I remember that he helped Russell with his batting when he was England assistant coach under Illingworth. 'How long can you coach me?' an appreciative Russell had asked. He continues:

I then started with Gloucestershire and county cricket in the early 1980s. I was playing club cricket in New Zealand in 1983/84 when England were there, and I saw the [third] Test at Eden Park in Auckland. That was the first Test match that I saw live. Bob was keeping. We had lost at Christchurch [the second Test] for the first time [the series was lost 1–0]. Tony Pigott made his debut; he had to cancel his wedding to play. It was exciting when I played a Test at Auckland myself, in 1991/92 [England won that series 2–0], ahead of the World Cup. At the end of that series in the draw at Wellington, Syd [Gloucestershire teammate David Lawrence] hurt his knee, which was wretched.

But Test cricket was also great in the 1980s. People cite so-called 'boring' players like Chris Tavaré, but batsmen like that did a job, they took the shine off the new ball … and believe me, Tav could smash it around if he wanted to. I saw him score a hundred in what seemed about an hour for Somerset at Taunton once.

I recall Ian Botham saying how grateful he had been for the role Tavaré played – 78 from 289 balls – when he scored his thrilling century – 188 from 102 balls – at Old Trafford in the Ashes in 1981, and Russell agrees.

I was there for Russell's England debut, in the one-off Test against Sri Lanka at Lord's, in 1988. He then played in the 1989/90 series in the West Indies, and although they lost 2–1, they were unlucky, and it was a monumental upturn in England's fortunes against West Indies, after a decade of misery. Gooch was determined that the under-achievements of the 1980s, despite having a team of talented individuals, would not be allowed to continue. Russell won 54 Test caps in total, suffering because he was competing with Alec Stewart, one of England's greatest all-rounders.

After harvesting his memories, we reflect on the plight that Test cricket finds itself in. He says:

I am a purist. It is the ultimate test. I have nothing against the white-ball stuff, though. Just do not let it take over completely, that is my beef. And do not prioritise it. Why do they do that? Test cricket still makes a lot of money. When England are doing well in the Ashes, the country unites; it is the first thing on the news at 6 p.m. You cannot get in the grounds. It still makes up most of the TV money, so it does not even make business sense to neglect it and undermine it. Why are the accountants allowing this to happen? Why are we putting it in danger?

When we started playing the T20 format in 2003, there were five group games, I think. I played in a couple of them for Gloucestershire. I joke that it just about finished me off, and I retired the following year. In 2005 they then increased the group games from five to eight. It was overkill. It killed it for me. Saturation.

Test cricket is special. I have not painted many T20 matches. I prefer painting the whites to coloured clothing. Test cricket has to pay its way, I understand that. And in some of the nations it does not, which is why they need their T20 tournament ... Sri Lanka, West Indies. But that is not the case in England. Maybe it is me being old-fashioned. Having played Test cricket, and understanding it ... the nuances of it ... but the spectators who I talk to still love Test cricket, and county four-day cricket. There is a real, deep passion. The crowds are decent, and it produces Test players. Why can't we have all the formats, and schedule it sensibly? Then you will not have the younger players facing such difficult choices.

The other thing that troubles me is people going straight into a Test match after playing only T20. It worries me to death. Because 'Lady Cricket' does not take any prisoners, and you will get found out. She will sort you out. If you do not prepare properly, if you take liberties ... she will chop you. She has chopped me a few times. The lad [Jason] Roy came in [against Australia in 2019] and did not have the basic defence. He nicked off and was bowled a lot. Look at Viv, and Brian Lara, Gordon Greenidge, Ricky Ponting, Matthew Hayden, the list is long... The most aggressive players, who could kill you, destroy you ... all had the best defence. You couldn't get them out. They kept the good balls ... or sometimes hit them for four. Viv's defences [Jack enacts a big forward defence] down the wicket like that. T20 is not preparation for Test cricket, unless the wickets are very flat.

With Bazball, we are going along that road a bit … scoring at four or five an over. I don't have a problem with the aggression. I would like to have played with freedom. It felt like we were in shackles: two bad games and you are out of the side. Even Chris Broad, who had done all sorts, an Ashes hero [1986/87]. There were no central contracts. I played in the six Tests at home in 1989, but only about three of us did. We used 29 players! It was pretty chaotic, and unnerving. You could not get any 'team thing' going. The day that we lost the Ashes [following defeat in the fourth Test] the rebel tour to South Africa was announced. I didn't have a clue that it was even in the offing. There were two dressing-rooms at Old Trafford and it was all done in the backroom. I wasn't asked and I wouldn't have gone if I had been. I was really cheesed off that the news broke the day I scored my century [128 not out]. Losing the Ashes was such a choker anyway, and I did not celebrate my hundred for a few days. I would like to have played for Brendon McCullum. He would have made me a better player. They were right to get rid of those shackles, but you do need some responsibility at times.

And what about draws, Jack? Apparently they are redundant…

Agh, Johannesburg 1995/96. People mention that and my [flowerpot] hat – those two things. Yes, I think England fans are proud of that draw against South Africa. Athers [Mike Atherton] batted two days, and I did just the one. It was enthralling. I suppose that it was not, or *is* not, everyone's cup of tea, but sometimes a draw is a good result if you have been in a bad position. Look also at the Ashes Tests at The Oval in 2005 and Cardiff in 2009, Matt Prior at Eden Park in 2012/13. Everyone was on the edge of their seats. They were thrilling.

Bazball is good, but not on its own. Bazball plus patience plus brain power is the solid combination. There are periods when you need to lay into the opposition, and others when you need to defend. Joe Root averaged 50 in Test cricket playing his natural game. He is like one of the older guys wanting to be in with the kids. When he started playing normally again [in India in the spring of 2024] runs came again.

It seems fair to say that Russell agrees with the premise of this book.

I feel guilty that I have taken up his time, when he should be painting. He replies:

> I like to be accurate about the recording of a particular moment
> in time. I always paint the weather on the day. I am trying to get
> you there in the moment. That is why I have to go on the day.
> I have painted most of the county grounds, and been to some
> places where the ground does not even exist any more – but I still
> want to get the feel of the place. Cameras are great but they don't
> always give you the correct colour, or perspective...

I say I will walk with him back to the Thames. We admire the buildings... Some look as if they could be in Amsterdam. It is clear that the light is not up to the mark, however. It has become gunmetal grey and gloomy, after a burst-fire of misty rain. He says it does not matter; he will return later that evening, when the lights are on. He loves Victorian streetlamps and is excited by the gap between the buildings on the south side of Putney Bridge. An artist with the gloves, and now with the paintbrushes; it is always a pleasure to spend time with him.

17

TEST CRICKET IN THE 2000S

'[England v India in 2002] was a high point in terms of technical excellence in the history of the Test game.'

The start of a new millennium did not offer immediate relief for Nasser Hussain, and – with a nod to Tony Blair and New Labour – his 'new England' project. They lost by an innings in the fourth Test at Cape Town, with those champion cricketers Allan Donald, who took five wickets in the first innings, and Jacques Kallis and Daryll Cullinan, who both scored first-innings centuries, bullying this fledgling outfit. It had been such a tough winter … but charity was about to come to the rescue. After three and a half days had been lost to rain in the final Test at Centurion Park, South Africa made 248 for 8, declared, and then their captain Hansie Cronje stunningly offered Hussain a lifeline: South Africa would forfeit an innings, England would be invited to reciprocate, and then have a target of 249 for victory. This was pre-Bazball, though, and the pragmatic Hussain nearly refused it. In the end, he decided that the terms were too good to be rejected. There was a reason for that … they were indeed too good. England chased down the target, not without drama, in a truly gripping afternoon of Test cricket. But it later emerged that Cronje was in the vice-like grip of bookmakers. He was ultimately destroyed by these parasites. Cricket will forever have match-fixing stains on its reputation as a consequence of this affair, and others like it. Looking at it sympathetically, being trapped like that must have been horrendously hard for Cronje, who then died in 2002 in a plane crash.

Elsewhere that winter, the Baggy Green was still dominant. There was no sign of the Indian resurgence that would come soon, as Australia whitewashed them 3–0 at home. This was in spite of the key avengers assembling – VVS Laxman, Rahul Dravid, Sachin Tendulkar (still underwhelming as skipper) and Sourav Ganguly. A line-up led by Steve Waugh and including Ricky Ponting, Shane Warne, Michael Slater, Adam Gilchrist, Mark Waugh and Glenn McGrath, who took five wickets in each innings in the SCG finale, was too powerful. Australia also went on to win 3–0 in New Zealand. Who was ever going to be strong enough to stop them?

Well, England would eventually, but not yet. They had taken three steps to put them on the right path, though. One was appointing Hussain as captain. The second was – finally – introducing central contracts in 2000, which meant that their fast bowlers no longer had to be flogged in county cricket. The third was introducing two divisions into the County Championship, injecting a much-needed catalyst of competitiveness.

In the case of central contracts, compare the cases of Australia's McGrath and the England trio of Graham Dilley, Neil Foster and Angus Fraser. Dilley, sadly now deceased, was superb in the 1986/87 Ashes. Alas, his career was hampered by injuries, including in his knees and neck. He delivered 8192 balls in Test cricket, out of a first-class total of 34,418 (a percentage of 23.80). Foster was plagued by back and knee problems. He sent down 6262 balls in Tests, out of a first-class haul of 45,833 (13.67 per cent). Fraser bowled 10,876 balls in Tests out of 56,281 (19.32 per cent). Compare this to McGrath: 29,248 in Tests, out of 41,759 (70 per cent). New South Wales's loss was Australia's gain. Among the first beneficiaries of England's new deals were Darren Gough and Andrew Caddick, who formed a potent partnership that did not shrink in comparison with Fred Trueman and Brian Statham. 'When I started with England, because we didn't have central contracts, players would come for a week of Test cricket and then go back to the counties,' said Mike Atherton. 'We didn't develop a cohesive sense of who or what the English team was. It was very difficult without them, because you are still playing lots of county cricket between Tests. Fast bowlers would arrive knackered, or often injured.'

Hussain, the beneficiary, said: 'Before central contracts, everyone turned up as county players – they might be there next game, might not be. You would get your £1200, play your game, usually lose and wait to see if your name was read out next time on the Radio 5 sports bulletin.' He continued: 'When you know you are playing for a team and you know your teammates, you can create so much more in terms of bonding and morale. You could turn up with bowlers who were fresh. Bowlers are like gold dust.'

Hussain had earned a reputation as intense and somewhat selfish. The best advice was to rush to the balcony to get out of his way when he was out and making his way back to the dressing-room. He recalibrated his passion and fire to be just the captain England needed at this time, however. He was inspirational, determined and fierce if necessary. He was like Neil Kinnock: they made England/the Labour Party fit for purpose, before Michael Vaughan/Tony Blair came along to finish the job (they also have the same birthday). Standing at mid-on instructing his bowlers, Hussain was like a soldier loading and programming a mortar launcher – 'Seven degrees to the left!' It was a bit much at times for Andrew Flintoff and a few others. Oh well.

Elsewhere that winter, there was no more potent bowler in Test cricket at this time than Muttiah Muralitharan. He took 26 wickets to help Sri Lanka win 2–1 in Pakistan, including 10 in the second Test at Peshawar, which was his 50th.

Back in England, with Duncan Fletcher's effective methods also starting to percolate, England defeated the strongest side Zimbabwe ever had, then faced West Indies, who they had not beaten in a series since 1969. The tourists looked vulnerable, but they still had three champion cricketers. Two of them, Curtly Ambrose and Courtney Walsh, found the up-and-down bounce on a length in the first Test at Edgbaston absolutely to their liking. Hussain was livid that the pitch had played into the visitors' hands, but he had assembled a fine attack by now. Darren Gough, Andrew Caddick and Dominic Cork – the latter when he had the ball swinging – helped England hit back; they also had Craig White reverse-swinging it, posing problems in particular for the West Indies' king, Brian Lara. He made a hundred at Old Trafford, but when he failed, England won at Lord's, Headingley (Caddick taking four wickets in four balls) and The Oval. The match at HQ was one of the most gripping of all time. The second day featured parts of all four innings. Then on the third, the Saturday, England crept over the line by two wickets. There were no reports of spectators gnawing their umbrella handles, but there should have been. What a day that was. I had started reporting on most Saturdays for the *Sunday Telegraph* that summer at county and international matches, but unsurprisingly the gig for that day was nabbed by a senior man.

The worry for Hussain was his own form: he did not make 100 Test runs in the summer, averaging 10. He came close to quitting. Scyld Berry had the story all written up next to me at The Oval in case. Thank goodness he did not need to run it, for Hussain's exit would have set England back considerably... and probably denied them one of their greatest winters.

In November 2000, Bangladesh joined the Test club, hosting India in their inaugural match at Dhaka. Also, that month, England were in Pakistan. Hussain's personal woes continued as the first two Tests were drawn, the teams jabbing and circling each other. Another admirable vigil of defiance from Atherton earned them a draw in the second at Faisalabad. Hussain did manage a half-century at Karachi in the finale, but his leadership was the instrumental factor in determining the result. Usually if a team posts more than 400 in the first innings of a Test in those pre-Bazball days, as Pakistan did, they should have been safe. Atherton helped England reach near-parity, although he was criticised for slow scoring, his 125 being chipped out painstakingly in nine hours and 38 minutes. As any student of Test cricket over a lengthy period of times knows, however, you don't have to play 'Bazball', or a form of it, to win matches. England chased down 176 in the dark, with umpire Steve Bucknor punishing the hosts, led by Moin Khan, for their time-wasting by preventing them from taking their ball home.

Part two of their winter of wonder came in Sri Lanka. This triumph was perhaps even more incredible for England, as they actually lost the first Test at Galle by an innings. Muralitharan claimed seven wickets in the match, but for once was outshone by Sanath Jayasuriya, his occasional slow left-arm twirlers pouching eight (he took only 98 in total in 110 Tests). Who on earth thought England could win the series from there? They did, however, with Hussain's streaky hundred giving them a handy lead at Kandy. He was reprieved twice by home umpire BC Cooray, with a local newspaper declaring 'BC bats for England'. Hussain had earned the luck for his courageous captaincy, however. Graham Thorpe was his key batsman in these conditions, helping England scrape over the line. Thorpe held his nerve again at Colombo, after a century in the first innings. Unfussy and dependable, he seemed the latest in a production line of quality and dependable Surrey batsmen who had served England so well, following Ken Barrington and John Edrich.

West Indies' demise was gathering momentum, alas. Ambrose had retired after the tour to England, and they lost 5–0 in Australia. India's batting line-up, on the other hand, had ripened, and they inflicted a stunning defeat on the Australians. It looked business as normal as Australia won by 10 wickets at Mumbai – their 16th successive Test victory. India produced their own 'Headingley 1981' moment at Eden Gardens, Kolkata, however. They trailed by 274 on first innings, but – following on – Laxman, with 281, and Dravid, 180, combined for a stunning, epic stand of 376. Harbhajan, the off-spinner with the fiery temperament of a paceman, finished Australians off, taking his wicket haul to 13 in the match. He recorded India's maiden Test hat-trick in the first innings. Credit to Australia for fighting so hard in the finale at Chennai; most sides would have been beleaguered after that. Matthew Hayden made 203 but could not prevent India establishing a crucial first-innings lead of 110, thanks to Tendulkar's 126. Hayden was a dream of an opener, free-scoring against the new ball: a player who certainly would have been to the liking of Brendon McCullum. Harbhajan was even more potent in this match, though, taking 15 wickets. He managed 32 wickets in the series – the next highest tally on his side was three. Then, fittingly, it was Laxman who played the crucial innings to take India over the line.

England supporters hoped that Australia were finally vulnerable to an Ashes assault, but they were the nut that Hussain just could not crack. He broke his finger in 2001 to miss the second and third Tests, and when he returned for the fourth at Headingley, England trailed 3–0 to Steve Waugh's side. They won at Leeds, with Mark Butcher's remarkable, unbeaten 173 taking advantage of stand-in skipper Adam Gilchrist's slightly benevolent declaration, but Australia clinched a 4–1 series result with victory at The Oval. Waugh defied medical advice after injuring himself playing squash – pool sessions, stretching, walking, gym and massages saw him return, and he scored 157 not out in the final Test, practically batting on one leg.

The Hussain era had peaked, but England continued to be competitive, the embarrassments of the recent boom-or-past past banished ... although as the Chancellor of the Exchequer at the time, Gordon Brown, was to find out when he promised financial stability, they would return. One of the most interesting Tests England played during this period was against New Zealand at Christchurch in 2001/02. Drop-in pitches had made teams reassess tactics. Instead of disintegrating gradually over five days, their extra grass at the start made them spicy, before they then became benign. Nathan Astle's 222, from 168 balls the fastest double-century in Test cricket, gave England the fright of their lives. Once again they had reason to thank Thorpe, who also made a maiden double-ton. From 231 balls, that was not slow, either.

This England side unearthed two fine batsmen. On his day Marcus Trescothick seemed like a left-handed Gooch, and he dominated the 2002 home series win over Sri Lanka. Duncan Fletcher had identified his promise when he was playing for Somerset, in an innings of 167 against a Glamorgan attack that included Kallis at Taunton in 1999. The season before, Trescothick had only averaged 31.37 in the first-class game. He had a terrific Test career, however, with 5825 runs at an average of 43.79. He was fearsome against fast bowling, and found an effective method against spin, using Fletcher's forward-press to smother Harbhajan, Muralitharan, Warne and co., and slog-sweeping them to relieve pressure.

Fletcher knew Michael Vaughan was special as soon as he saw him bat, but in the summer before he was called up (1999) he averaged 27.10 for Yorkshire. He proved himself to be exceptional before knee injuries hampered him, with six Test tons in 2002 (seven if you include the New Year Test at Sydney). Radiating elegance, he made a hundred against Sri Lanka at Lord's, three in a superb home rubber with India, and then was England's hero, in vain, Down Under with three more in yet another emphatic defeat to Australia (technically, the third was in 2003).

The 1–1 series at home to India in 2002 was a joy to report on. Test cricket was still the dominant format at this stage, no doubt. Just quality batsmen v fine bowlers, and no need for rebranded gimmickry, or players trying reverse scoops or ramps to show how clever they were (danger was imminent, however, with the 2003 Twenty20 Cup arriving in England the following summer). India had Virender Sehwag in their line-up by now. Low-achieving openers had been moved aside to make way for this brilliant, belligerent batsman who was Bazballing before the word had been invented. In his first innings of the series he pummelled 84 from 96 balls (actually he never fared that well against England, averaging 29 compared to 49 overall, but he was the quintessential new type of opener). Hussain's 155 helped England win at Lord's, and they had the better of the draw at Trent Bridge, thanks to Vaughan's 197. Dravid secured the draw on the final day, in front of a full house. Tons from Dravid, Tendulkar and Ganguly allowed India to hit back at Headingley, and the final Test at The Oval was dictated by Vaughan's 195 and Dravid's 217 – these two chess grandmasters ensuring a stalemate. That series was a high point in terms of technical excellence in the history of the Test game.

Warne dispelled all doubts about his longevity after all the injuries and setbacks he had that winter, taking 27 wickets in a 3–0 series win in Pakistan. He was ready for England again in 2002/03. The tourists badly missed the injured Gough, and with Vaughan not firing at the Gabba, Warne helped Australia bundle them out for 79 in the second innings. Hayden scored 300 runs in the Test; if Dravid was the Wall, Hayden was the dam. Vaughan looked a cut above his England team-mates, his cover drive and swivel-pull having us all purring. He made 177 at Adelaide, but Steve Waugh's men won there as well. If Vaughan looked as good as Ponting, who made 154, that year, sadly injury and possibly later the weight of captaincy did not allow the Englishman to shine as long. England surrendered the Ashes 11 days into the series at Perth, and lost again at the MCG, despite Vaughan's

145, with Justin Langer making his highest Test score: 250. England did take a thrilling Test at the SCG for their customary consolation victory. It was a match memorable for skipper Steve Waugh silencing his critics who said that he should quit, making a century with a four off Richard Dawson's final ball of the second day, which was ever so slightly wide. Vaughan made 183, but never ruled the world as a batsman again; he did become a fine captain, however, and then, later, a ballsy commentator.

The following summer Vaughan took over the one-day captaincy of England; Hussain, worn down by the politics surrounding the 2003 World Cup and whether his side should play in Robert Mugabe's Zimbabwe, felt that the tectonic plates had shifted. He handed over the Test brief to Vaughan too, after the draw against South Africa at Edgbaston. I knew it was coming; I just did not have the clout to write it (*see* Chapter 25 on journalism). The tourists were, as ever, a tough outfit. They had a leviathan of an all-rounder in Jacques Kallis, whose bulwark batting ground out runs and whose whippy swing bowling chipped in with useful wickets. In addition, they were led by Graeme Smith. His technique may well have been limited to a few highly effective shots, but he knew his game inside out, and he made 277 at Birmingham, then 259 in an innings win at Lord's. That Test was a tough baptism for Vaughan, although it did indicate England had a new Botham-esque star, Flintoff, whose 142 in the second innings cleared the bars and had the red-top headline writers salivating. It was a terrific series, with Hussain's hundred helping his new captain chalk up a first win at Trent Bridge, the South Africans hitting back at Headingley and England squaring the series at The Oval. Trescothick, who had once been the heir apparent to Hussain, made 219 in that Test, masking a slight unease that Vaughan had been quiet with the bat in his four Tests in charge so far.

There was one more chance for India's fabulous five to prick Australia's pomposity. Tendulkar, Dravid, Laxman, Sehwag and skipper Ganguly – who deserved enormous credit for moulding such a teak-tough side – helped secure a 1–1 draw against Waugh's men. Dravid, who was on the field the entire match, made 233 in the win at Adelaide. Ponting was ready to assume the captaincy by now, his gambling problems under control, and his 257 at the MCG ensured that his predecessor would avoid defeat in his final series. Waugh's 80 clinched a draw at the SCG, but India yet again showed how much they had changed by defying the scriptwriters and bossing the match.

Australia founded a national cricket academy in 1987. It was a joint initiative of the Australian Institute of Sport (AIS) and the Australian Cricket Board (now Cricket Australia or CA). The idea was to have a batch of elite young cricketers training and playing together, learning the game and life skills – cooking pasta, doing the ironing, and so on – under mentors like Rod Marsh. It took 14 years for England to follow suit, and they even appointed the charismatic Marsh – a fusion of geniality and iron – to take charge. A permanent facility was built at Loughborough University from 2003. In 2007, following the Schofield Report into the disastrous 2006/07 Ashes, the National Academy was renamed the National Cricket Performance Centre. It consisted of a state-of-the art £4.5m indoor training complex. Facilities included lanes enabling full run-ups for seamers and wicket-keepers standing back, Hawk-Eye cameras and advanced biomechanics analysis equipment. The England Lions, 'the next generation', were based here. 'There is no comparison between the facilities that we have here and those in Australia,' said Marsh. 'These are far and away better. Australia will now be aiming to follow what we will be doing.' I got to know Marsh. What a brilliant man he was.

England had a fast bowler by now who was the most potent weapon in Test cricket, but alas, this accounted for a relatively brief period. In the 2003/04 series in the West Indies, Steve Harmison dealt a series of revenge blows after years of suffering at the hands of the Caribbean quicks. His 7 for 12 in the series opener at Sabina Park was the stuff of make-believe. It would have been a 4–0 whitewash for England if Lara had not conjured another of his ridiculously epic knocks, 400 not out at Antigua. He had craved the captaincy for so long, and when it came he did not prove especially adept at the task, but boy could he still bat (OK, OK, some say this knock was selfish, and stopped the hosts trying for a win).

That winter there was also a rare series between Pakistan and India, the first for five years. It seemed to signal a detente, for they visited each other three times in the next three years. India's hosting in 2007/08 was, to date, the last bilateral Tests between the sides, though.

Something exciting was happening to England. Vaughan was an adept leader. Like Mike Brearley before him, he had a 'degree in people'. He was brilliant at coaxing the best out of someone, equally adept at patting someone on the back or kicking another up the backside, depending on what was needed. From mid-on he would chat to Steve Harmison about anything – football, where they were going that night – as long as it was not about his bowling. He caressed Kevin Pietersen's ego, reassured Simon Jones, knew how to deal with the oldies Graham Thorpe and Nasser Hussain, and wound up his Australia counterpart Ponting while pretending to be matey. It was artful stuff.

Fletcher was not so proficient in coaching the seamers, but struck gold with the appointment of Troy Cooley, an Australian who had the insight to get the best out of Flintoff, Harmison, Jones and Matthew Hoggard: the 'Fab Four'. Jones had raw pace and was capable of bowling reverse-swing. County cricket, which can provide a fertile feeding ground for mediocre seamers, was not seeing the best of him. The summer before he was picked by England (2001) he took 17 wickets at 52.17 for Glamorgan. Fletcher insisted upon his selection, however. He had such insight.

In the summer of 2004 England astonishingly won all seven Test matches: three against New Zealand, who were no mugs under the fine captaincy of Stephen Fleming, and four against West Indies. Trescothick was consistently excellent for England at this time except at the end of tours, when he became a bit jaded and homesick; and he had a new opening partner in the organised and industrious Andrew Strauss, who worked out what sacrifices were needed to reach the top, as opposed to his county counterparts who loved beer, curry and nightclubs. England waved goodbye to Hussain, who signed off with a match-winning century against New Zealand at Lord's, making amends after he had run out Strauss, to take up a successful career in the Sky commentary box. Vaughan made back-to-back centuries in the first Test against West Indies at Lord's; Trescothick did the same at Edgbaston.

A trip to South Africa was always an arduous assignment, but victory there ensured that no momentum was lost ahead of the eagerly awaited 2005 Ashes. Strauss had a seriously good series, with three centuries. The hosts did unveil dazzling talents in AB de Villiers and Dale Steyn in this series, though.

And so it arrived… One of the greatest, if not *the* greatest teams ever to play Test cricket, landed to face a resurgent England. McGrath and Warne were not having a bean of it, hogging wickets in the win at Lord's. The one bright spot there was Harmison's bowling in the first innings. He hit Australia captain Ricky Ponting in the face, leaving the Australians in no doubt that England meant business. There was also a hugely promising debut for the maverick Kevin Pietersen, who made a pair of impudent half-centuries. England enjoyed an astonishing stroke of luck at Edgbaston, however, when McGrath stood on the ball before the start of play. England subsequently took advantage, 'Bazballing' their way to 407 on the first day. The great Australian left-handers, Justin Langer, Matthew Hayden and Adam Gilchrist, and the not great but still effective Simon Katich, were wary of Flintoff's pacy, probing bowling at their off stumps. Harmison's slower ball that bowled Michael Clarke was one of the greatest I have seen in the flesh.

Despite a first-innings lead of 99, England were under huge pressure in the second innings with Warne doing his stuff (he took 10 wickets in the match); but Flintoff's fearless 73 calmed their nerves. Australia needed 282 to win, and despite slipping to 220 for 9, they came within three runs of victory, in one of the greatest Test matches of all time. I count myself so blessed to have seen every ball of this match in the ground, working for the *Daily Express* and *Sunday Telegraph*.

Vaughan's 166 so nearly gave England another win at Old Trafford, and Australia's celebrations after securing a draw in Manchester showed how England had finally closed the gap on them. That was a central point of Vaughan's pre-match speech next time around. Flintoff struck a century at Trent Bridge as England won another thriller. Simon Jones was superb in the first innings there, taking five wickets, but injury saw him sit out the second innings; sadly no one knew that this 18th Test cap would be his last. England played a batsman in his place at The Oval, which was a mistake in hindsight; fortunately Flintoff and Hoggard bowled their hearts out there to keep their side in the match, with Harmison starting to look burned out and Australia not overly respectful of the slow-leftie Ashley Giles, as nuggety all-rounder as he was. Pietersen's series had hinted at greatness, and this was the match that saw him confirm that England had a special talent. Yes, he rode his luck, but his 158 in the second innings was the ultimate illustration of the adage, 'the best form of defence is attack', and he secured the draw – with a bit of help from Giles – that ignited a period of national rejoicing. It felt like everybody was talking about cricket. English cricket was at the crossroads. The sky seemed the limit. Sadly for many, Sky TV did limit the renaissance as they were allowed to assume full control of the television rights.

England were not on top of the world for long either. The subsequent tour to Pakistan was a car crash. Vaughan hurt his right knee and was never the same again. Trescothick was locum leader and made 193 in the first Test at Multan, but reckless batting saw England lose there. Mohammad Yousuf was a wonderful player, and his 223 also saw England lose the third Test at Lahore, again their batting collapsing. Comedy writers could reintroduce that into their repertoire once more.

Vaughan's knee trouble resurfaced in India again, and Trescothick's mental health problems came to light for the first time. His wonderful international career was essentially over. England had found another left-handed player who would go on to become a great, however. Alastair Cook made a debut century in the draw at Nagpur after flying in at short notice from the A tour in the Caribbean. He did not have time to be nervous, but he was always a pretty phlegmatic character anyway. Flintoff was skipper, and this series was his captaincy high. Anil Kumble had many times been a thorn in England's side and was still a threat. Initially dismissed as 'not much of a bowler' when scouted by coach Keith Fletcher ahead of the 1992/93 series, the zippy leggie took nine wickets in the win at Chandigarh, and he took 92 against England and 619 in Test matches in total. Flintoff forged a fine steam spirit, though, and inspired a magnificent win at Mumbai. That the theme for the win was Johnny Cash's 'Ring of Fire' owed something to *Inbetweeners*-style humour, but the banter had a bonding effect.

By the following summer Flintoff was also injured, though, so up stepped Strauss as skipper. He made two centuries against Pakistan and it all went rather well, even taking into account the tourists forfeiting the final Test at The Oval; umpire Darrell Hair said they had tampered with the ball, and Inzamam-ul-Haq's side refused to take the field as a result.

England had a tricky choice for captaining in Australia that winter, with no Vaughan or Trescothick available: Flintoff v Strauss. Alas, two things were starting to affect the situation – Duncan Fletcher's judgement was beginning to fail, and Flintoff's ego was becoming problematic. Fletcher and Flintoff did not get on, and ultimately the coach chose Flintoff for the wrong reasons. Watching a motivational DVD, a message flashed up on the screen: 'The team has to be together to beat Australia.' Fletcher concluded: 'It had to be Flintoff... I was not confident that we were making the right decision, but I also knew that if Flintoff was not captain he would be a huge hindrance to the side.' Ouch. Flintoff was a huge star, managed by the former England batsman Neil Fairbrother and part of 'Chubby' Chandler's International Sports Management (ISM) stable. Perhaps the stardom got a bit too much.

With Ponting hell-bent on revenge, the series was disastrous for England. Australia's captain set up wins at the Gabba and Adelaide with scores of 196 and 142 respectively. A glorious driver and timer, has Test cricket seen a better puller? The latter innings was the one that broke Flintoff and England. They made 551 in the first innings, thanks to Paul Collingwood's 206 and Pietersen's 158. They could not lose from there. Could they? Alas, they were like rabbits in Warne's headlights as they slumped to 129 all out in 73 overs, the blond trickster taunting and turning them inside out. They could have done with a bit of Bazball then ... anything to break the shackles. Flintoff turned to the booze on the tour by all accounts, and a whitewash was inevitable. Gilchrist's 57-ball century at Perth was cruel. A decent keeper and blistering batsman, he made the role of specialist stumper who was not expected to make many runs redundant. Warne bowed out after victory at Sydney, 195 of his 708 Test wickets coming against England. Fletcher also departed. Arguably he had been England's finest coach, just pipping Micky Stewart. He was replaced by micro-manager Peter Moores, a fine example of the Peter Principle, the observation that 'in most organisational hierarchies, employees rise in the hierarchy through promotion until they reach a level of respective incompetence'. Perhaps that is a little harsh. He resurrected the international careers of Graeme Swann and Ryan Sidebottom, knew when the time was up for Steve Harmison and Matthew Hoggard, got the best out of James Anderson, and blooded Stuart Broad.

Like Hussain, Vaughan fell on his sword after a home defeat to South Africa, in 2008. His unlikely replacement was Pietersen, chosen because he was a guaranteed pick in all three formats. Predictably his brashness saw his relationship with the selectors fracture. He told them that 'either Moores went, or he went'. They both went, the selectors punishing him for it. Such an almost uniquely gifted, divisive, tactless, yet sensitive and misunderstood character was never going to be in the job long.

Strauss finally had his chance to take on the captaincy permanently, and with Moores also going, having irritated some of the senior players with his tinkering, assistant coach Andy Flower stepped in. It was a temporary appointment at first, for he felt disloyal replacing Moores, but he gelled with Strauss, and great things were around the corner. As is so often the case, however, the 'Andocracy', as it became known, got off to a spluttering start, England losing 1–0 in the West Indies. The tourists had the chance to level the series, but cautious declarations held them back. It showed West Indies had not completely given up the ghost in Test cricket.

The turnaround for England really began in the Welsh capital, the unusual venue for the first Test of the 2009 Ashes. James Anderson and Monty Panesar were the unlikely batting heroes as England held on for a draw, their siege-defiance worthy of nearby Cardiff Castle. It was thrillingly tense. Thinking back to it, you wonder why Stokes would say that he has no interest in Test match draws. It was deeply frustrating for Ponting, who thought he had set up victory with his 150. Strauss then led from the front with 161 in the win at Lord's, and although England's batting misfired horribly at Headingley, they clinched the series at The Oval. Jonathan Trott made a hundred on debut and looked a great discovery; Broad produced one of his memorable spells – when he got on a roll – that so delighted English crowds; and the building blocks were in place for possibly England's greatest Test side to take the field over the next couple of years.

18

MERV HUGHES COMING IN OFF HIS LONG RUN

'[Test cricket] is tricky at first [...] It has rules and laws all
of its own. Its genius is that as you live with it, you keep
finding new things. There are layers on it that make it last forever.'

With his handlebar moustache (with a hint of beer foam), imposing
torso, slightly mincing gait and catapult delivery, Merv Hughes was
a throwback to the W.G. Grace days. He turned the air blue with
his insults at batsmen, often leaving them stunned, but, somehow,
he remained likeable with it. Certainly, off the pitch he was/is most
genial. He engaged with the crowd, who admired his big-heartedness,
grinning as they joined in with his ostentatious warm-ups, making
them laugh as he tamed a canine pitch invader at Trent Bridge
in 1993. Dramatis personae like him make the Test game. It is no
surprise, therefore, when I discover that he feels strongly that its
survival is imperative.

Hughes was born in 1961 and says the first Test match that he has vivid memories of watching, to the point where he can name it, was the 1977 Centenary match at Melbourne in the March of that year. He admits that he was a 'bit of a latecomer', and other recollections are a bit hazy. He was certainly playing a lot of cricket in his summer, and Aussie Rules in the winter. He does recall listening to the Ashes Tests from England on the radio in the middle of the night (so I am surmising that was the 1975 and 1977 series). He said to me that Bob Willis, Clive Lloyd, Ian Chappell, Dennis Lillee and Rod Marsh 'were the guys that I loved watching'. Then it was 'Kerry Packer's circus, and Bobby Simpson coming out of retirement to lead the official Australian side at that time.' He also watched a lot of Sheffield Shield cricket. 'I lived half an hour out of Melbourne,' he told me. 'On Fridays and Mondays I nicked off school early and went to the MCG by train to watch the last two sessions of Victoria's matches, especially the fast bowlers, Maxie Walker, Alan Hurst and Alan "Froggy" Thomson.' The Australian rebel tour to South Africa in 1985/86 opened up a vacancy for him, and he made his Test debut – the first of 53 caps – against India at Adelaide in December 1985. Although his match figures were modest – 1 for 123 – his next Test was actually more painful (even though that time he took 5 for 162 over both innings). At the Gabba in Brisbane 11 months later, Ian Botham took 22 off one of his overs. He had started well, dismissing Mike Gatting, Allan Lamb and John Emburey. Hughes later revealed his thoughts at the time. 'I can't let him get away with that,' he said to himself. 'Not wanting to be taken lightly, I let him have a bouncer next ball. He hooked it again. The ball struck the fence [at midwicket] with such force that it bounced most of the way back to the middle. "Well done, Merv, nice thinking," I screamed silently to myself. "For God's sake, pitch the next one up."' The result was the same, another four through the same area. Botham then completed the over with a rasping drive over mid-on. 'It was hard to watch,' said Hughes's teammate Steve Waugh. 'A mauling like that can ruin a career.'

'It was certainly a baptism of fire,' Hughes told me. 'I had David Gower dropped early on and he got runs. We copped it that winter, so it was satisfying when we did it to England in 1989, when *they* were distracted by a rebel tour.' Hughes, not for the first or last time, showed indomitability to bounce back, however, and in early 1988 his maiden five-wicket Test haul came against Sri Lanka at Perth. At the same ground later that year, when Geoff Lawson had his jaw broken by Curtly Ambrose, Hughes took 13 for 217 in a desperate effort to avoid defeat (in vain).

Merv delivered a verbal bumper at me when I suggested that West Indies' dominance was coming to an end by then. 'I wouldn't say that – I'd say West Indies were still bloody strong… Desmond Haynes, Gordon Greenidge, Viv Richards, Richie Richardson, Gus Logie, Jeffrey Dujon, Malcolm Marshall, [Curtly] Ambrose, Patrick Patterson and Courtney Walsh…' I take his point; what I meant was, Australia were getting stronger, and about to take their crown as the No. 1 side in the world. 'Steve Waugh, Ian Healy, myself, Dean Jones and Tim May had played a fair bit of cricket together by the 1989 Ashes. We still had AB [Allan Border] as skipper, and we added Trevor Hohns and Carl Rackemann … and Terry Alderman was available again after his ban ended for being on the rebel tour. In English conditions he was pretty good, wasn't he?' He sure was. He took 42 wickets in the 1981 Ashes, and 41 wickets eight years later, helping Australia to a 4–0 win in the latter (Hughes took 19). Australia used 12 players, England 29 (including those who defected to the rebel tour, thus missing the final two Tests at Trent Bridge and The Oval). Hughes also had considerable success in 1993, stepping up when Craig McDermott was ruled out with a twisted bowel. Over the six Tests, he took 31 wickets, helping Australia to a 4–1 victory. Alas, he played only two more Tests, a knee injury striking him down, and he finished with 212 Test wickets at 28.38 apiece. He later became a selector and is now an instantly recognisable figure among the tour groups, becapped and clad in canary yellow – sorry, Australian Gold – in the crowd on Ashes tours and at World Cups.

He says:

When I speak to people about Test cricket they can remember stuff from 30 to 40 years ago. I was sitting on a plane talking to a guy from Pakistan recently and he was recalling a series in which Wasim Akram and Imran Khan both made centuries in the second innings [Adelaide, January 1990], and I thought, 'How do you remember that?' [Merv should have remembered it: he took

5 for 111, his fourth of seven times he took five wickets or more in a Test innings]. And then he started talking about Ijaz Ahmed's 121 in the series opener at Melbourne. That is the difference. People remember what happens in Tests – 1981 at Headingley, Ian Botham; 2019, same ground, Ben Stokes – no one forgets that. They can tell you the year, and exactly what happened.

Compare it to one-day cricket, now that is a bit sketchy. It happens too fast. Apart from World Cups: the blood pumps through the veins when a World Cup is on… India v Pakistan at the MCG in the 2022 T20 World Cup in front of a crowd of 90,000 people – now that was amazing. But apart from that, all the series morph into one for me. Look at those Australia v England ODIs that soon followed. The crowds were not interested. You can recall stuff, but you wouldn't know what year it was. The people who watch and follow Test cricket are cricket lovers.

T20, The Hundred… Everybody will be sick of T20s as they go on too long… T10s … it will be T5s soon. It is the attention span of people these days: now they want everything on a platter, in a hurry. It's all takeaways, while Test cricket is sitting down in a restaurant for fine dining. Only two countries actively promote Test cricket: England and Australia. All the others are pushing towards T20. The IPL, all the franchise cricket … players turning their backs on the longer game, it is a real concern. We should go back to promoting red ball and pushing Test cricket.

What people don't understand is that you might be good enough to win a Test match, but you can also be good enough to stop the other team winning it. Some people can't understand how a game can go on for five days and end up with no result. Some of the best games have ended up in draws, though, and they are some of the ones that I remember the most … because of the heroism of the players. Allan Border batting for five and a half hours for 53 not out against India at the SCG to get the draw [in January 1992]. Things like that hit back.

The best analogy I have heard about the situation was from [former Australia leg-spinner] Stuey MacGill. People who drink wine will understand this. Everything has a place. T20 is the equivalent of people going to a winery and having a taste, as they do not know what they are looking for, and if you like the taste, you buy a bottle. The people who are wine buffs know what they want, though, and buy a case… That is Test cricket.

That analogy is reminiscent of a similar one by James Anderson. He said:

Cricket is [the album] *Revolver* by the Beatles. T20 is 'Yellow Submarine'… catchy and instantly recognisable. It doesn't matter what age you are; you get it. Test cricket is 'Tomorrow Never Knows'. It is tricky at first, irregular and at odds with the other song structures on the album. It has rules and laws all of its own. Its genius is that as you live with it, you keep finding new things. There are layers on it that make it last forever.

And Anderson's message is: they both belong on the same album.

Hughes is right to say that Australians still appear keen on the Test game. Like England, though, I find their tinkering with the schedule annoying. In the 1980s, they seemed to prize all cricket – Tests and ODIs. Each Ashes Test seemed like a major course, with succulent palate cleansers slotted in between, when the players put on their pastel pyjamas and smashed white balls into ink-black skies illuminated by towering floodlights, to the pleasure of adoring crowds. The Australians were initially sceptical of T20. They sent the format up when they played the New Zealanders in the first ever T20I at Eden Park, Auckland, in 2004/05. They wore retro gear, wigs, John McEnroe-style headbands and fake moustaches. Soon they acquired a taste for it, though, and the Big Bash, sponsored by KFC, appeared in 2005/06. From seven matches a tournament to 13, 16, 17, 20, 31, 35, 43, 59, and finally to 61 in 2022/23, it swelled like a genetically modified chicken … until common sense prevailed and it went back to 44.

The history of the Australia Test team is rich. From the first captain, Dave Gregory, who is said to have looked like an 'Old Testament prophet', to the indefatigable seam bowler Fred Spofforth… 'This thing can be done.' There was captain and all-rounder Warwick Armstrong, the 'Big Ship' who circumvented an unbeaten path around England in 1921. Don Bradman's bountiful feats will likely never be matched, but his contemporaries Bill Ponsford, Bill Woodfull, Stan McCabe, Arthur Morris, Neil Harvey and Lindsay Hassett were superb batsmen in their own right. Then there were the spinners who gave it a rip and evoked such mystery, Clarrie Grimmett and Bill 'Tiger' O'Reilly, and sturdy and skilful pacemen like Ray Lindwall and Alan Davidson.

Keith Miller was a great all-rounder and a magnetic character, a surefire guest for your dream dinner party. Richie Benaud was a superb cricketer, but his sagacious commentary transcended that, and he was loved and admired around the world. Bill Lawry was another whose distinctive broadcasting eclipsed his cricket, as good as that was. The 1970s team were a teak-tough and talented crew, with the Chappells, Greg and Ian, leading from the front with the bat, and Lillee and Jeff Thomson hurling down Exocets to Rod Marsh. Their 'taches glistening with Tooheys, the testosterone flowing from every pore. The 1980s gang took a few years to rescale the heights, but Border was always a defiant and courageous batsman – someone you would pick to bat for your life.

Alongside him, Jones exuded confidence and flair. In 1989, I had never seen an off-spinner give the ball such a rip as May, bowling an attacking line outside off stump, and 16 years later, Nathan Lyon picked up his baton and ran with it to carve out a prolific career. Then Shane Warne resurrected leg spin, his skills with the ball combining with bedazzling chutzpah and cheekiness. The runs were posted by the unflinching and indestructible Steve Waugh, his stylish brother Mark, and the counter-punching Ricky Ponting, who would relieve pressure by emerging amid a starburst of strokes. Mark Taylor was a well-organised batsman and gracious leader, and in Glenn McGrath he had a brilliant seamer, the best ever really, clinical and calculating, with the uncompromising aura of Clint Eastwood. Adam Gilchrist, meanwhile, redefined the role of the wicket-keeper/batsman, adept at dismantling attacks, ruining things for inferior candidates whose batting did not cut the mustard, however good their glovework, for generations to come. Matthew Hayden, Justin Langer, Michael Clarke, Mike Hussey and Steve Smith all achieved brilliance with the bat in their own ways.

Finally, the quicks… Mitchell Johnson was the butt of the Barmy Army's jokes in 2010/11. He took 15 wickets in that series at an average of 36.93, but nine of those came at the helpful, bouncy Waca in Perth, at only 9.33… The rest of the time he was like a crop sprayer. The England travelling fans sang:

Who bowls to the left and
Then bowls to the right?
Mitchell Johnson
Who bowls for his side
Then the umpire calls 'wide'?
Mitchell Johnson

In the Ashes series three years later, however, Johnson rammed their words down their throats, taking 37 wickets at 13.97 each. 'His pace forced my body to do things I'd spent my whole career training not to,' Joe Root admitted. For Johnson, that was quite a redemption arc.

That terror has been taken on by Johnson's successors in recent series. Fellow southpaw Mitchell Starc, Pat Cummins, the clean-living Superman lookalike who has also been skipper, and Josh Hazlewood have formed a trio who have exposed England in some ways to the shock and awe of 1974/75. All this in legendary venues that are so distinctive: the gemlike Sydney Cricket Ground with its mint-green grandstands – an emerald city for the wizards of Oz; the colosseum that is the Melbourne Cricket Ground; the boutique Adelaide Oval; and the imposing and intimidating Gabba in steamy Brisbane. Anything or anybody that jeopardises that incredible history and its legacy needs their heads examined.

19

TEST CRICKET IN THE 2010S

'The journey from rock bottom to No. 1 Test team in the world had been long and winding, but Strauss, the calm diplomat, and Flower, the driver, made it happen.'

An anocracy is a form of government that is part democracy, part dictatorship. Whether the 'Andocracy' – the regime of Andrews, Strauss and Flower in charge of the England cricket team – conformed to that is a matter of debate. They certainly pushed their England players to the limit, however, and the results were unprecedentedly good.

Strauss was sensible and collegiate, led by example, and had a strong-minded and able ally in coach Flower. They were the men to make England the best Test side in the world. The journey from rock bottom to No. 1 Test team in the world had been long and winding, but Strauss, the calm diplomat, and Flower, the driver, made it happen. From winning the Ashes at home in 1985, and gloriously so again in Australia 18 months later, to being bottom of the Test rankings in 1999, after a home defeat to New Zealand, Nasser Hussain, Michael Vaughan and Duncan Fletcher laid the foundations for the gradual recovery, then Strauss and Flower finished the job.

Flower, like Fletcher, came from a big family – the former was one of six siblings, the latter five – and they were both shrewd, hard-working, calculating and ruthless when they needed to be. It was Flower who hauled England on the last leg to the summit, combining Fletcher's eye for detail with his own Stakhanovite work ethic. The 2009 Ashes triumph was followed by a truly remarkable one in Australia in 2010/11. Then, in August 2011, England were ranked No. 1 in the world, after a 4–0 home hammering of India.

Key to this renaissance was England eventually, even reluctantly at times, cottoning on to what was going on in Australia. Central contracts created a 'Team England' ethic; an academy was built to match Australia's; and there was an increasing focus on data and insight. Those central contracts were a component of the ECB generally starting to spend more on Team England: in 2005 it was £10.9m, but by 2010 it was £24.8m, according to *The Plan*, a book by the former Glamorgan batsman Steve James, who had played two Tests for England in the Fletcher era.

England treaded water under Peter Moores, a terrific county couch whose micro-managing ways floundered at international level, although he deserves praise for bringing back Ryan Sidebottom and Graeme Swann after they had been frozen out by Fletcher. So the England chiefs turned to Flower. Another good thing that Moores did was bring Flower in as his assistant. Initially reluctant to take on the main job after the way that Moores had been treated, Flower was won round. He was a meticulous planner with a fierce work ethic, and he saw a like-minded cricketer in Strauss.

Strauss was the calm diplomat, Flower the driver. Micro-meetings were crucial in forming winning strategies. Strauss said of Flower:

He's a guy who prefers to lurk in the shadows. He's not good at smiling for starters. He has been immense... incredible... little conversations he has with people, little thoughts he puts on to paper. The way he works with the backroom staff is as good as I've seen in county and international cricket.

A camp in Bavaria was said to be pivotal in forging the team spirit and work ethic essential to winning in Australia, even if Chris Tremlett did break Anderson's rib while boxing (Flower resented the way that it was described as a 'boot camp' by the media). The planning of tours was meticulous. This was especially true of that 2010/11 tour to Australia. The modern way is for tours to be short, to avoid the warm-up matches of old, pandering to player power, ceding ground to franchise leagues, but that winter England had three-day matches, against Western Australia and South Australia, then a four-day match against Australia A at Hobart. The first and third matches were won, the middle one drawn. It paved the way for a 3–1 Test series triumph, winning an Ashes series in Australia for the first time in 24 years. The English team found a way to nullify Australia's captain Ricky Ponting, who was restricted to an average of just 16.14. Flower's insightful work had been pivotal.

When Moores departed, Kevin Pietersen was stripped of the captaincy. After all, he had instigated the mutiny. Upon his return to the ranks, Pietersen needed careful handling. A brilliant, unorthodox batsman in all formats, he was a weird hybrid of arrogance and insecurity. He played breath-taking strokes like the switch-hit and 'the flamingo', which had not been seen from an England batsman before. Strauss and Flower set out a detailed programme to harness his talents and get the rest of the team to accept him. It was successful until the dire 2013/14 Ashes. There were signs that Pietersen was no longer the dominant force he had been. In 2011 in Test matches he averaged 73.10, and in the two subsequent years that slipped to 43.88 and 36.10. The management considered his behaviour to be not worth tolerating any longer, and they discarded him.

Swann was also a quirky character, somewhat hyperactive. He had infuriated Fletcher in South Africa in 1999/2000 with his poor time-keeping and drinking, and was discarded. He admitted that he had not been ready for the international game, and his behaviour had been immature. But after working hard at Nottinghamshire, Moores wisely brought him back. Swann had learned to bowl more defensively when necessary – and developed away-drift. His county captain, Chris Read, told him: 'Stop looking for the dream ball every ball.' He proved, with 255 Test wickets at an average of 29.96, to be the best off-spinner England had had since Jim Laker (193 at 21.24, from 1948–1959), his record even better than that of Fred Titmus (153 at 32.22, 1955–1975) and John Emburey (147 at 38.40, 1978–1995). Swann had a strong action with a powerful shoulder that enabled him to generate plenty of revolutions on the ball (2000 per minute – the same as India's Ravichandran Ashwin. This technology gave England crucial insight). Swann's 1370 Test runs were a handy bonus.

James Anderson had been one of bowling coach Troy Cooley's few failures. The Tasmanian tried to remodel his action to help him avoid injuries, but in doing so risked losing what made him so brilliant – prodigious swing and accuracy. Under Flower's insightful guidance, Anderson reverted to what he knew. He took 24 wickets in the 2010/11 Ashes and has become England's leading Test wicket-taker – an extraordinary 704 wickets putting him third on the world list – the highest seam bowler, behind spinners Muttiah Muralitharan and Shane Warne.

Flower's belief in intensity of focus also brought the best out of Jonathan Trott – England's finest No. 3 for four decades. The insight of selector Ashley Giles from their time together at Warwickshire identified Trott as a Test cricketer. He made 41 and 119 on debut against Australia in the pivotal fifth Test at The Oval in 2009, and in 52 Tests overall averaged 44.08. There had been modest summers for Warwickshire – he averaged only 22.52 in 2007 – but Giles was right to identify technique and temperament as factors that could transcend numbers.

Flower helped everybody. He brought in the maestro, Graham Gooch, and the sturdy Australian David Saker as batting and bowling coaches respectively, and both did fine jobs. He hired Richard Halsall as fielding coach, and subsequently England's fielding was excellent in the 2010/11 Ashes – 66 out of 90 wickets came from catches, with four run-outs to Australia's none. The work of psychologist Dr Mark Bawden was lauded. Flower forced Ian Bell to be fitter, after bringing in the excellent Huw Bevan as fitness coach. He helped Alastair Cook with his backlift during a lean spell. He knew that Strauss needed a rest, so he missed the tour to Bangladesh in early 2010 (Cook stood in as skipper). The attention to detail was extraordinary, even down to the husbandry of the ball that allowed reverse-swing.

When Strauss reached the end in 2012, Cook was anointed on the basis that he was a batsman of the right age, and he certainly looked the part: 'very much the sort of people we want the England captain and his family to be,' said ECB chair at the time, Giles Clarke, in a statement that many labelled as snobbery. Cook was hugely respected for his phlegmatic personality and focused batting, which perhaps explains why he was allowed to plough on for a record 59 Tests as skipper. Winning a series in India in 2012/13 and defending the Ashes at home the following summer were the highlights. The 2013/14 whitewash in Australia that annoyingly followed on immediately – not the finest hour for administrators who wanted to avoid having the Ashes and 50-over World Cup in the same winters – nearly broke him, however. That campaign highlighted the unbelievable scrutiny that comes with the role, especially in Australia. Mark Butcher said of Cook on that tour: 'He seems to be able to do nothing about the outcome of the game once the boulder starts running down the hill. He has no real feel for the nuances of the game.' Ouch.

There was also a surprise 1–0 series defeat to Sri Lanka the following summer, which put him under real pressure. Muttiah Muralitharan had retired in 2010, but the tourists did have one of the finest No. 3/4 duos in Test history in Kumar Sangakkara and Mahela Jayawardene. It did not help that Cook then had his leanest spell in Test cricket. From 2013 to 2015, he went 19 Test matches without a century.

He regained the Ashes in 2015, however. During this decade, Anderson and Stuart Broad profited greatly from central contracts, bowling two-thirds of their first-class deliveries for England. It upset their county fans, but England's Test results were better from 2000–2020 than they were in the preceding 20 years. Broad's spell of 8 for 15 at Trent Bridge was one of the highlights of that Ashes win in 2015. Australia's total of 60 in Nottingham was the shortest opening innings in any Test – 18.3 overs, 111 balls, so a wicket every 11.1. The look of disbelief on Broad's face said it all, when Ben Stokes took an amazing, one-handed catch at gully. England took nine catches in the cordon, surely their greatest close-catching performance of all.

Cook's greatest fans will admit that he was not an imaginative captain, but he was sure and steady, indefatigable really, and his batting overall allowed him to lead by example. The long-term predecessors before him had greater success, however.

As is generally the way, the selectors turned to the best batsman to succeed him. Joe Root will also not be recalled as one of the great captains, although the way that he maintained his brilliant batting form was admirable. He is one of the nicest people to lead England in recent memory, and I admired the way that he tried to put on a show on benign surfaces in the West Indies in 2022 to entertain the travelling thousands, but things drifted at times in the five years that he was in charge. He will be remembered for the 4–0 defeats in Australia (2017/18 and 2021/22), even if administrators, especially in the latter series, may as well have broken his bat, such was the inadequate schedule they presented him with. Take the red-ball neglect of the tenure of England and Wales Cricket Board, whose chief executive was Tom Harrison, add in a woeful pre-Test series fixture list, sprinkle on top players who are jaded by an overdose of 'bubble' life during the Covid pandemic, and … voilà! At least Root managed a 2–2 draw at home to Australia in 2019, thanks to Stokes' brilliance, especially in that nail-biting Test match at Headingley. In 2017, 2019 and 2020 England won every series under Root, but there were times when he and his attack lost the plot, such as against India at Lord's and The Oval in 2021: testosterone-charged short-pitched bowling that tossed away match-winning positions.

So that was England in the 2010s. What about the other countries? Australia continued to dominate India at home but could not master them away. The 2010/11 series in India was a weird two-Test affair. It had been hurriedly scheduled, and although its skimpiness did not set the pattern for encounters between those two nations, it did for others, sadly. The first Test was a thriller at Mohali, won by the hosts by one wicket, and they took the series 2–0.

India actually hosted a longer series that winter against New Zealand, which they won 1–0. The first Test at Ahmedabad was notable for the emergence of Kane Williamson, who made 131 – the beginning of an illustrious career for the Kiwis.

Australia then welcomed India back to their shores again in 2011/12. The tourists had a new star in Virat Kohli, but his maiden Test century at Adelaide in his eighth match could not prevent a 4–0 whitewash. Ponting, now a year away from the end of a wondrous career – as a batsman, anyway – and his successor as captain, Michael Clarke, showed imperious form during the series. The latter made the highest Test score of his career at Sydney: 329 not out. Australia had also found a worthy spinner to succeed Shane Warne. Nathan

Lyon went from working on the Adelaide ground staff to being in the Test squad 12 months later. An attacking bowler who has a command of flight, he became only the second off-spinner to take 500 Test wickets, behind Muralitharan, in the winter of 2023/24.

The Australia/India home-dominance pattern continued in 2012/13: India 4, Australia 0. Mahendra Singh Dhoni was captain of the Indians by now, and made his highest Test score, 224, in the first Test, at Chennai. India at least managed to keep the score down to 2–0 in the four-Test rubber in 2014/15. Steve Smith was starting to make a name for himself. Who was this skittish kid who shuffled around the crease and bowled unimpressive leggies, England fans thought in 2013, at least until he made his maiden Test century at The Oval? Seven centuries in 14 Tests followed, however, including one in each of those Tests against India: 162 not out, 133, 192 and 117. It was an amazing sequence, and thinking about it makes me feel a bit sad to see him struggling so much of late.

Pakistan were being forced to play their 'home' Tests in the United Arab Emirates on benign surfaces that did not make for great Test cricket. It was a tough place for touring sides to play, and Pakistan had a strong middle-order, with the gifted Younis Khan and admirable captain Misbah-ul-Haq, who had waited a long time for his chance, making his Test debut at 26. He went on to enjoy a superb career, making 10 centuries before finally retiring just before he turned 43. The regal Younis made back-to-back tons at Dubai and the 213 at Abu Dhabi as they beat Australia 2–0 in in 2013/14. New Zealand did well to draw a series there in 2014/15, and it was a sign of things to come for England fans in the match that the Kiwis won in Sharjah. New Zealand's captain, Brendon McCullum, reached three figures in 78 balls, and went to make 202 (receiving support from Williamson, who made 192). Really, we should not have been surprised by Bazball.

West Indies were hanging in there; they drew 0–0 in Sri Lanka in a series recalled for Chris Gayle making his Test best score, 333, at Galle. South Africa had a strong decade, thanks to a potent middle-order of classy craftsman Faf du Plessis, the silky Hashim Amla and the belligerent AB de Villiers. England beat them 2–1 on their own patch in 2015/16, however. The passage of play at Newlands, Cape Town, when Stokes made a pulsating 258 from just 198 balls, was one of the most thrilling and satisfying for England's travelling fans in the history of the overseas expeditions. Jonny Bairstow joined in the fun with 150 not out, in an extraordinary stand of 399. For once the beauty of Table Mountain was overshadowed, and the nearby brewery was drunk dry, even if that Test was actually the one that was drawn thanks to Amla's more sedate double-century – 201 from 477 balls – in reply.

With Smith in charge of Australia, they were embarrassed 3–0 in Sri Lanka in 2016. The hosts had another match-winning spinner by now in Rangana Herath. An orthodox slow left-armer, he lacked the mystery of Muralitharan, under whom he had served a long apprenticeship, but he took 28 wickets in the three-Test series on his way to a grand haul of 433 in Tests overall.

Smith did dominate the 2017/18 Ashes, though. He began the series with an unbeaten 141 at the Gabba, and made his highest Test score, 239, at Perth as the series was secured after three matches. Poor Root, captain of England, was poleaxed by the heat, 41°C (105.8°F), in the final Test at Sydney and took to his sickbed.

Later that winter Australia could not maintain that form, though, succumbing 3–1 to hosts South Africa, now led by tough guy Du Plessis. The series will not be recalled for the result, however, but the deep shame of Smith, who lost the captaincy when television cameras picked up the batsman Cameron Bancroft sandpapering the ball – one side shiny, one side scuffed, wait for the reverse-swing. Smith was sent home along with the instigator, his at-times roguish vice-captain David Warner. It instigated a period of deep soul-searching for the Australian nation as a whole and provided considerable comedic material for England fans in forthcoming encounters. Warner will be recalled for his part in the affair, and his later refusal to apologise for it. He should also be remembered as a destructive opening batsman, however: good enough to make 26 Test centuries, even if only three of them were against England.

The IPL, which started in 2008, started to dominate the world scene through the 2010s. The television rights went from £47.5m in its first year, to £910m by 2023. The warning signs were increasingly there for Test cricket.

20

RICHARD HADLEE, THE PRINCE OF NEW ZEALAND

*'[The all-rounders] didn't want to get out to each other;
we had ding-dong battles, and often the media would build
it up prior to the Tests. It lifted things, and it gave the
spectators more interest. They were exciting times.'*

New Zealand's tours to England in my formative years, the 1980s, were low-key compared to those of their boisterous trans-Tasman neighbours Australia but were enjoyable affairs, nevertheless. The Kiwis, in their powder-white, homespun-looking sweaters inflicted some excruciating blows on their hosts.

Sir Richard Hadlee, their main man in that decade, joined me to recall New Zealand's first Test win in England, at Headingley in 1983; their first series victory, at home in 1983/84; and then the first time they took a series in England, in 1986.

The 73-year-old told me in an online interview:

I did not take a wicket in that Test at Leeds. All the wickets fell to bowlers whose surnames began with C – Cairns [Lance, who took 10 in the match], Chatfield [Ewen, six] and Coney [Jeremy, four]. I was a bit unlucky ... but in the book it says, 'RJ Hadlee, no wicket in each innings', for the first and only time in my Test career.

(He did score 75 and six not out in the match. And, actually, there were three other Tests when he did not take a wicket: two against Australia, one of which was rain-affected, at Wellington in early 1982; and another against England, when he was injured in the second innings at Christchurch, in early 1988.) England won the 1983 series 3–1, however, despite Hadlee taking 21 wickets and scoring 301 runs.

Then, that winter, New Zealand beat England 1–0. For the tourists, the trip is recalled as 'the sex, drugs and rock 'n' roll tour' (the part of the latter was overplayed ... allegedly). There were two drawn matches, with England losing at Lancaster Park, Christchurch. They persuaded Sussex seamer Tony Pigott to postpone his wedding to win his only Test cap. England's tactics were disastrous, with Ian Botham persuading them to bump the home batsmen at every opportunity, despite the pitch favouring line and length – Hadlee took 3 for 16 and 5 for 28 as the visitors were bundled out for 82 and 93; he also top-scored with 99 in his side's total of 307.

As well as the aforementioned players, New Zealand had a determined opening batsman in John Wright, brilliant middle-order technician Martin Crowe, and the feisty wicket-keeper/batsman Ian Smith among their notable players. They all played their part in New Zealand winning 1–0, again, in 1986. The only positive result came at Trent Bridge, where Hadlee played for Nottinghamshire. He recorded match figures of 10 for 140, with England dumbfounded at the pitch prepared by Ron Allsopp.

About this time, *The Cricketer* magazine called Hadlee, then aged 35, the 'sultan of swing and seam'. It was a joy to watch him probe the technique of batsmen; only those who played the new ball determinedly straight would survive. Hadlee said to me in an interview:

As a 21-year-old, I didn't have much idea really about tactics, strategy and skillsets ... my performances were very inconsistent. My first 10 Test wickets came at 51 apiece. So things had to change. I really had to work on my fitness and learn a little bit more about adapting to conditions, and getting the ball in the right areas consistently... I had to take more notice of what batsmen were doing, their feet position, and so on ... how they picked up the bat, whether they played straight, or whether they played across the line.

My breakthrough came in England in my first year in 1978, and after that I played county cricket for 10 years. During that time, I fine-tuned my skills, as I was doing it day in, day out. I learnt about my body, trained a lot, played a lot. My record at Notts, if I can say, was pretty outstanding really: 622 first-class wickets, plus quite a few runs [5854] ... and I took 1490 first-class wickets in total, including 431 Test wickets... But for me the stat that really highlighted my role was taking five wickets in an innings on 102 occasions... I know a lot of players in county cricket exceeded that but, for me, coming from New Zealand, in an 18-year first-class career, I think that is pretty good going. I did my job. And if I couldn't get batsmen out, then I denied them scoring runs. There were days when they tore me apart, that is the contest between bat and ball, but there were other days when I was in control. Obviously it is the bowler who controls and dictates the game – where they pitch it affects the outcome.

Sir Richard was continuing the family legacy. New Zealand played their maiden Test against England at Christchurch in early 1930, and his father Walter made his debut in 1937, at Lord's. His final Test was against the same opposition at Wellington, in 1951. Hadlee continued:

Dad captained the famous '49-ers' in England in 1949. They played 32 first-class games, winning 13 and losing only one. They drew all four Tests, which was a considerable achievement compared to what came before. He only won 11 caps; the War years denied him more. He made one century: 116 against England at Christchurch in March 1947. He was the godfather of New Zealand cricket. Remember it was an amateur game in the 1930s through to when I was playing, when a lot of us were semi-pro. Dad was a player, captain, selector, administrator, chair of board and president, and managed the 1965 team to England, India and Pakistan. He also represented New Zealand at ICC level. His involvement,

experience, knowledge and love for the game shone – he is owed
a tremendous amount of gratitude. I also played with my brothers,
Barry and Dayle, in the 1975 World Cup, and Dayle and I played
a number of Tests together. I think the Hadlee family overall has
made a significant contribution to New Zealand cricket.

Sir Richard will also be recalled for being one of a mighty quartet of
Test all-rounders in the 1980s. He took 431 wickets at 22.29 apiece in
86 Tests and scored 3124 runs at an average of 27.16; Ian Botham hit
5200 runs at 33.54 and took 383 wickets at 28.40; Imran Khan made
3807 runs at 37.69 and took 362 wickets at 22.81; and Kapil Dev struck
5248 runs at 31.05 and took 434 wickets at 29.64. Hadlee went on:

That was a great era, often referred to as the 'Battle of the
All-rounders'. Beefy [Ian Botham] and I started playing against each
other in 1978. Kapil Dev came on the scene more in the 1980s, and
Immy [Imran Khan] about the same time. We did have tremendous respect for each other. We always knew what each other was
doing around the world, although we did not have the technology that we have today, so we had to rely on newspapers or radio.
The one-on-one contests were very competitive ... the adrenaline
flowed because you wanted to outperform and outskill each other,
and often if the all-rounder had the better of his opponent it would
affect the outcome of the game. We didn't want to get out to each
other; we had ding-dong battles, and often the media would build it
up prior to the Tests. It lifted things, and it gave the spectators more
interest. They were exciting times. Clive Rice [Ricey] was also a
fantastic player and if South Africa were playing, he would have
made a huge impact too. Ricey's battles were in county cricket,
when he was playing against West Indian bowlers in opposing sides.
That is how he measured how good he was.

I would like to think I was the better bowler of the four, and I
think my record would probably suggest that, with average, strike-
rate and number of wickets. My batting was the weaker part of
my game compared to the other three. Imran was the pick of the
all-rounders because he was a more consistent performer than
the rest of us. He was a potent strike bowler. He swung it and
was quite vicious at times, with express pace. He certainly made

the Australians jump around in the 1980s. It would vary, though. Beefy was a showman ... a very good bowler, with inswing and outswing ... he got a lot of his wickets through freebies [laughs affectionately] ... through experimentation. He could also be very destructive as a batsman. Kapil, considering a lot of the time he was bowling in [unhelpful] Asian conditions, his performances were quite phenomenal, and he broke my record [for Test wickets]. So we had different skillsets, some stronger than others.

Sir Richard was capable of free-flowing, swashbuckling innings, though.

Notts really helped me because they gave me responsibility to bat at Nos 6–8, but mainly 7... Previously I'd been a tail-ender, batting 10 and 11. I liked to hit bowlers back over their heads. When I switched, I was still positive, but more selective as I couldn't give my wicket away. Helmets made a difference, because I was a target. I did not have too many problems with West Indies, actually, as they bowled either too short or too full against me. One of my best innings was in March 1985 at Trinidad: I only got 39 not out, but I batted a couple of hours and helped to save the Test. I got hit and peppered, and that was a courageous innings... I had never been more determined. My batting stats improved considerably from that point on.

So, to the crux of this book – does Sir Richard like T20? And is he worried that it is swamping the Test game? We speak soon after news has broken that New Zealand's greatest Test batsman, Kane Williamson, has declined a central contract, allowing him to pick and choose various franchise leagues no doubt. Sir Richard replied:

I predicted that this would happen 10 years ago. Kane is following in the footsteps of Trent Boult, Martin Guptill and Colin de Grandhomme. I am not saying it is wrong. Everyone is faced with a set of circumstances. The money and opportunities are around with T20 to secure your life's future. You have to do what is right for your family. They can pick and choose, which is fine, and it creates opportunities for other players to be exposed to international cricket, although the problem is that it potentially weakens your international team. We have to live with what is happening. There are so many T20 franchise games, and a player cannot play Tests, ODIs and T20s, giving full commitment to his country as well. The leagues are enticing them out of the international games and rewarding them very well for their skills. Players should remember, though, that it is their country that has given them the opportunity and exposure to perform. Where is the balance? I don't know the answer.

I do really enjoy T20. When it first came about I was a bit frustrated about what it was doing to the game... I used the word 'butchering'. I have always believed Test cricket was the foundation upon which the game was based, the pure game. People growing up and wanting to play Test cricket was the ultimate goal. Then 50-over cricket came about, and that was a good spectacle, and the World Cup was good, and now there is T20, and it is proving to be the game's greatest revolution, even more than Packer. It is high-risk and entertaining. A six-ball innings of 20 can win a team the game. One over can lose you the game. I enjoy it... The fact it goes for three hours, I can sit down and watch it. It is a technical, strategic game – fascinating to watch.

I would like to think Tests can survive, though. If we lose it, we will never get it back. It is up to the ICC and the countries to protect and preserve it. To their credit they tried to revitalise the game with the World Test Championship, but then you see South Africa send their C team to New Zealand [in early 2024]. That loses credibility. That potentially is the death of Test cricket.

Don Bradman sent me a lovely letter when I received my knighthood, congratulating me and offering me a little bit of advice. It said: 'We are all custodians of the game, and while we still play, we need to respect the game, and ensure it survives, and do everything we can to protect the values and history.' That will always live with me.

New Zealand now stage Test matches at boutique grounds like Mount Maunganui, Hamilton's Seddon Park, Hagley Oval (Christchurch), Nelson, Napier, the Basin Reserve in Wellington and Dunedin ... the ones with embankments, marquees and lovely pavilions, with families and picnics and youngsters, and crowds of about 7000/8000. Away from what Sir Richard described in an earlier interview to me as 'concrete jungles', i.e. the rugby stadiums. By doing so, they have perhaps developed a blueprint for Test cricket's survival. We can but pray.

21

2020 TO ... BAZBALL AND BEYOND

'The danger is that Test cricket is moulded into a homogenous T20-cloned, one-size-fits-all, fast-scoring product that lacks the depth and nuance that we have seen in the past.'

And then there was Bazball. That was the name that journalist Andrew Miller coined for the style of Test cricket that England have been playing under coach Brendon McCullum and captain Ben Stokes since they assumed control at the start of the English summer of 2022. And it has well and truly stuck.

Stokes is clearly a fabulous motivator. He appears even more alpha male than his mighty predecessors in the ace all-rounder/captain category: Tony Greig, Ian Botham and Andrew Flintoff. He obviously makes people feel like a world-beater. No one wants to let him down. McCullum looks seriously chilled out, his feet up on the table even in the most desperate situation, and that rubs off on his charges. As a player he batted belligerently – and brilliantly – himself.

Initially results were incredible: in the home summer of 2022, 3–0 against New Zealand, winning the one-off Test against India at Edgbaston, then defeating South Africa, with some extraordinary second-innings run-chases along the way. Just a year after Joe Root had decided to batten down the shutters and go for a tame draw against New Zealand at Lord's in 2021, now no second-innings target was out of reach. They used to flash a card up on the telly with record fourth-innings run-chases; India's 406 for 4 at Port of Spain always stood out for me. It was a warning: however hopeful you are that England can pull off an improbable win, save yourself the energy. Now the Bazballers could produce miracles, though. Three times England chased successfully against New Zealand (yes, they were visiting again ... do not ask me; talk to the schedulers). In the second Test at Trent Bridge England made 299 for 5 in only 50 overs, Jonny Bairstow making 136 not out from only 92 balls. In the following Test Bairstow pummelled 71 not out from 44 balls on his home ground as England made 296 for 3 in 54.2 overs. India were next, to play the match that they had missed in 2021. Desperate to stay Covid-free ahead of the resumption of the 2021 IPL, they refused to play the final Test at Old Trafford. It should have resulted in a forfeit, but England decided it was best not to get on the wrong side of the Board of Control for Cricket in India, so it was replayed (sort of: it was switched to Birmingham). This time fearless England stunned India, reaching their target of 378 in only 76.4 overs, Root and Bairstow both making brisk centuries. England then made light work of a more modest target in the final Test against South Africa at The Oval, winning the series 2–1. Stokes and McCullum thought they were the saviours of Test cricket. Some feel that they were right, others that they were a tad conceited. I am in the latter camp, I am afraid.

Stokes expressed his frustration at those who were not getting with the programme, those of us who said that there was more than one way to win a Test match. He called for cricket writers to go easy on him after the final Test of that summer of 2022, at The Oval. It seemed naive. 'Me and the team ... have a responsibility for upcoming cricketers who aspire to play for England... If you look at 10-, 11-, 12-year-olds, things will be different ... there will be a new way of playing ... we are trying to inspire them ... but for all the positive stuff we've done this summer, I feel there's an added responsibility on people who comment on the way that we play as well. Because we're in the day and age now that social media is so accessible in a certain way ... if we play in a certain way and are saying that's what we want to do and we believe in it ... to be ... almost ... criticised for that – what type of message is that sending to the next generation?' In other words, do not complain, do not analyse. Undoubtedly some are happy to be client journalists, but for others, his request goes against everything that we learned in our training. His sensitivity on this subject resurfaced during the UEFA Euro 2024 football championships, actually. England were being heavily criticised after a tepid 1–1 draw with Denmark. Their right-back, Kyle Walker, defended the display on television, and Stokes posted on X (formerly Twitter): '... get behind the team and leave the hindsight and negativity to the pundits ... come on England.'

The good news continued for the England cricket team in the autumn of 2022, though: not only winning, but winning in stunning style in Pakistan. I really thought that their attacking cricket would not work there, as Pakistan had always been the final frontier for England. They won the first Test because they scored at 6.73 an over. To think that Steve Waugh's Australians recalibrated Test cricket by scoring at *four* an over... Surely never has a Test been so hard-won as that in Rawalpindi, and never have the tactics and style of play been so adventurous to negate such a benign surface. They took the series 3–0, maintaining a run-rate of 5.50 per over – a stunning and unprecedented achievement.

It was one of the greatest transmogrifications in sport. England had won only one of the last 17 Tests that they played under Root, culminating in a 1–0 series defeat in the Caribbean in 2022. Everyone now appeared imbued with self-belief. The fear of failure had seemingly been removed. Players knew that they would have a good run in the side. They would not lose their spot for one injudicious shot. The most pertinent comparison I can think of was West Indies under Clive Lloyd. Battered by Dennis Lillee and Jeff Thomson's bumper and sledging barrage in Australia, West Indies went down 5–1 in 1975/76, with racist barracking by spectators rubbing salt into the wounds. Lloyd decided that the way ahead would be to double that level of firepower with four quicks of his own, unleashing a blitzkrieg back at the bullies. Lloyd led his side on a run of 26

Tests undefeated between early 1982 and late 1984. As mentioned, Waugh's Australia side (1997–2004) upping the scoring rate to four per over (although under Mark Taylor they were already a top side). Outside of cricket, there was Nick Faldo's transformation in golf; baseball side Oakland Athletics' incredible improvement under the alchemic powers of Billy Beane in 2002; Greece winning the Euro 2004 football championships; and Leicester City taking the Premier League title in 2015/16...

Since that triumphant tour to Pakistan, though? Not so good. A 1–1 draw in New Zealand in February 2023. The declaration in the second Test at the Basin Reserve, Wellington, backfired as the hosts levelled the series with a one-run win. It was a shame for Harry Brook, who made 186 from only 176 balls. Stokes insisted the defeat was not a disaster, however, and it was a privilege to be part of such a great contest. That Olympian detachment was becoming a common theme. A reckless 2–2 draw at home to Australia followed. Zak Crawley struck the first ball of the series for four at Edgbaston, and England's first innings was pulsating: they had reached 393 for 8 in 78 overs, with Root contributing 118 not out. Stokes stunned almost everyone by declaring, however, with Root dismantling the bowling. It was an insult to those followers of Test cricket who believe it is a game where you have to grind your opponent down and do what they least want you to. The Australians must have been delighted. Yes, Usman Khawaja and David Warner had a few tricky overs to negotiate, but they managed that, and Australia went on to win the Test, by only two wickets.

This was followed by England's heedless batting at Lord's. They crashed from 188 for 1 to 325 all out, and it was shabby. I really do not want to keep seeing Ollie Pope trying to hook the ball out of the ground as we saw at Lord's (or Root trying to reverse-scoop the first ball of the day as he did in the third Test at Headingley against Pat Cummins of all people). Stokes, after a year of 'setting the tone of belligerence' (i.e. reaching 50 only once in 18 innings) actually batted sensibly at Lord's. The headline on *The Australian* newspaper website said it all, however: 'Australia crush England after Kamikaze Bazball shambles'. Some younger writers said us oldies were missing the bigger picture, and even months later, Lawrence Booth, the editor of the 2024 *Wisden Cricketers' Almanack*, wrote in relation to the declaration and Lord's batting, that Bazball is the 'Test revolution that has thrilled everyone bar the po-faced and one-eyed.' He said that criticism of such things 'reflects the conservatism that lurks close to the surface in this country.' He carried on: 'Test cricket will survive only if it keeps us interested.' Well, of course, but one man's meat is another's poison.

Rod Bransgrove expressed similar sentiments in Ben Bloom's book, *Batting for Time*. 'There's a form of intellectual snobbery about the game that watching Geoffrey Boycott bat for six hours is far more interesting than watching Ben Stokes slog 100 against the Australians in two hours,' the Hampshire owner said. Frankly, that is a weird interpretation. Nobody is saying that they do not enjoy watching Stokes smash the bowling around. What we are saying is that sometimes you need a roundhead to support a cavalier. Ian Botham may have made a thrilling 118 against Australia in the Ashes Test at Old Trafford in 1981, but he remains immensely grateful to Chris Tavaré at the other end for carving out 78 in 289 balls in support. Andrew Strauss at the time was critical of England's approach in that Lord's Test, on Sky:

> Any cricket needs to be smart cricket ... adaptability is crucial ... hubris and ego have come into it at times at Edgbaston and Lord's. Over the last year the tactics have resonated with the public and it has been brilliant, but the level of scrutiny in the Ashes is that much greater.

England clearly did recalibrate their tactics after falling 2–0 behind: keep the positivity, ditch the recklessness. They played brilliant cricket, with Mark Wood and Chris Woakes coming into the side and making us wish that they had been there from the start. Yes, England did do well to claw back the 0–2 deficit, and yes, they probably would have won if it had not rained at Manchester. They only had themselves to blame, though. Stokes and McCullum seemed hell-bent on playing a daredevil game of 'how far can we get behind in the series only to hit back and win it?' The baddies in *Scooby-Doo* 'would have gotten away with it too, if it weren't for you meddling kids', and England 'would have gotten away with it [winning] too, if it weren't for the Manchester weather.'

Then England lost in India 4–1, despite winning the first Test at Hyderabad. A considerably weakened India side at that, without Virat

Kohli and a host of other players. So, after winning nine of their first 10 Tests under Stokes and McCullum, they won eight (including one against Ireland, at Lord's) and lost seven. Results were no better than they had been under the Chris Silverwood-coached regime, before the pandemic. There were no draws, by the way. Stokes and McCullum do not like draws.

That England's results have plateaued does not invalidate this side's achievements, I suppose, but it does show that there is not a one-size-fits-all formula for transforming a Test team, or the Test game. You can be a huge admirer of Stokes as a leader and cricketer, but still dare to question his tactics. Mike Brearley did. In an interview with *The Daily Mail*, he said:

> I'm full of admiration for Ben. What he seems to have done is release people to be freer to be themselves. ... The second thing he has done is make people less worried about losing.

Brearley had 'caveats', however:

> I hope it doesn't mean there will never be another Geoffrey Boycott opening the batting for England, or another Alastair Cook. And one of the great things about long cricket is there is a possibility of a draw if you can't win.

A bit of background here. ... Stokes had absurdly said Cook would not be picked by England if he was still available for selection. Personally, I prefer Australia and India's positive and *intelligent* approach.

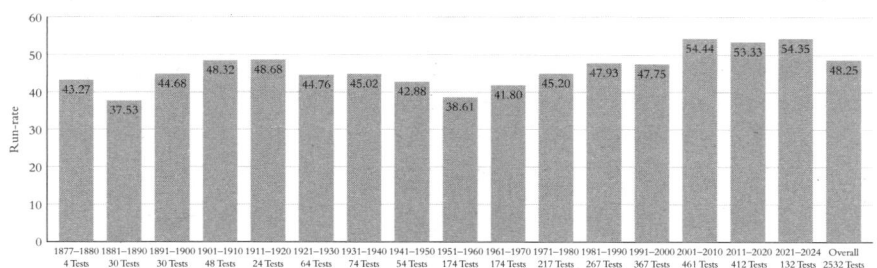

Figure 21.1. Test run-rates across the decades.
Graphic taken from the May 2024 issue of *The Cricketer*

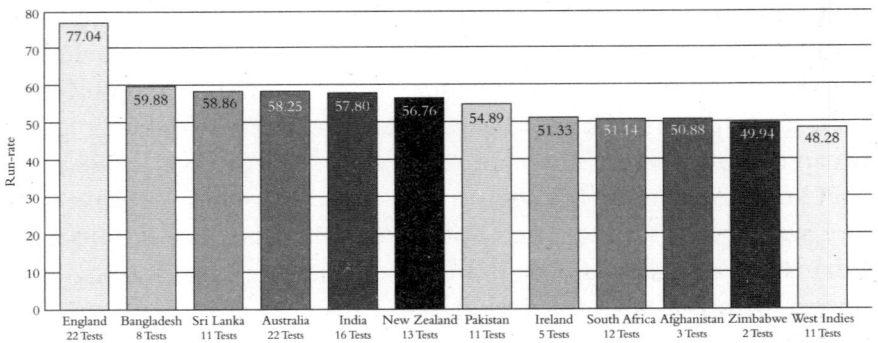

Figure 21.2. Test run-rates in the Bazball era (ranked since 1 June 2022).
Graphic taken from the May 2024 issue of *The Cricketer*

So has Bazball run out of gas? As of spring 2024, run-rates had risen a little in this decade on the previous one, thanks to England's belligerent batting, but it was not the fastest-scoring decade (well, so far) according to data provided by Cricket Archive, the sister company of *The Cricketer*. That decade was 2001–2010. Steve Waugh was Australia captain from 1997 to 2004 and is credited with driving his side on to score more rapidly. T20 also began as a professional format in 2003 in England and soon spread worldwide, inevitably leading to riskier strokeplay. India opening batsman Virender Sehwag's strike-rate from 2001 to 2013 was notably high (82.23). West Indies were known for their powerful and entertaining batting style in the 1980s, but actually the overall run-rate by teams was under three an over, and it stayed that way through the 1990s. There was a big rise in run-rate in the 1970s from what is recalled as the somewhat dour 1960s. That is down to two things: the big upturn in form of West Indies, and the introduction of limited-overs cricket, attacking batsmanship permeating into all forms of the game. Some captains did try to jazz things up in the 1960s, though. In the 1960/61 series between Australia and West Indies, the captains, Richie Benaud and Frank Worrell, made a vow to play cricket that was sporting and full of intent to win. The tour was a triumph. The tied Test is legendary. The 1950s saw the introduction of India v Pakistan Test series with the latter's arrival. With national pride at stake, their batsmen favoured a cautious approach, hence the dip in overall run-rate.

Cricket scholars recall the 1910s as having its entertaining moments, most notably South Africa's tour of Australia in 1910/11. The increase to 48 per 100 balls by the Great War (1914) could have been labelled 'Vic-ball', the impact of dashing Australia batsman Victor Trumper in an age of chivalry.

Looking at the table of scoring in the Bazball era, England really are way ahead of everyone else. The others are yet to embrace this format-saving elixir. Great stuff, eh? Well... The trouble is, you are either with Bazball, or against it. You either understand it, or you do not. It all seems such a binary argument. I cannot deny that scoring more runs per 100 balls is entertaining, but a Test is played over five days, and the primary focus of players and teams has to be to win.

When England lost the Test series in India in early 2024, Bazball fanatics were saying to the sceptics: 'I suppose you are happy now. You wanted them to lose so that you could be proved right.' And so on. Well, no, no one who is English *wants* England to lose. At the very least, fans of cricket in general would surely have felt it would have been splendid if the tourists had won the fourth Test at Ranchi, so that it was all to play for in the fifth and final Test at Dharamshala. There is something a little irritating about this team and their ethos, however. It is fine that they have decided on a style of play. Attacking, enterprising, bold. They then have chosen the players who fit that mould. For instance, Zak Crawley (Test strike-rate 65.59 runs per 100 balls as of 9 December 2024), who had a pretty good series even if he did not convert eight promising starts into a biggie, ahead of, say, Keaton Jennings (Test strike-rate 42.49), who has made Test centuries at Mumbai and Galle. Fair enough. For the most part Stokes and McCullum have got these players expressing themselves with flair and confidence. And while we are being positive, the selection of the spinners for the trip, Tom Hartley and Shoaib Bashir, of Lancashire and Somerset respectively, was inspired. Stokes has also handled them brilliantly, as he did with Jack Leach in the last year or two. These are the things that grate, though...

Root was having a poor series after three Tests, with 77 runs in six innings. Most sensible people could see that he should be playing his normal game, not trying to reverse-ramp Jasprit Bumrah, as he did in the third Test at Rajkot at such a critical juncture. When he fell for 18 at 224 for 2, after India had made 445, the possibly apocryphal quote from Gubby Allen to Walter Robbins sprang to mind. At the MCG in 1936/37, Robbins dropped Don Bradman before he had reached 50, and he went on to make 270. 'Oh, don't give it another thought,' said Allen, the England captain. 'You've just cost us the Ashes, that's all.' The modern equivalent might be: 'Oh, don't think about that reverse-ramp, Joe. You have just cost us the Test, that's all.' Although Stokes would never do that, because he is an excellent leader, not a spiteful snob.

Root also seemed to have had a similar epiphany 12 months before. A lean spell of 242 runs in 11 Test knocks saw him make an acknowledgement in New Zealand that he was 'trying to find out what [his] role [was] within the team', and the 'tempo' he needed to bat at. He then made 153 not out and 95 in the second Test at Wellington.

Root did knuckle down in the fourth Test in India at Ranchi, making a masterfully controlled 122 not out. Afterwards, however, rather than admitting that that is how he should nearly always play, unless there is a race to declare, for instance, he insisted that he had not been wrong, and that he might yet revert again… Rather like a pupil having the last word to a punctilious teacher.

If you do not want to listen to me, then this is what Ian Chappell said. He played for Australia between 1964 and 1980, leading them impressively between 1971 and 1975, before becoming a hugely respected commentator. 'Root had a bloody fine record playing normally, and he was a quick scorer playing normally. I don't see why he's trying to change things drastically, and I've never believed you should play premeditated shots.' Somebody more modern? OK, try South Africa's master blaster, AB de Villiers after the Ranchi Test. He said: 'This is the Joe Root mode that wins you Test matches! Glue mode. Let the rest play Baz Ball [sic].' It was so blindingly obvious that it was infuriating.

Stokes certainly upped the aggression with the bat at the start of his captaincy tenure. CricViz said he attacked 41 per cent of balls in 2022 compared to 24 per cent in 2019. The fear was that he was underselling his talents, but he buckled down and played well in the 2023 Ashes.

Then there are some of the things that the players are saying. Take Ben Duckett in India claiming that Yashasvi Jaiswal had learned to play like that – 655 runs at 93.57 in this series – from being inspired by England and watching Bazball. It was utterly absurd. No wonder it sparked a fiery reply from Nasser Hussain, who said: 'He [Jaiswal] has not learned from you, he has learned from his upbringing and all the hard yards he has put in while growing up, he has learned from the IPL. If anything, I would look at him and learn from him.' Of course we do not want players to stop speaking. By all means, go for it. It is just worrying that people actually believe this stuff. It really was starting to sound just like a cult.

Attacking Test cricket has been around a long time, fellas. Like these innings, all against England: Gordon Greenidge's 214 not out at Lord's in 1984; Viv Richards' 110 not out from only 58 balls on his home island of Antigua in 1985/86; India's Kapil Dev saving the follow-on at Lord's in 1990 with four successive sixes over long-on off Eddie Hemmings; Nathan Astle's 222 at Christchurch in 2001/02; Adam Gilchrist's 57-ball century at Perth in 2006/07; and Virender Sehwag's run-a-ball 117 at Ahmedabad in 2012/13... Those are six examples I can think of, just off the top of my head. And if you want an Englishman in that list, add Ian Botham, whose 138 against Australia at Brisbane 1986/87 was unforgettable.

Barry Richards, the former South Africa batsman, feels that the whole notion of Bazball has been overhyped anyway. 'The press always coin a phrase,' he told *The Cricketer* in September 2023.

> I think Brendon McCullum likes positive cricket rather than Bazball, which gives the feeling of slogging every ball for six. His format is nothing to do with that. Brendon and Ben Stokes are playing positive cricket, the fans love it and are prepared to pay. Stokes is aware that entertainment is part of Test cricket. You can encourage positive cricket as long as your technique doesn't go out of the window. Joe Root is a classical player. I sometimes worry when he plays the shots which are reserved for the IPL. Joe's good enough to score fast enough without doing that.

There is also the blatant disregard for practices that have been the bedrock of the game since it started. Warm-up matches are a good way to prepare. Not training camps in Abu Dhabi. (An exchange about that on X did make me laugh, by the way. Kevin Pietersen posted on X after England started the first Test poorly: 'If you're that person who's now blaming England for warming up in Abu Dhabi, please give yourself an uppercut!' To which Alan 'Dad of Mark' Butcher, a fine county cricketer with an England cap, and later coach, replied succinctly: 'Oh f★★★ off @KP!') And bowlers need overs to prepare. Ollie Robinson had not bowled in a match since last July (the third Ashes Test at Headingley). Sussex were desperate to pick him in the summer of 2023 after he had recovered from back trouble. There was no sign of him after May, though.

Yes, Bazball has been entertaining, but it is not going to save the Test game around the world. Let's face it, nothing is going to stop the IPL owners buying up cricket teams like an annoying older brother hoovering up houses and hotels in a game of Monopoly. Test cricket will find its place, even if it is inevitably condensed and diminished. And winning *is* important, despite what Stokes said. The declaration in Birmingham, the reckless batting at Lord's, and, yes, the rain at Manchester, all played a part in denying England fans the Ashes triumph that they wanted in 2023.

The fact is that Test cricket is fabulous, though, and should stand and fall on its merits over the decades, not on two years of Bazball. There is more than one way to win. There is more than one way to entertain. High-octane, five-an-over scoring with reverse-ramping is not the sole option. Can so many old great players be wrong? Like Mudassar Nazar, for instance. A senior player said to him, 'Yes, get a hundred, but actually stay there for two days, that means that you belong,' he told me in *The Cricketer* in September 2023.

Stokes' man-management in general is brilliant, to be fair – he is a bit like the former Liverpool manager Jürgen Klopp. Tactically, he is terrific too. Just stop the messianic stuff about saving Test cricket, and everyone will be happy. In the winter of 2023/24, I met a man in a pub who tends the grounds at a Surrey cricket club. He rarely plays any more, but did for decades, studiously opening the batting, prizing his wicket. He finds Bazball disrespectful. 'Getting out *does* matter.' 'Losing *does* matter.' I am sure that he speaks for many.

Simon Barnes, the former chief sportswriter of *The Times*, touched on this same point in *The Cricketer* in July 2023.

The point of courage is that it cannot exist without fear: without the urge to do the complete opposite. In traditional forms of cricket the focus of fear is the batter. You are concerned with your own doubts, and the effort to conceal them; you are also concerned with the possibility of getting hurt. You are surrounded by 11 enemies, every one of whose day would be improved by your failure. Batting is one of the most intense personal examinations any individual can go through in sport. Bazball is the much-resented label for the policy of all-out attack that is pursued by England under McCullum and Stokes. Don't worry! It doesn't matter if you get out! It doesn't matter if you don't make any runs! Just go out there and have FUN! Sometimes I think that Bazball and the abolition of fear is just what Test match cricket has always needed ... and sometimes I think Bazball will do what T20 has failed to do and make Test match cricket not so much out of date, as ridiculous. I can only pose the questions, though: I really don't know the answers. Bazball is about transplanting not just the techniques but the mindset of T20 batting into Test cricket. If Test match cricket is just a bit of fun, all part of the entertainment business, then it is rather less interesting than it was when we all took it much too seriously. I have greatly enjoyed the sensational Bazball victories England have pulled off as a result of fearless batting. It is just that I keep wondering if there isn't something lacking. If a wicket is no longer a personal or a corporate disaster, something is lost in the eternal dispute between bat and ball.

There is also a sense of a superiority complex with Bazball. 'You cannot criticise us', and 'You don't understand what we are doing.' And an inverse logic. Take the 'Nighthawk' nonsense. Instead of a lower-order batsman going in late in the day as a nightwatchman to play cautiously, to protect a better player so they can go in the next day, they play belligerently from ball one. Stuart Broad did it in New Zealand in 2023 at Mount Maunganui and should have been out second ball after playing a daft shot. David Gower on commentary duty had not heard of the 'Nighthawk' concept and could not understand it ... and there was a good reason for that – it is silly. Too clever by half.

There is also a weird obsession about everyone playing golf. Essex batsman Jordan Cox described how he was informed of his call-up to the England team. McCullum told him: 'I just want to get you around the group, see what you're like in the environment because we want aggressive cricketers, which is what you have been doing. Oh, and bring your golf clubs.'

From my perspective, I think that the approach – 'attacking cricket, don't worry about getting out' – is disrespectful to all the great Test cricket that has gone on before. Test cricket has endured for nearly 150 years, and there is more than one way to skin a cat (just as there was more than one way to spin out Gatt). And after all, it is not really going to save Test cricket, is it? The Indian billionaires are not going to be thwarted because Test batters are scoring at five an over, are they? The danger is that Test cricket is moulded into a homogenous T20-cloned, one-size-fits-all, fast-scoring product that lacks the depth and nuance that we have seen in the past. A bit like making chess into draughts. And then even something that now seems exciting and enthralling becomes samey and dull.

22

INTERNATIONAL WHITE-BALL CRICKET

'Floodlit cricket in Australia was wonderful [...]
The costumes, the imposing stadiums, the over-excited
Channel 9 commentators, Daddles the Duck, the
New Horizons *theme tune – it was out of this world.'*

Considering there was talk about one-day international cricket eclipsing, and even exterminating, Test cricket in the 1990s, the 50-over game has been a remarkably transient format: initially unwanted by the players, then all the rage, now an endangered species.

The Gillette Cup, introduced in 1963, and the Sunday League, which followed six years later, gave county cricket shots in the arm. The first ODI at the MCG, hastily scheduled on England's 1970/71 tour to Australia after the third Test had been rained off, was seen as insignificant by Ray Illingworth and his touring side. 'Neither side took it too seriously,' he told me.

The proprietor of *The Cricketer* magazine, Ben Brocklehurst, who had captained Somerset as an amateur in the early 1950s, had the idea for an ODI World Cup. The Imperial Cricket Council, as it was then known, were not interested, until they had the idea themselves. The 1975 and 1979 competitions were skimpy, fun affairs, held over a fortnight, predictably staged in the 'mother country', England, and predictably won by the enforcers at that time, West Indies, thanks to their exciting blend of belligerent batsmen and rapid bowlers. Innings lasted 60 overs in both. The 1975 one is often recalled for India's Sunil Gavaskar 'blasting' 36 not out from 174 balls, as he opted for 'practice' (in going strokeless). It infuriated an Indian supporter so much that he punched two policemen and was jailed. Lord's was sold out for the final on the summer solstice. Captain Clive Lloyd made 102 from 85 balls, out of a West Indies total of 291. His counterpart Ian Chappell made a half-century in reply, but three run-outs by Viv Richards proved pivotal. After two false alarms that led to pitch invasions, the final wicket was taken at 8.43 p.m. to give West Indies a 17-run win. They won £4000 – yes, that is all. In 1979 West Indies won again, thanks to a rare example of Mike Brearley getting his tactics wrong as England captain, but this tournament was a party that celebrated peace after Kerry Packer's World Series Cricket breakaway. Brearley and Geoffrey Boycott thought they had laid the foundations for victory in the final when they posted an opening stand of 129 in 38 overs, 'chasing' 286 for 9. Their teammates did not share that view, though, and West Indies admitted that they did not want either man to get out. Joel Garner's toe-crunching yorkers – he took 5 for 38 – secured a 92-run victory. This time West Indies received £10,000.

The 1983 tournament, again 60 overs per side, provided one of cricket's greatest shocks, however, when India, defying odds of 66 to 1, beat West Indies in the final, again at Lord's. If T20 does eventually consume Test cricket, then 25 June 1983 might be seen as a point of singularity. Their great all-rounder Kapil Dev had spared India from an ignominious exit in the first round, peppering the rhododendron bushes at Tunbridge Wells with six sixes and 16 fours in a then World Cup-record 175 not out against Zimbabwe after his side had slumped to 17 for 5.

Australia also overcame the odds by winning on the subcontinent in 1987, with the tournament now seeing sides bat for 50 overs per innings. No one had given them a chance, but captain Allan Border used the triumph as a springboard for a resurgence in limited-overs and Test cricket.

That was when the ODI format came on my radar, and I enjoyed the games through the decade. There were usually three, the Texaco Trophy, coming before the main event, the Test series. I liked England's jumper, having just the one lion on it compared to the Test sweater's three, in a lighter shade of blue, and I liked the games because my hero and role model, Derek Pringle, usually shone in them. He could not stop Viv Richards at Old Trafford in 1984, however, in that inaugural Texaco Trophy. I vividly recall my cricket teacher, Mr Riley, arriving with spring-back stumps, the reliable old Clipper bat that had been sitting in the school's store cupboard for half a century, and tennis balls for our lunchtime game in the playground. He told us that England had reduced the mighty tourists to 102 for 7. It must have injected some vim into our collective efforts to dislodge him from the crease, but inevitably the scoreboard would be something like: Riley 96 all out (i.e. for 1), the rest of us, 23 all out. Sometime later that day, we discovered that Richards had made 189 not out from 170 balls with 21 fours and five sixes – Pringle 11–0–64–0. England usually did pretty well in that trophy, however. They beat West Indies 3–0 in 1988 for instance, Pringle really starring this time.

The 1991/92 World Cup is considered by many to be the best, and I certainly enjoyed it the most. I was a student at the time, and there was a match every morning, which meant I could not possibly do any work. The format was deemed to be pleasing, with everyone playing each other in the first round, although that does not provide guaranteed entertainment – see the 2023 tournament. England had the best squad in the competition but there was a twist in the tale, with Pakistan close to being knocked out before hauling themselves off the canvas and taking the trophy under the inspirational leadership of Imran Khan. Their method in the final was the polar opposite of the one that turbocharged England to the endgame in 2019. Slumping to 24 for 2 in the ninth over, Imran, with 72, and Javed Miandad, who made 58, patiently rebuilt, laying the foundations for a bit of welly in the last seven or eight overs. That said, England did have to rebuild in the 2019 final, thanks to a Lord's pitch that demanded circumspection.

Floodlit cricket in Australia was wonderful, I thought. I had seen a bit of it watching the highlights on BBC2 of the 1982/83 Ashes tour by England, and four years later I could not get enough of it. The costumes, the imposing stadiums, the over-excited Channel 9 commentators, Daddles the Duck, the *New Horizons* theme tune – it was out of this world.

The 1996 World Cup on the subcontinent was interesting, for it signalled Sri Lanka's coming of age, and a shift in tactics. Enter the 'pinch-hitter'. Forget 'taking the shine off the new ball'. Now it was 'if the ball is there to hit, hit it', even if it is the first over. Old-fashioned England, marshalled by a now fuddy-duddy Ray Illingworth, thought they had posted an adequate total of 235 for 8 in 50 overs. Opener Sanath Jayasuriya had other ideas as he smashed 88 from 42 balls. Then, in the semi-finals, Indian fans at Eden Gardens, Kolkata, set fire to some areas of the stands and threw fruit and water bottles on to the field when their side looked as if they had all but lost; the match was abandoned, sending Sri Lanka into the final, where they thumped Australia.

The next World Cup in 1999 was back in England. The opening ceremony was a shamefully tepid affair, Prime Minister Tony Blair looking embarrassed to be there. It was a foggy morning, something had gone wrong with the fireworks, and no one could see anything. Then the hosts were knocked out in the first round, one day before the official World Cup anthem, 'All Over The World', performed by Dave Stewart, was available to buy. England's minds were never on the job after a pay dispute. Shane Warne, Glenn McGrath and Steve Waugh showed how much they loved playing in England again as Australia won for a second time.

Australia retained their title in southern Africa in 2003, Ricky Ponting bossing the final with an unbeaten 140. England were shot in the foot by the Blair government, not actually ordering them to boycott the first-round game in Robert Mugabe's Zimbabwe, but essentially not giving them much option. Poor Nasser Hussain, the England captain stuck between a rock and a hard place by posturing politicians. They did not go to Harare, and the forfeiture cost them their place in the tournament. Australia played a far cannier PR game, hinting that they would not go to Zimbabwe until the last minute, realising that they had to, and so ducking quickly in and out of Bulawayo and retrieving the points.

The 2007 World Cup in the Caribbean was pivotal in terms of format. Four groups of four in the first round looked neat and mirrored the football World Cup. India were knocked out after three matches following defeats to Bangladesh and Sri Lanka, however, to the despair of their billions of followers, and the ICC made a mental note: 'Never again.' England were an utter shambles once more, in a campaign best recalled for an inebriated Andrew Flintoff finding himself in a spot of bother out at sea in a pedalo at 4 a.m.; and Australia were imperious, with this time Adam Gilchrist, who made 149 not out from 104 balls, proving their champion in the final against Sri Lanka.

In 2011, India's second World Cup victory was the first by a side on home soil and signalled the start of their reign as *the* cricket superpower. The tournament is also seen as a return to form for the 50-over game. These things are subjective, of course. Once again the format of a first round of two groups of seven resulted in a month's cricket to produce a predictable last eight (the Associates as well as Zimbabwe and Bangladesh missing out). And like 1996, there was a lot of travel with games in India, Sri Lanka and Bangladesh (although not Pakistan, because of the 2009 terrorist attack on the Sri Lankan bus in Lahore). The game needed a successful tournament after so many damp squibs, though. And Ireland's first-round win over England at Bangalore was memorable, with Kevin O'Brien thumping 113 from 63 balls. India's increasing power on and off the field was also emphasised. England's Ian Bell looked plumb lbw but he was given not out as the ball had struck him more than 2.5m (8.2ft) from the stumps, a point at which the accuracy of the decision-tracking system Hawk-Eye was said to be below acceptable levels. India captain MS Dhoni complained, and the TV umpire lbw rules were revised more to his liking mid-tournament. He went on to score the winning runs (91 not out) in the final against Sri Lanka. It was a memorable occasion also for Tendulkar, played in his home town of Mumbai, at the Wankhede Stadium. To emphasise what it meant to Indians, the triumph inspired a film: *M.S. Dhoni: The Untold Story* (2016).

In 2015 Australia won their fifth World Cup, England flopped once more, and the T20 game started to make a serious impact on 50-over batting. 'You'd have to have an absolute stinker not to make the quarter-finals,' said Stuart Broad. England did not make them. Tickets for the now obligatory India v Pakistan match (the ICC ensures this happens at every World Cup, which is A) refreshing as they do not face each other at other times, but B) a bizarre flaunting of all known sporting principles) at the 50,000-seater Adelaide Oval were sold out within 12 minutes of going on sale. India won by 76 runs. The final broke Australian cricket's attendance record, with 93,000 seeing the hosts beat New Zealand at the MCG.

So England had never won the 50-over World Cup, and Andrew Strauss was tasked with doing something about it in 2019. The man who took England to No. 1 in the Test rankings did an incredible job in such a short space of time. He kept faith in skipper Eoin Morgan, whose methods were: 1) identify the best players; 2) if in doubt, always take the positive option; and 3) keep things simple. After losing the group game to Australia at Lord's, the campaign looked doomed, but England regrouped and won impressively, Jos Buttler and Ben Stokes playing the testing conditions expertly in the final at Lord's.

A bit like 2005, when England won the Ashes and sold out to Sky, they won the World Cup and then turned their back on the 50-over format. From 2021, the domestic tournament was scheduled at the same time as The Hundred, thus ruling out the best 100 or so white-ball cricketers, and England played precious few matches in the warm-up to the 2023 World Cup. Their ageing squad made a wretched defence of the title that they had waited so long and fought so hard to win. Hosts India looked to be cruising to a third title, while Australia looked down and out after losing their opening two matches. You can never write the Australians off, though, and captain Pat Cummins capped an incredible year by leading his side to seven group wins on the trot, a semi-final victory over South Africa, then a stunning, surprise victory in the final for their sixth title. He chose to chase against the Indians, sparking a collective gasp of incredulity from his compatriots. His tactics proved spot on, however. One match in particular stood out for me: Australia against Afghanistan. They looked set for ignominious defeat when they crashed to 91 for 7, chasing Afghanistan's 291. Glenn Maxwell's finest hour saw him smash 201 not out from 128 balls, essentially standing on one leg because of cramp. For me it illustrated the power of the format. The match was turned on its head like a sand timer. T20 does not allow for the epic like that.

If the 50-over World Cups are likely to carry on until at least 2031, bilateral series look imperilled. The three-match ODI series England played in Australia in front of sparse crowds, with the tourists fielding a depleted squad, was an embarrassment – a travesty for those of whom recalled the thrill of 50-over international cricket in Australia in the 1980s. 'England white-ball captain Jos Buttler said that he was not too worried about meaningless matches like that and he is probably right,' said Glenn McGrath in *The Cricketer* in March 2023.

> Every game has to mean something. Test cricket is the ultimate, T20 is so exciting, all-happening and popular, and 50-over cricket is under the pump. We need to find ways to protect it, otherwise it could fall by the wayside. The crowd in the last match at the MCG of all places was especially disappointing. There is so much cricket these days, with the IPL and all the T20 tournaments. They have crunched international cricket into a smaller period. I still think that the 50-over World Cup is more important than the T20 World Cup, but maybe I am biased as I played in them. Whether three forms can continue to co-exist, time will tell.

Another Australian great, batsman Dougie Walters, suggested to me in *The Cricketer* (July 2022) that ODIs should now be reduced to 40 overs per side.

The future of the T20 World Cup is more guaranteed, you would think. In fact, the five-year gap between the 2016 and 2021 editions, partially caused by the Covid pandemic, proved so insufferable to administrators that they doubled down on their commitment to run it every two years. The first one in South Africa was a skimpy eight-team affair that proved chastening for Stuart Broad, who was hit for 36 in an over by Yuvraj Singh at Durban. The India batsman had been wound up by Flintoff, which is never a sensible thing to do to players who hit a long ball. Yuvraj reached his half-century in just 12 balls, a taste of the carnage to come in T20. Chris Gayle also became the first centurion in T20Is. The final was exciting, with Pakistan pipping India by just five runs. Pakistan were not to be denied two years later in England, however. It was another embarrassing World Cup for the English hosts, who lost to the Netherlands at Lord's.

In 2010 England at last ended their agonising wait for a major limited-overs triumph, however, taking an enjoyable tournament in the West Indies. During it, Pakistan's Mohammad Amir bowled one of the most destructive overs in cricket history. He took three wickets, and there were two run-outs, against Australia at St Lucia. He is an interesting case study. Burdened by the scandal of bowling no-balls to order in the Test against England at Lord's in 2010, the gifted left-arm quick has won only 36 Test caps. At the time of writing he had played 305 T20 matches as a professional (after being banned for five years between 2011 and 2016 for spot-fixing).

The 2012 World T20 saw a predictable increase to 16 teams. West Indies won that one in Sri Lanka, ending a 33-year drought for a World Cup, and another in India four years later. For all Stokes' incredible successes, one over of ignominy in the latter will be recalled for a long time, when Carlos Brathwaite hit him for four sixes in the last over in the final at Kolkata to take his side over the winning line. Those West Indies' successes kick-started a love of that format that is seriously imperilling their participation in the two others.

Sri Lanka caused a shock in the 2014 edition, defeating India in the final. It was heartening to see Bangladesh, one of the world's least-wealthy nations, be given the chance to put on a good show. Would football do that to such a nation, I wonder? The 2021 tournament in the United Arab Emirates was seriously poor; playing the matches in the evenings to satisfy subcontinental television audiences all but decided the games by the toss of coin, due to the difficulty of defending totals with a wet ball, thanks to the dew. England won the tournament again in Australia in 2022, and this will go down probably as Jos Buttler's finest hour in an England shirt, just pipping the 2019 50-over final. The seriously talented batsman may seriously have underachieved as a Test player, with two centuries, even though his average of 31.94 is respectably Graeme Hick-like (31.32); but in this World Cup he was skipper, and made four half-centuries, including an unbeaten 80 in the final against India. Curiously, at the time of writing he has only made one T20I century for England, compared to seven in the IPL.

The 2024 World Cup saw matches in the United States, which proved to be an interesting experiment. There is no denying the attractive adaptability of the T20 format to take cricket to parts that other formats cannot reach. I cannot claim that a huge number of memories of these tournaments will live in my head, but they have often been succulent, crowd-pleasing affairs.

23

AT HOME WITH THE TOPLEYS

*'The fandom in India is incredible, almost on a par
with football here. Everything the IPL seems to do works …
it is growing exponentially, and going from strength to strength.'*

A common insult these days is that you 'live in an echo chamber'.
With that in mind, after interviewing a number of Test cricket
aficionados, I thought I'd better find some folk who are enthused
by T20 and the franchise fiesta. After all, it must have something
with so many people loving it; and it is giving a great many young
cricketers a fabulous lifestyle. Don Topley had a successful career
bowling seam for Essex before becoming head of cricket at the
Royal Hospital School in Holbrook, a spectacularly beautiful school
with naval roots – like Don himself – on the Shotley Peninsular, in
Suffolk's 'Constable Country'. It hosted the evening newspaper, the
Ipswich Star, in the Ipswich Inter-firm Cricket League when I was
a cub reporter there in the mid-1990s. We hit it off, with him soon
telling everyone I was a 'front-foot lunger'. Presumably a few years

back he would have pinged one around my ears to pin me back into the crease. Don's son, Reece, attended the school, then became a professional cricketer, first at Essex, then Hampshire, Sussex and Surrey; he is now a key member of England's white-ball squads. At 2.03m (6ft 8in) tall, he is a real handful, and has enjoyed sought-after, and lucrative, stints in the Indian Premier League and other global franchise competitions. He has shown incredible stoicism and bravery to fight back from a series of injuries, especially five stress fractures in his back.

Don and I do not agree about what is best for the future of cricket. He would like to see a reduction in the red-ball game in England and Wales, which would improve its quality, and he appears to positively embrace the expansion of T20. I would rather watch Surrey v Yorkshire all day long, than Oval Invincibles versus Northern Superchargers. I admit I am sentimental, romantic and probably old-fashioned. When people say that Don is looking at things through the prism of the needs of his son, which would be understandable, he is vehement that it is not his motivation, saying that he has always held modernising views. He would like to see the County Championship reduced from 14 rounds to 10, and he thinks that new sides like London Spirit and so on will attract more youngsters and new fans into the game than established teams like Essex and Surrey.

Don has four teams listed on his ESPNcricinfo page: Norfolk, for whom he played Minor Counties cricket in 1984; Surrey (one match v Cambridge University at Fenner's in 1985); then Essex (115 first-class matches and 155 List As between 1985 and 1994); and South Africa's Griqualand West (where he spent the 1987/88 winter). Reece, on the other hand, has more clubs than – cue *badum-tsh* – Tiger Woods: 13 in total. He started off with Essex in 2011, 17 years after his father stopped playing; and as well as his four counties there is the Royal Challengers Bengaluru, as well as teams in T20 tournaments in Australia, Pakistan, South Africa and the United Arab Emirates (I think we should not bother ourselves for too long with 'Team Moeen' and 'Team James Vince' – improvised teams to make up for proper tour warm-up matches).

Reece kindly allowed me to come into his exquisitely decorated and furnished modern home in a quiet corner of South London not far from The Oval to talk about his career. I was determined to be open-minded and accommodate his views. He played one match for the Royal Challengers in the 2023 IPL, and four more in 2024. Life became harder in that latter edition, with the addition of 'the substitute batter'. 'You just have to be careful,' said Nasser Hussain in the June 2024 issue of *The Cricketer.*

> The moment that you make a change, there will be repercussions. In T20 or white-ball cricket most of the changes have favoured batters, whether it is bringing the boundaries in, the size of bats, limiting bouncers and wides … and this is another one. We had Dinesh Karthik on the Sky podcast and he pointed out that teams simply do not ever have to rebuild any more, as everyone is told to go at it as hard as possible.

Reece insisted that he enjoyed the experience, however. 'The Indian Premier League has a different feel to any other cricket competition I have been involved with,' he told me as he sat back on his sofa, still feeling the effects of his flight from India the day before, his RCB luggage unpacked.

> The fandom in India is incredible, almost on a par with football here. Everything the IPL seems to do works, though … it is growing exponentially, and going from strength to strength. The tournament becomes more and more glamorous. The fans just flock to it. It is all carefully thought out. The social media side of it was particularly impressive. Teams are making a lot of money out of that, and it is another source of revenue. The atmosphere is amazing. I love playing there. Although it is a tough place to bowl, it is a good challenge. If anything, there is nothing to lose as everybody expects the batters to score runs and the bowlers to get hit.
>
> Off the field, there are times when we go out with various players and we get absolutely swarmed. There was one time in Dharamshala just now when Faf du Plessis got on the back of somebody's moped and the guy just sped off, which was hilarious. People just deal with it in different ways. I am thankful that I am not such a big name, and I do not get it as much as some of the other guys. I do not envy them as it is a difficult experience. Playing alongside Virat Kohli was an amazing experience. Seeing

what he does and how hard he works hopefully rubs off on us. It is a chance to get inside his mind and see how such a legend in the game goes about his business. I try to absorb his knowledge and know-how. There is always stuff to learn. Virat is a terrific bloke. He is always willing to chat to anyone or offer any information, but I found the best way to learn was just to observe how he went about his life. We were lucky that the Bangalore changing room was filled with great characters, though.

I asked Reece to compare the coaching in a franchise tournament like the IPL to being with a county throughout the English summer.

In county cricket, when you have an 18- or 19-year-old, coaches can occasionally look for a reaction from a player. They can grill them. Players can be annoyed at them, but then they can rebuild the relationship. It is almost like a character arc in a movie, where they learn and develop over a period of time, and then you reap the rewards at 21, 22, down the line. In the IPL a coach only has eight games to work with a player in a month. A franchise coach has to ask, 'How do I get the best out of this player for eight games?' You don't have the long-term relationship. A lot of time players are out of form, and the coach has to keep morale up. There is no chance to change technique in mid-competition. In the Blast there are rarely training days, let alone days off. Surrey are playing back to back twice in the Blast this year, so it is not like, 'How do you actually coach someone with a technical issue?' or whatever. If they have got a duck, you need to pump their tyres up literally for the next day.

Travel varies too. In India there is a lot of long distances. In the SA20 it is 'play, fly, play, fly'. In the Blast there is a lot of road travel. One time I played an ODI for England, day off, then another ODI, then I flew to South Africa the next morning and played a T20 that evening, the first of three games in four days for Durban. So, it was six games in eight days. So, the franchise tournaments are all very different in their own way. You can have a bad tournament or two, but there are so many games, you can still have a good year. Playing for the Royal Challengers, or Surrey at The Oval allows me to play in front of a good, animated crowd. It is not any more pressure playing in front of a big crowd. You just hear one big roar, a wall of noise, as opposed to when you play in front of only 100 people, you can hear 100 individual voices. You can hear what the Leicester fan, for example, is saying to you at smaller grounds. That is a strange thing that people who play club cricket will never find out.

Reece only has a couple of nights in his new place, before the T20 circus leaves town and he is off again, this time with England, to play a four-match series against Pakistan ahead of the T20 World Cup in the Caribbean. So I want to leave him in peace. He and the other England players had to depart from the IPL early. 'It's my personal opinion that there shouldn't be any international cricket that clashes with the IPL,' said England captain Jos Buttler. Yes, Jos, we know the way things are now … and how they are going to be.

Don and I go for a pizza to reflect on what his son has said. Don has a brother, Peter, who is 13 years older than him. He was Derek Underwood's spin-bowling understudy, playing for Kent in 19 first-class matches between 1972 and 1975. He helped Don develop a passion for the game. Between 1982 and 1985 Don was on the MCC Young Cricketers programme, based at Lord's. He had a fleeting moment of fame when he was 12th man in the second Test against West Indies at Lord's in 1984, when he 'caught' Malcolm Marshall off Bob Willis, but stepped over the long-leg boundary. 'Bob was fuming, but I thought it was a good effort!' He then had trials at Kent, Surrey, Sussex, Middlesex, Derbyshire, Northamptonshire, Gloucestershire and Glamorgan, then finally spent an entire pre-season with Essex in 1985 as a net bowler, at last winning a county contract. Competition was fierce at Essex. They had John Lever, the Ponts (Keith and Ian), Norbert Phillip, Neil Foster and Derek Pringle, among many others, but he went on to take 367 first-class and 197 List A wickets for them. There were no lucrative T20 stints for him. 'I'd go away most winters and play all over the world, but predominately South Africa,' he told me.

I had a good season in 1989 and was hoping at least for an England one-day call-up, so I thought rather than court controversy, I will go to Zimbabwe instead: play a bit less than normal, relax a bit, do some coaching. Straightaway, Dave Houghton wanted me to help the bowlers, and I became more and more involved, eventually landing the head coach's role for the World Cup. We beat England at

Albury, Australia, in the 1992/93 World Cup [the first with coloured clothes and a white ball]. Richie Benaud asked me if I would be reminding my Essex captain Graham Gooch, who was also England skipper. I said: 'If there are 200 days in the English summer, I'll be mentioning it on 198 days.' Goochie replied: 'No you won't, as I won't be watching any 2nd XI cricket.' He was a man of his word.

Despite a playing career that fizzled out, county cricket gave Don a good living. I ask him: 'Why don't you defend the county clubs and try to block the advance of these new outfits?' He replies:

Look, I love county cricket. I played in the old era of three-day games, with the John Player League game on a Sunday 'sandwiched in between', and it was lovely, and it was romantic ... but it was an absolute circus. It bore no resemblance to the professional game as it is today. We took the game to the people with outgrounds and so on, but we were running on empty; we were knackered. In those days we would cover for people, so if, say Pring [Pringle] had a back niggle, Fozzie [Neil Foster] and I would bowl more, or John Lever or Norbert. Today, the seam bowlers are all finely tuned race animals. It is the way that they have grown up. From Alex Tudor onwards, they have muscular physiques and spend much more time now in the gym.

Yes, I reply, but it doesn't seem to be helping them much – do they not get injured a lot more?

I think that is because they have to obey people who have the keys to the next level: strength and conditioning guys. People are pushing them to play too early. I also think that they are breaking down more as they are not used to bowling a lot of overs, after only being allowed to bowl four overs as juniors. People say that there is too much franchise cricket, but every season more and more counties are taking bowlers on loan as they have so many injuries. It is ridiculous. You cannot play weekly on the rock-hard wickets we have now. Yes, the likes of Fred Trueman and Fred Rumsey broke down less, but the pitches were softer. I mean in the 1970s they still had uncovered pitches! In the 1980s and 1990s bowlers like Angus Fraser, Andrew Caddick, Pringle and David Graveney were lethal as they could make the ball talk. It was art, it was skilful, but it bore no relation to cricket today. Now wickets around the world today do not change much, especially in white-ball cricket: they are all rock-hard, flat shirt-fronts. It hardly nibbles; it hardly swings. Batting hasn't changed as much. I would have 10 rounds of the County Championship. It would allow us to start later, spread the matches out better, allow for more rest. They would fit the season better, coinciding with the Test matches. You cannot compete with the IPL: it is the ultimate, the No. 1 world tournament. We also now need to facilitate the American T20, Major League Cricket; county players will want to be part of that as they are offering so much money.

As our pudding arrives, I bring up The Hundred, a topic on which we clash often… I ask him, why does he love it so much? He replies:

I met you, Huw, when we played 15 eight-ball overs in Ipswich. I thought that was a great format, and The Hundred would adopt it. I was surprised with what they came up with. It is not the end of the world, though. I have wanted change in our domestic cricket for years, because I am afraid county cricket has lost its relevance on the world stage. County cricket in its present guise does not do it for youngsters, and ethnic minorities. We need an eight-team elite tournament… certainly no more than 10 teams, for you don't want it to be any longer. It has to be played at the larger grounds, as they have the bigger squares, and so therefore have better T20 pitches. For those reasons I really hope that The Hundred survives.

At his old school in Holbrook, Don organises a festival for National Counties (formerly Minor) teams at under-11 and under-12 age groups. He has been doing so for 25 years.

I am seeing more and more Hundred shirts being worn by youngsters there – honest! The key for me is enthusing the youth. County cricket has not done it for years. Declining numbers in recreational cricket prove that. We have to entice, enthuse, excite and engage with the next generation to watch and ultimately play, as they are the future of the game. I am not the future and nor are the county members.

24

MY LOVE OF CLUB CRICKET

*'Playing alongside older men taught you
things that equipped you for adult life.'*

Outside of being married and having three wonderful children, and becoming the editor of *The Cricketer* magazine, I can firmly say that playing club cricket from about the ages of 15 to 25 was the most profoundly satisfying and enjoyably fun period of my life.

Playing alongside older men taught you things that equipped you for adult life. You learned about marriage, fatherhood, divorce, death and redundancy – how to keep the show on the road amid adversity; how cricket improves mood and enables people to bounce back. How, also, to cope with people who are richer than you; how to act humbly to people who are poorer; how to manage obnoxious creatures, and – as captain – how to imbue people with confidence.

I had several years at my local club, Halesworth, in north-east Suffolk, a short drive from the coast. It is a tragedy that it is now defunct, one of a tranche of sides that have bitten the dust in the county, and no doubt across the country. Smaller clubs have tended to disappear, or be absorbed into 'super clubs', those with the best facilities, with their own bars.

Halesworth had some tremendous characters, none more overpowering than Dick Clarke. 'Lad, come next to me at second slip … come closer, so close that if I fart, you can smell it.' He was a powerful ally, but he was not to get on the wrong side of. He was fiendishly accurate, and on wet wickets, he was a spiteful bowler. When the ball reared off a good length and welted an opponent, he was not one to show concern. When I left to go to a bigger club, he was not best pleased and it took him many years to forgive me. His sidekick was Terry Driver, a gentler and kinder man. I was in awe of him, for his powerful hitting, and he later said he was in awe of me, for my technique. 'I cannot give you advice; you have just played a couple of shots I have never played in my life!' It takes all sorts. There were quite a lot of these burly, muscular men in Suffolk cricket. Bub Grant, of Tuddenham, hit the ball harder than any player I have fielded to. They must have been of farming stock, or labourers; they wielded their bats, heavy things, like railway sleepers, often handcrafted by Baronet's Bernie Facer, like clubs. Dick Bond, of Lakenheath and Suffolk, was another. Brawny and belligerent, he reminded me of a Cossack. At Halesworth there was also David Lawn. I could not understand how David could play cricket because, I was told, most of his stomach had been cut out. He was a miracle man in my young eyes.

As my Woodbridge School days came to an end, I joined Deben Valley, the side for pupils, old boys, teachers, parents and friends (they changed their name to Woodbridge later on). The home school pitches were a vast improvement on those that I'd encountered at Halesworth, and it is a lovely ground; we also played at some exquisite venues on our travels, including Mildenhall, Worlington, Bury St Edmunds' Victory Ground, Easton, Yoxford and Southwold (by the sea, the home of Adnams – what is not to like?). I was spoilt really. I made sufficient runs to be asked to play a couple of matches for the Suffolk second team. It was also handy for my sportswriting with the newspapers based in Ipswich. More important was the comradeship, though. The younger players at Deben Valley were brilliant on Saturday, with a win-rate of about 80 to 90 per cent; but after a heavy night of pubs, Marlboro Lights, curry houses, nightclubs and 4 a.m. bedtimes, we would often turn up the worse for wear on the Sabbath. The older players noted wryly that our win-rate would drop to about 50/50.

The older players fascinated me. The traffic cop, Geoff Spencer, who smoked cheap cigarettes from the Co-op that we would cadge if we were desperate, and who bowled the loopiest, wiliest left-arm spin that anyone could imagine. The scientist, Peter Taylor, who celebrated yet another half-century by buying everyone a jug of orange squash. There was an orchard farmer, Charlie Parker, who was cut from the same cloth as Dick. He had a scathing tongue when riled, but was nevertheless good, intelligent company off the field. His polar opposite was a kind, playful, gnomic figure, Barry Spall, who liked nothing more than cutting quick bowlers off middle stump, and teasing opponents. A 160kg (25-stone) behemoth of a batsman would shuffle out to the middle, to be greeted by Barry shouting, 'Here he comes, no more quick singles now, lads!' 'Shut the f★★★ up, Barry!' was the furious reply. There was also Mike Barden. Anything short or back of a length, and he blocked it. You could contain him for over after over. Anything in his own half, and it would disappear into the next postcode, however.

My goodness, I miss those days. I had to move to London for my job, though, and then did not play every Saturday again for 20 years. Instead, I ran my own side, the Carpediems, and we found like-minded wandering sides, playing every three weeks or so, which was just about acceptable to wives and girlfriends. It was wonderful playing with old school teammates again, like Nick, and also seeing those who had not embraced the game when young, like Morgan and Simon, taking the chance to do so in their later years. We hired pitches in Dulwich, including the Trevor Bailey Sports Ground, owned by the private school. It was a pleasure to tell the great man that, when I went to interview him in 2010, for my book, *The Toughest Tour*. We tour Suffolk every July, and Corfu in the autumn.

In choosing a club, it is best to follow the words of Peter Andrews, chair of the Bank of England CC, as reported by Paul Edwards in *The Cricketer* in July 2017. 'Choosing to play for a team, after the first few games, is a statement that their values are compatible with one's own (not necessarily the same, but not so dissonant as to make playing uncomfortable). That embraces both how we play the game (attempt to be competitive, attempt to give everyone a reasonable go, show courtesy to opponents and officials) and socially.'

I look back at my club days when I was a young man with great fondness and find it sad that the format in jeopardy in world cricket – the 50-over game – is the one most similar to what is played by recreational cricketers at weekends. I would love the club game to go on forever, but sadly nothing does.

25

CRICKET JOURNALISM

'I saw history being written not in terms of what happened but of what ought to have happened according to various party lines.'

'What are cricket journalists like?' I have been asked. They are a generally courteous bunch. Less conceited and intimidating than the football hacks. When I spent my first sustained spell for national newspapers in press boxes from 2000 to 2006, most people were friendly; some were up themselves, as if they thought they were Tolstoy; some, well, one, were hideously haughty and spiky. Some local ones were horribly proprietorial about their areas and did their best to make you feel thoroughly unwelcome. Generally most people were OK, though.

These days the modern cricket writers – they seem young to me as a rule – appear earnestly liberal; they want to save the planet and play their part in fighting social injustice. Do not call them 'woke', as it annoys them. When I started out, some sports journalists were promiscuous and roguish … now they are more likely to be puritanical. It has all become a bit Presbyterian, even prudish. Many of them also seem defensive about franchise cricket. 'You represent everything I hate about old cricket writers!' one notoriously idealistic youngster who I had never met before told me a short while ago, after I had offered my hand by way of introduction. Ouch. I could only conclude that it is because I champion the red ball. I always make an effort to be friendly in the press box, whoever I am dealing with. I would never tell anyone what one reporter said when asked for advice on how to get on in journalism: 'F★★★ off!' To be fair, my protagonist offered an apology via WhatsApp the next day, which I accepted. This new generation want to change the world through journalism, ignoring inconvenient truths, whereas I was brought up to report on them. As George Orwell wrote: 'I saw history being written not in terms of what happened but of what ought to have happened according to various party lines.'

I always found Billy Birmingham's comedy creation 'The 12th Man' spoof cricket commentaries, *Fawlty Towers* and *The Inbetweeners*, to be hilarious… I am not sure the modern cricket writer would. The former has been deemed racist, for instance, for changing names like Mohinder Amarnath to Cuttiz Hisarminarf.

I will give you an example of earnest modern-day cricket writers: I was surprised that some journos were talking about the late Shane Warne not that affectionately (I loved him as a cricketer and always found him genial and helpful in person), focusing instead on his libido and his sexual shenanigans. Lord Botham is another. Asked to sum him up, a young journalist described him as: 'Unelected member of the House of Lords … Brexiteer' and so on. Now I know Beefy is not everyone's cup of tea, but come on, you have to acknowledge that he was a wonderfully entertaining and talented cricketer whose heroics in the Ashes galvanised the nation during the 1980s, and who, after despairing at seeing young leukaemia sufferers, raised more than £20m for research into the cancer – money that has helped transform survival outcomes. One thing that has not changed, however, is younger journalists naively wanting to give authority figures a free pass. World-weariness and cynicism have not been acquired, yet.

I have known that I wanted to be a sports journalist since I was in single figures. I used to make newspapers and distribute them to the neighbours. I had some good feedback. My breakthrough came at the Ipswich newspapers, after studying a degree in English and sport studies in London. I wrote and wrote to the sports editor of the *East Anglian Daily Times*, Tony Garnett, and he eventually visited me in the East Suffolk pub where I was working to raise money to travel to watch the Ashes series in Australia in 1994/95. He had a sandwich and a pint and put me on the spot by asking me a question about one of Ipswich Town's opponents in the FA Cup that weekend. I guessed the player's name – Andy Impey – and that was my initial test. Luckily, he liked cricket. He had been secretary of the Suffolk Minor Counties side who took the 1977 and 1979 titles, playing, he tells me, a prototype form of 'Bazball'.

Suffolk, like Ben Stokes, found draws anathema. Timur Mohamed, of Demerara and Guyana, was a batsman in that side. What Tony really wanted from me was for someone to sit next to him, answer the phones, type in the greyhound cards (some with smutty names), open letters and then, when all that was done, write some stories if I so wished. The penny eventually dropped that he just wanted to be left alone when he was busy; we worked on our relationship, how to co-exist and so on, and we became pretty good friends. I never turned any assignment down – show jumping, BMX, boxing – and he gave me a tremendous stepping stone into journalism. In Ipswich I learned what to do, and what *not* to do… There was a pleasing amount of cricket to cover. I followed the Suffolk Minor Counties team around the country in the 1998 season. Derek Randall was the professional, and told the players some amusing tales, which then found their way to me over a beer. Captain Phil Caley was in the top drawer of Minor Counties cricketers. Ray East was at nearby Ipswich School, so was always good for a yarn or two.

The last 18 months of my four-year stint in Ipswich was on the evening newspaper, where I learned a lot from my colleagues about racism, divorce and misogyny. I was never bored, though. Never once did I clock-watch. What a shame that these local newspapers are a shell of what they once were, if they still exist at all. And yes, the BBC's all-engulfing website is at least partially culpable.

The lure of London eventually made me leave. I joined the sports desk of the *Sunday Telegraph* as a sub-editor under the avuncular Jon Ryan and did some cricket and football writing. The highlight was being the news and quotes gatherer alongside Scyld (pronounced

'Shild', the first recorded name in English, from the poem *Beowulf)*
Berry, the cricket correspondent; I was his 'bag man' (like Endeavour
Morse to Fred Thursday, I like to think). It was so exciting. I was like a
jack-in-the-box. I was up and down out of my chair so often, it used
to infuriate the legendary scorer Wendy Wimbush, who sat behind
me. I adore Scyld. Once, he handed me his laptop and requested
that I recommend five ways of improving his article. How daunting
was that? He also taught me how to analyse the game more closely.
England lost to West Indies by an innings and 93 runs at Edgbaston
in the Test series opener in 2000. What did I think of it, he asked? I
was cross at what I saw as England's ineptitude. 'Terrible! Dreadful!'
'No,' urged Scyld. 'The surface was uneven, particularly on a length
at either end. It played directly into the hands of Curtly Ambrose
and Courtney Walsh, who had that crucial extra height, as opposed
to Darren Gough and Ed Giddins, shorter and skiddier.'

Of course, I should have known that, recalling the treacherous
surface that faced Mike Atherton's side in Birmingham against the
same opposition five years earlier. West Indies won that one by an
innings and 64 runs. He was confident that England would go on to
win the series under Nasser Hussain, and they did. While Scyld was
in his 'zone' after 4 p.m., honing his match report, I was despatched to
press conferences. When I played the tape back, he had an observation
to make. He told me to keep my questions short. Long questions
allow the interviewee to reply with short answers, which are not
as much use when you are trying to fill an 800-word slot. I can
claim one thing, mind you: I did teach him how to use Statsguru on
ESPNcricinfo... I was a teeny bit more au fait with the internet and
technology (although my family and colleagues would laugh at that).

One 2002 summer Saturday, England were playing a Test against Sri
Lanka at Edgbaston and news arrived in mid-afternoon that shamed
former South Africa skipper Hansie Cronje had been killed in a plane
crash. We looked at each other with that sense of anticipation/dread
(and a degree of sadness at Cronje's demise, of course), knowing that
almost everything we had been preparing would have to be consigned
to the desktop wastepaper bin. 'Events, dear boy, events!' Scyld is so
generous with his time. He proofread my book, *The Toughest Tour*, in
2010. He did not want any payment. 'I enjoyed it,' he insisted. He also
wrote the foreword. The label 'deep thinker' does not quite do Scyld

justice. In hotels after a day's play, he can be spotted in the corner of the restaurant with a notebook and pen, perhaps mulling over the best fields Jack Leach could set to left-handers.

I even had the chance to go abroad, as Scyld's locum. The Sunday newspaper journalists in those days were known as 'the bucket and spade brigade', as they only had to file once a week, on the Saturday. Because they had all week to think about it, though, their articles were expected to have a bit more to them. My maiden trip was to Zimbabwe in 2001. I went to visit the teenage duo of Hamilton Masakadza, who had just made a century on Test debut against West Indies at Harare, and wicket-keeper Tatenda Taibu, also making his bow that series, at the school, Churchill High. It was an exclusive interview. The mauve jacaranda leaves were in full bloom, and all seemed idyllic... Robert Mugabe's regime had not yet erupted into violence. We had a dinner at the end of the tour, which had seen Zimbabwe host England for five one-day internationals. I was suddenly told that because it was my first assignment overseas, I had to make a speech. Unlike the other debutant, the BBC's Jonny Saunders, I had been given no notice. I said: 'I can't possibly say anything with no preparation.' Saunders then did his speech. By now I had plucked up the courage, thought of some material and realised that it was too good an opportunity to miss. I banged the table. 'What's this, a second innings?' asked Jonathan Agnew. I had played tennis in a press tournament that day, and my best quip was: 'I never thought I'd be beaten for pace by Angus Fraser.' David 'Bumble' Lloyd looked bemused and mortified in equal measure but, in the circumstances, I think that they respected my efforts.

It was a struggle to make ends meet in those days. When it came to paying my hotel bill, I had to pay in a combination of US dollars, Zimbabwean dollars, and put some of it on my credit card. It took a while and I had to make way for the rather grand Agnew and his *Test Match Special* producer, Peter Baxter. 'Bloody hell, Turbers,' said Agnew. I let them through. Then they had trouble communicating with the receptionist. 'Now listen here, Clifford. We work for the B–B–C...'

The cricket press box can obviously be an intimidating place for youngsters. In 2003 on the fifth morning of the Test against South Africa at Edgbaston, I told the press box that Hussain was going to quit as Test captain.

'Bollocks!' I was informed. 'Why?'

'Well, I work with him on the *Sunday Telegraph* and I have been studying his body language and picking up on his mood. I reckon that he feels that he has lost hearts and minds to Michael Vaughan, who had taken over the one-day side with success.'

'Bah, load of rubbish,' snorted the red-top men.

An hour later an email arrived from England press officer Andrew Walpole: 'There will be an announcement regarding Nasser Hussain at the close of play.' I gave out a little chuckle and felt a delicious sense of vindication ... although crucially I had not had the hard facts – or perhaps balls – to write up the story the night before.

Those red-top men liked to flash their teeth at times. When I covered the one-day series in New Zealand for the *Sunday Telegraph* in 2001/02 the opportunity came up to interview Chris Cairns. He appeared and I walked over to him. There were three correspondents from English tabloids, standing in a pack.

'What do you want?' said one.

'To interview Chris Cairns.'

'Well push off.'

'What do you mean? Why?'

'You'll crowd him.'

It was ridiculous. As daily journalists they were published six times a week; I just had the one window, on a Sunday. They clearly had a huge advantage over me, and their article would go to press before mine. I wish I'd had the guts to tell him where to go. That is how old-school journalists survived in Fleet Street. I appreciate that now.

The editor of the *Sunday Telegraph* was Dominic Lawson, the son of the former Chancellor of the Exchequer, Nigel. He writes a terrific column now in *The Sunday Times*. He was a somewhat scary man, but he loved cricket. I wrote a story, against the clock, with the same word – 'whether' – in successive paragraphs one week. He was furious, ringed it on the table with a felt pen, and I was taken off cricket writing for a month or so. The first task when I was eased back in was to interview Lancashire and England fast bowler Sajid Mahmood. His upbringing; what he had done before he became a cricketer; how he impressed Rod Marsh at the academy. Lawson slipped into the sports department... 'Did you write that?' All eyes in the office were on me. Everyone breathed in. Time seemed to freeze. 'Y-y-yes,' I stuttered... 'It was very informative!' he barked. And walked out. I was back.

The 2005 Ashes was, of course, a highlight. On the Saturday at Edgbaston, Berry and I huddled together, frozen in slightly foetal positions. Andrew Flintoff played so boldly, so brilliantly. Helping Michael Kasprowicz over midwicket for six with power and timing. Hitting Brett Lee straight for six. 'Hello!' proclaimed Mark Nicholas on Channel 4. Simon Jones supported him valiantly. Scyld and I occasionally looked at each other in disbelief, like youngsters thrilled at the generosity of Father Christmas. The tense atmosphere was all-consuming. It was the best day in a press box ever. I covered all five days of the match and when Geraint Jones took the winning catch off Steve Harmison a young reporter, Wayne Veysey, stood up and roared in excitement. His senior colleague at the *Evening Standard*, David 'Toff' Lloyd, looked mortified, grabbed his arm and pulled him back into his chair. That was a big no-no.

At Trent Bridge during that series I had a scary/fun clash with Australia opening batsman Justin Langer. It was at the press conference on the Saturday, after substitute fielder Gary Pratt's run-out of captain Ricky Ponting. The use of substitute fielders had irked the tourists all series (and rightly so: England had exploited the system), and the hosts' coach Duncan Fletcher did not help by standing on the balcony grinning at Ponting as he came off. On this occasion, though, Pratt was on as a genuine replacement – Simon Jones was crocked (in fact, sadly he never played a Test again).

I asked: 'Justin, do you think it's because this series is so close after so many years of Australian domination that your team are getting overly upset about small incidents like this?'

'Mate,' came the reply, 'that's the dumbest f***ing question I've ever been asked.' One had to laugh. Stephen Fay, of the *Independent on Sunday*, reassured me that it was actually a good question, and when I reached the corridor immediately afterwards, Langer apologised. Then when I returned to my desk at the other side of the ground, Langer rang me and said sorry again. What a legend!

Another great highlight of those days at the *Sunday Telegraph* was being invited to the planning meeting, on a Tuesday. It was in Davy's Wine bar in Canary Wharf and lasted from midday to 6 p.m. *Hic.*

I also wrote for the *Daily Express*, where Colin Bateman was another good mentor. I had many evening shifts subbing badly written stories by football hacks. We all drank too much beer and ate too many takeaways. Many of those colleagues have sadly 'not made old bones', as my mother used to say. Desmond showed David and Victoria Beckham around our offices on the banks of the Thames in Blackfriars one night; she latched on to every word he said, whereas I thought Becks looked mortified.

Desmond was clearly not a tennis fan. He marched into the newsroom on a summer's day in 1995 and said that 'he wasn't paying us to sit there watching tennis.' He switched the telly off ... with Goran Ivanišević serving on match point in the men's final. A wag created a television out of cardboard with a picture of the Serb celebrating. It was put up on a wall and stayed there for years. Desmond was not without a sense of humour.

I did bits of cricket tours when Berry and Bateman needed a break. In Sri Lanka in 2003/04 a cobra crept into a packed crowd and it parted like the Red Sea. I phoned my copy through. 'With a cobra in the crowd, England needed Rikki-Tikki-Tavi, but alas all they had was Rikki Clarke...' The sub-editor had never heard of the mongoose from the *Jungle Book*, however, and to my disgust took it out. It was criminal.

I have ghost-written many cricketers – taking down their thoughts and writing them up as if they were doing it (ghosting means something else to youngsters these days). Chris Cairns – I finally got to talk to him! – was the best. It was for *The Sunday Telegraph*, and he knew how to go straight for the jugular. It was the summer of 2004. New Zealand had the first three Test matches of the summer, then West Indies had four. 'England have made us second billing to West Indies this summer. We intend to punish them for their impertinence!' he said. The sports editor was delighted. As it happened, Michael Vaughan's England won all seven.

Allan Donald was not quite so riveting, although perfectly competent and pleasant. The most exciting thing about that experience was that I accidentally sent him a romantic text message that was intended for my wife. 'Please ID yourself,' was his reply. As a *News of the World* reporter would have said: 'I made my excuses and left.'

I have ghosted Hussain for the *Sunday Telegraph* and *The Cricketer* magazine. During the 2001 Ashes he had broken his finger (again) and England were getting hammered (again). Ryan told me to ring him, and we did his column. Ryan then said he also needed a story for the front page. 'Well,' I said, 'Nasser told me that he intended to carry on as skipper until 2003...' Ryan was delighted and relieved. The front-page story said: 'Nasser to carry on until 2003'. The next day the proverbial hit the fan. Dermot Reeve, Ian Smith and co. took him to task on Channel 4. 'How dare he say that? It's not up to him how long he stays England captain, it is up to the selectors, etc.' In the *Daily Mail* the next day Nasser attempted to clarify the situation via his old mate Paul Newman. I had probably been naive, not seeing the trap that lay ahead. It never occurred to me that it would be a problem. He was a great captain, one of England's finest, doing a tremendous job. I thought that everyone would be delighted. Nasser never harbours a grudge, and I carried on ghosting him, as I do today for *The Cricketer*.

With most players, they say things, and you put them in the order that you see fit. I had the most extraordinary time with Geoffrey Boycott, however. This is the procedure with him: he dictates to his wife what he wants to say. She types it out and prints it off. He reads it out to you down the phone. You write it down, then type it in, and send it back. So he phones me up. 'For f★★k's sake, this is not what I said!' I had literally only changed the odd word, and I was mortified, but then his kindness shone through: 'Never mind, lad, this is the first time we have done this together...'

Ray Illingworth was a favourite interviewee, but he could be hot and cold. My book, *The Toughest Tour*, had a chapter on every Ashes series in Australia since the First World War. Illy gave me chapter and verse on the 1970/71 tour, John Snow et al. It felt like we were on the phone for two hours. A while later I phoned him to talk about England's home series with India in the 1971 tour, the one with the elephant, at The Oval. England lost... 'No thanks. I don't want to talk about that!' And the phone went down.

From 2008 to 2015 I had opted for a staff sub-editing job at the *Daily Telegraph* to provide security for my young family. The sports editor who appointed me, Keith Perry, was also wonderfully supportive of my writing, and the first few months went well. I ghosted George Cohen about the 1966 football World Cup triumph and came up with a couple of good cricket scoops, including the dire decision to phase out England's iconic woolly pully. That made the front page of the main paper. Alas, Perry was moved upstairs shortly after I started, and with the internet already threatening the hegemony of print, it was obvious that there was going to be some cuts. Several sports journalists declined the chance to head the department, so a news man called Mark Skipworth came in from *The Times* as head of sport and he wielded the axe.

I was news editor quite a lot and answered the phone when these cuts were taking place. I spoke to a bewildered Graham Taylor, the former England football manager, who asked me what was going on. Writers were frightened about losing their jobs and were being kept in the dark. Some did not help themselves, though. One athletics writer had filed nothing for a fortnight. Perry instructed me to ring him and ask him to cover an athletics meeting the next day. 'How dare you!' he replied. 'Tomorrow [Saturday] is my day off!' Perry and I knew that time for such dinosaurs was running out. The production department did not escape the treatment. A week before Christmas in 2008 we knew that something was afoot when the secretary stayed behind after 5.30 p.m., their usual departure time. Five staff sub-editors started the shift that night, and by 10 p.m. when the paper was sent to the printers, two – including me – were still sitting there. There were so many good cricket writers at the *Telegraph* that my chances were limited once Perry had left. Only on a few occasions did they need me as a cricket writer in an emergency. They required my services to bang out 1000 words in under an hour when Kevin Pietersen did a video revoking his decision to quit one-day internationals, slap-bang in the middle of Mo Farah's glory at the 2012 London Olympics; and the other time was when Graeme Swann quit cricket midway through the 2013/14 Ashes series in Australia, at 9 p.m., when the edition went an hour later.

The culls happened every two years until I left after securing my dream job at *The Cricketer* in 2015. Good things come to those who wait. During those years, I had all but given up. 'You might never get a job in cricket writing,' I was told by a cricket writer. Luckily, another one, Bill Day, said: 'You cannot keep a good man down.' Those words stayed with me.

My saviour was the magazine's managing director, Andy Afford, the former Nottinghamshire left-arm spinner. I had the best interview I have ever had until the final question, a curveball: 'What are the last three non-cricket books you have read?' I was not expecting it, but I quickly regained my composure and luckily at the time I was a member of a book club. *Dracula*, *The Prime of Miss Jean Brodie* and Julian Barnes' excellent *Metroland* were reeled off, and my dream job was mine. Afford gave me some advice: 'Always be positive about cricket. Readers of *Caravan Weekly* do not want to be told how rubbish caravans are.' I do bear it in mind, although sometimes my education in journalism, cynicism and traditionalism dictates that I do otherwise, I daresay. I was initially hired as a sub-editor, before rapidly being upgraded to deputy editor. From 2016, I became managing editor working with editor Simon Hughes. 'Does that mean you do all the work and he gets all the credit?' a journalist asked me. Simon was always graceful around us, though, and was good enough to acknowledge the work of me and my colleagues James Coyne, later my deputy, and Geoff Barton, the art director. Simon called me 'joint editor' when speaking to the public. He is a bit of a maverick, he cuts a few corners, but he is funny and engaging and is good at opening commercial doors. He was popular with our readers.

I became editor myself in 2021, a hugely proud moment. I wish my parents had lived to see it, but Dad died earlier that year, and Mum two years before that. The job is incredibly fulfilling – a mixture of writing, sub-editing, proofreading and commissioning. Another hugely enjoyable aspect of the role has been that two cricket writers who, in one case, treated me as invisible and another who treated me with disdain, now had to talk to me.

In 2021 we also celebrated our anniversary, and I had the pleasure of writing up the magazine's history. Founded by Sir Pelham Warner, the former England captain, *The Cricketer* was based in Fleet Street. Arthur Conan Doyle, A.A. Milne and C. Aubrey Smith were among the famous, early contributors. Warner stayed editor until 1963. In the 1932/33 'Bodyline' series he had a dilemma. Warner (known as Plum, of course) was manager of the England team. He famously disapproved of Douglas Jardine's 'Bodyline' tactics but could not be too scathing about them in the magazine – after all, he was part of the England squad... He did not resign or anything like that, so *The Cricketer* tried to ignore the whole brouhaha.

The magazine was produced by a husband-and-wife team, Arthur Langford and his wife, Meg, in Surbiton, and a man called E.L. Roberts drove their pages to Bermondsey to have them printed up. All through the war years and the London Blitz this carried on. E.W. Swanton started writing for the magazine, from shortly before the start of the Second World War, just before he famously became a prisoner of war of the Japanese. I wonder if he met my grandfather, who was forced at knifepoint to serve on the Railway of Death in Burma. Swanton wrote for *The Cricketer* up until his death in 2000. The editorial staff tried to slash his word count once. 'Dear boy, my words are golden!' There is also the story of when he was in the press box at his beloved Canterbury in 1996. Matt Walker was batting against Somerset, coming close to beating Frank Woolley's 270, the record score by a Kent batsman at the St Lawrence ground. As Walker entered the 260s, Swanton ran down the steps, waving his arms at him, imploring him to leave the record intact. Walker refused to walk and went on to make 275 not out.

In the 1960s the American company who owned *The Cricketer* wanted to close it down. Ben Brocklehurst, the former amateur Somerset captain (he averaged 15 with the bat between 1952 and 1954 and did not bowl) persuaded them to give it to him as his redundancy present. He and his wife Belinda, and son Tim, ran it from their home in Ashurst, Kent. They were commercially savvy. They created The Cricketer Cup for schools in 1966, the National Village Cup in 1972 (*The Cricketer* still runs this), and *Cricketer* holidays to Corfu. Editors included David Frith (a slightly fierce Anglo-Australian who I used semi-regularly as a writer) and Reggie Hayter, who founded the legendary journalism agency named after him. Christopher Martin-Jenkins became editor in the 1980s, when I started reading and loving the magazine. 'I would be walking on the shoulders of giants,' I said to Afford at my interview. I feel that way still. We must strive to keep this beautiful thing going.

Sometimes we might seem a bit traditional and earn the disapproval of the young liberal journalists who work for other organisations. When the ICEC report came out in 2023, 'to drive equity, diversity and inclusion forward within cricket', young journalists' instincts seem to be that it was heresy to analyse. 'You! Do! Not! Debate! Racism!' Of course, we were doing no such thing – we were debating if it was a good report or not. There were some good things in it, and the 2000-plus people who say that they have been racially abused on the cricket field is a saddening, damning statistic. There were leaps as well, however, suggesting that the entire English game was riddled with racism. There was also quite a bit of revisionism. To say that England captain Mike Gatting's argument with Pakistani umpire Shakoor Rana at Faisalabad in the winter of 1987/88 was prejudiced ignores the facts: the Pakistani umpires showed clear bias towards the hosts. Mudassar Nazar, the Pakistan all-rounder, admitted that to me. He said that he was embarrassed about the officiating in that series. During the 1970/71 Ashes in Australia, England did not receive a single lbw and West Indies also lost their cool in New Zealand in the 1980s when they never got a decision in their favour. That was bad umpiring. Biased umpiring.

The other tricky group I find in the press box are the former players. There are sweet people like Steve James, who used to work with me at the *Telegraph* and now works for *The Times*, and Vic Marks, who wrote for the *Guardian* and the *Observer* for 31 years. We are now lucky enough to have him on *The Cricketer*. Angus Fraser, who became cricket correspondent of the *Independent*, is another good guy.

Michael Vaughan is a bit of a blunt instrument. I wanted to remember him as some sort of modern-day Walter Hammond, stroking three superb centuries off Glenn McGrath and Shane Warne – half of one of the finest attacks of all time – in the 2002/03 Ashes series, with majestic cover drives and crisp swivel-pulls. It felt like *him* alone against Australia. He then became a universally well-regarded captain, with perceptive man-management skills. Building on the great work of Nasser Hussain, he took England to the promised land: beating Australia after an agonising 18-year wait. Shane Warne called him 'England's greatest captain'. 'When Vaughan is in charge, he is relaxed and chilled out and encourages people to express themselves,' Andrew Flintoff said. 'Nasser was totally different. I don't think it is any accident that I have played some of my best cricket under Michael simply because he encourages you to enjoy your cricket without fear of failure.' Vaughan knew the players who wanted an arm around their shoulders, and those who needed a kick up the backside. He became a bold, strident pundit. He was highly entertaining. *The Cricketer* did an evening with him, and he was indiscreet.

I digress. Vaughan was a media star – he was also popular on Australian television. Then something was invented that was the making of him, but almost the destruction of him: Twitter (now X). I won't go into all that here, but he has said some things, and apologised for some things. He is still always the first to know what will make a good headline, always the first to try to appear progressive. 'It's time to lose a day and have four-day Tests!' 'Replace counties with franchises!'

In recent times, the cricket correspondent of the *Daily Mirror*, Dean Wilson, was made redundant. That is sad news. Now the *Mirror* and the *Sun* do not have one – although John Etheridge fulfils the role for the latter as a freelancer. It feels like a grave development, for newspapers and for the game of cricket. It is because stories about football's Premier League, specifically the top six clubs, attract far more readers than anything else. That is also why broadsheet papers like *The Times* and *Telegraph* do not cover county cricket so much anymore. They used to have a reporter at every match. Now, often everything is shovelled into a round-up. Newspapers have also had to cut costs drastically. The *Independent*, which used to have a healthy dose of cricket with writers such as Stephen Brenkley, David Llewellyn, Fraser and Stephen Fay, folded as a print product and is now available on website only. 'You can read everything online now' is a popular notion.

There are obvious comparisons with the battle between the red (traditional) and white ball (progressive) in cricket. People predict what the landscape will look like in 50 years, and then they want it now. They destroy something that remains profitable, and gives people pleasure, but they are cutting their noses off to spite their faces. They also make something's extinction a self-fulfilling prophecy.

T20 does not lend itself to great cricket writing. In August 2023 and 2024 *The Times* barely had a word on The Hundred. What a spectacularly bland future it threatens to be.

26

CRICKET AND MY FAMILY

3 September 1945

'We are depositories of our memories, and those of our forebears.'

It was like looking at a stranger. I had not seen my wife for three years. How could I even begin to explain what I had gone through? How could we pick up the pieces again? All those shared experiences, in eight years of marriage, and then a relationship cut in half. I was on the other side of the world, in hell. She was at home, trying to carry on. Of course it must have been hard for her too. Wondering what had happened to me. Raising two children on her own. The country, the world, wracked with uncertainty. As I looked through the train windows, she was at the front of a large crowd on the platform at Milford Haven station, as far west as the British Isles stretched. I wish I had not had to return to Wales by train. I never wanted to see a damn railway again in my life, after Burma. She looked thinner, obviously. Rationing had seen to that. Not as thin as me, though. I was now back up to nine stone, from six, after six months of slow rehabilitation at, first, a repatriation centre in Bangkok, Thailand, then Rangoon in Burma, then Bangalore, India. My head and body ached. All that malaria, I guess. I wondered if it was a permanent sensation.

The train had finally come to a standstill now. The next few minutes were a blur, like an out-of-body experience. I had had enough of them in the camp. One long bout of panic. Japanese guards screaming at us. What were they saying? The agony of hunger. Rice and dirty water. Rice and dirty water. Rice and dirty water. The brutality. All for what? To build a railway that the Japanese never even ended up using.

We hugged, her embrace pushing all the air out of me. We were then swept along by the cheering mass. I recognised many of them. They patted and clawed at me. There was my old car. That was a welcome sight. Margaret and I had many happy times in that, weaving around the winding roads of Pembrokeshire on the way to its beautiful beaches.

My friend, Keith, was at the wheel. He smiled warmly. 'Let's get you out of here, get you home, get a cuppa inside you.' Ha, the old cuppa – the answer to all life's ills. As he turned the key, the engine tried to splutter into life. Several attempts later a look of panic spread across Keith's face. 'Sorry, Raymond ... it got us down here all right ... I'm not sure what the problem is...' Then we started moving anyway. Twenty people started pushing the car. We were over the bridge, then up St Lawrence Hill. It is extremely steep. I didn't think that they would make it. We started rolling back at one stage, and more people joined the push. All the time my head was elsewhere. Margaret and I looked at each other but did not say much. We finally made it to Waterloo Road. Keith hurried to the back door and helped me out.

'We'll come and see you later, Raymond. Get settled in first.'

'All the best, Ray ... it's wonderful to have you back!' We rushed back into the house and the big oak door slammed shut. I looked at Margaret. She looked at me. Then she burst into tears.

As you hopefully realised, that was me putting myself in the shoes of my grandfather, Raymond Picton Turbervill. The incident really happened. It must have made for an incredibly evocative scene. After the railway, from Nong Pladuk in Thailand to Thambuzyat in Burma, was completed in October 1943, Raymond was kept on as part of a maintenance team, repairing bombed bridges. They worked from 4.30 a.m. to 8 p.m. They lost 20,000 men – about one in three – from cholera, malaria, beriberi, dysentery ... and brutality. There were eight regulations; break them and it would result in 'immediate death': disobeying orders; being antagonistic; showing egoism; talking without permission; walking and moving without orders; showing signs of running away; trying to take extra food; using more than two blankets.

Raymond's job was to burn the bodies of his friends. He was a miracle man. He caught cholera but recovered from it. The Japanese scientists wanted to know how he had done it. They pored over him, carrying out numerous tests. If Raymond got better, maybe the others could too... so they could get back to work.

Another close shave came when Raymond and his friend Syd broke out of camp to see if they could find some supplies. They would trade their cigarettes for food with the locals. Horrifically, as they broke back into the camp, they ran into a Korean guard. He would inform his Japanese masters, and they would be punished with death: shot or bayonetted before being allowed to bleed to death. Raymond and Syd had no choice: they overpowered then strangled him.

When my grandfather was released, he tried to read up on what he had missed. The period when he had been a prisoner, 1942 and 1943, had been a blank when it came to world news. Of course, he did not recognise his children, Gordon, my father, and Lilian, upon his return. Life for Raymond was, of course, horrendously hard after the war. The memories, the flashbacks. He resumed his work as an accountant. He took refuge in the men-only members' drinking club over the road, the Waterloo, where he was secretary. He drank too much, though – who wouldn't? – to drown out the pain, to try to dilute the nightmares. A courteous, modest man, he was reluctant to talk about the war. His wife's patience was tested. He passed away at the age of 67, his remains committed to the waters of Milford Haven Waterway, one of the deepest natural harbours in the world.

When I was caring for my parents – as an only child I was responsible for organising care rotas in an area of Suffolk known as a 'black hole' for that sort of thing – I turned to therapy. It was a rewarding yet arduous, and frankly terrifying period of my life. I was anxious, struggling to sleep, fearful of the future. I did not know if I would be able to hold down my job. One of the many interesting things my therapist told me was how we carry the memories and experiences of our forefathers. My grandfather's war scars would have had a profound effect on Gordon. A French teacher at Halesworth Middle School, he was quite an internationalist, but – understandably – he was wary of the Japanese. For years he refused to buy their cars and electrical goods, if they could be avoided. Except, curiously, Sony televisions. For some reason he always insisted upon them. And then he had an epiphany moment, in 1994. His school twinned with one in Japan: Shirakawa High. Now initially this prospect filled him with dread but he struck up a close friendship with the visiting teacher – a true gentleman. He was an ornithophile, and Dad took him to watch the birds and the breaking of the dawn together at Minsmere Nature Reserve. Dad was invited back to Japan in return, and had an enjoyable, cathartic time.

Where is this all going, you may well wonder? This is a book about cricket. It is just what my therapist said: we are depositories of our memories, and those of our forebears. Could that blind spot about Japan of my father (at least until he went there, and it would not be a wild leap of imagination to assume, of my grandfather, though I never heard that) have transferred to me when it comes to formulating my world and life views? I certainly have a deep reluctance to let go of things in my past that have given me such pleasure. I enjoyed school. Mainly the cricket. Others seemed to be only too happy for it to end, to move on. Not me. The same with my love of cricket. The 1980s were magical for me, the England characters colourful and flamboyant: Beefy, Golden, Lambie, Goochie, Gatt… Ditto county cricket. The sticker album. Gooch and Pringle at Chelmsford; Imran and Garth Le Roux at Hove, and Paul Parker and the Wells brothers. Wonderfully warm memories.

I always find it astonishing when people I know and like, who actually played county cricket, do not have that same sentimentality for their former clubs. Instead, they talk about the expansion of The Hundred.

I also enjoyed cricket in the 1990s, if perhaps not quite as much. Mike Atherton, Alec Stewart, Angus Fraser and Devon Malcolm were super cricketers to watch.

I enjoyed working in the game in the 2000s. Nasser Hussain is a good man. Marcus Trescothick and Paul Collingwood have always been helpful. Michael Vaughan has been on a journey.

I no longer see people like Joe Root and Ben Stokes as my heroes, even though they are wonderful cricketers, who I have loved watching. Root especially seems complicit in rejecting my beloved county cricket. He suggests cricket keeps the Northern Superchargers in The Hundred, and scales back – or even eradicates, the Yorkshire T20 side. This seems like heresy to me. In many ways it would be easier just to go with the flow, to embrace change, to not be a 'middle-aged guy lecturing younger generations'... but you have to believe in some things in life, don't you?

CONCLUSION: LET'S TALK UP TEST CRICKET

'"Cricket must remain relevant to the next generation." ... but you don't have to euthanise the first-class game in the process.'

'Don't kill Test cricket for the rest of us!' They were the words of David Gower after he attended World Cricket Connects, an event organised by MCC and hosted by Mark Nicholas. The Long Room of Lord's hosted a century of cricket's leading lights in July 2024 for a symposium to discuss the future of cricket. I was one of the journalists waiting in the adjacent, resplendent Reading Room, but spotted inside were Jos Buttler, Kumar Sangakkara, Graeme Smith, Ramiz Raja, Rob Key, Heather Knight, Clare Connor, Brendon McCullum, Andrew Strauss and his old friend Kevin Pietersen. Mike Atherton helped host it, and big names from the world of cricket administration were in attendance, including ICC and ECB chairs Greg Barclay and Richard Thompson. Oh, and some business people, like Rajasthan Royals owner Manoj Badale and Sanjog Gupta, Star TV head of sports. Some might say that they have the real power; I couldn't possibly comment. The timing seemed appropriate, after the T20 World Cup in the Caribbean and the USA (the new frontier), won by powerhouse India, ahead of the long-awaited first Test of the English summer, England v West Indies at Lord's, James Anderson's 188th and final Test.

Mr Nicholas ... he has so many qualities. Energetic and effervescent, he was a terrific host of Channel 4 cricket. He did not spin it when I asked if fans of Test cricket would feel better after the day's chat, however. After a bit of a pause, he admitted to me in *The Cricketer* (Summer 2024):

> Not much... The world is reacting to − not England, I agree − the short form. If you go to a ground, that is where the children are; T20 is the behemoth that everybody wants... It's where the new market is; it's where the fans are; it's where the money is. In cricket, money is seen as a dirty word, but it shouldn't be, as it is the only way to sustain the game.

He was enthralled by Rajasthan Royals owner Manoj Badale's presentation:

> Manoj's take on where we are was one of the highlights ... the importance of the fan, that the fan drives the market ... and how we easily forget that ... because we have established traditional views which don't really reflect the modern fan.
>
> Sanjog Gupta was also crystal clear on the fact that only the fan drives the market. There are probably no more than 20–30 players in the world who make it worth the TV rights ... which is a very interesting point: how many superstars actually are there, who make it worth investing billions of dollars in cricket? And that is what happens if you don't constantly upgrade your access, interest and response to fans.

At least the controversial ICC distribution table for 2024–2027 was discussed. It is projected that there will be surplus funds − or dividends − of $600m from the sale of media rights. Of those, Full Members will receive 88.81 per cent, with the Associate nations the remaining 11.19. And of the 88.81, India will get 38.5, with England, the next highest, 6.89, and Australia, 6.25. Afghanistan will get 2.3, the least amount. It was acknowledged that more must be done to ensure West Indies and others keep playing Tests.

As the event ended, Sky TV put up a graphic from a waterlogged Kia Oval (Surrey v Middlesex in the Blast, match abandoned) that showed the ludicrous amount of white-ball cricket England's men face between now and spring 2026: the ICC Champions Trophy in February 2025, masses of bilateral series, culminating in another T20 World Cup, in India and Sri Lanka. Cricket's powerbrokers just can't seem to get enough…

Gower – who had to ask for an invite from his old Hampshire team-mate – was frustrated. 'Although the matter was indeed discussed, the overall impression that I took away from the day was that the decline of long-form red-ball cricket is just an inevitability,' he wrote in *The Cricketer* in the Summer 2024 issue. 'We were told, "Cricket must remain relevant to the next generation." Well, fine, but you don't have to euthanise the first-class game in the process.' Gower also made a fascinating analogy with the new Labour government.

> Badale warned us that change was coming – he said: 'Just look at Labour.' What struck me about that analogy was that our new government had just been elected on 33.7 per cent of the vote and needs to reflect not just the core support of its 'fans', but the interests of others who might not have voted for them.

Gower implored his friend Kumar Sangakkara not to meekly accept that T20 will continue to proliferate and eventually smother Test cricket, but to fight it… For otherwise it becomes a self-fulfilling prophecy.

> People will listen to the recent greats, of which he is certainly one. Virat Kohli made it clear that he values it as the pinnacle. If the world's best players stand up for Test cricket, then its demise can be slowed.

Thankfully, Pat Cummins and Ben Stokes sent video messages to the event that did give Test cricket their full support. While the Australia Test captain admitted that he could be away from his family for much less time playing purely franchise, Cummins said: 'Test cricket ties the cricket world together. It's where people learn their craft. It's so important. It gives context to the other formats. It's where a deep love of cricket comes from for most fans. A world where international cricket and franchises working in unison is what we are all striving for.' He wants windows for Test cricket. Stokes called Test cricket 'incredibly vital', and said, optimistically, that 'there would always be a place for it'.

Alas, the first Test series of the summer, featuring the visit of West Indies, was one-sided, with England winning 3–0. At Lord's after the first Test former paceman Colin Croft highlighted to me how ludicrous it was that Shamar Joseph had not bowled a ball in first-class cricket since being West Indies' match-winner at Brisbane in February. Of course, it all comes down to money, with former captain Jason Holder telling *The Times*: 'We don't make money from any home series apart from England or India. We lose a significant amount when we tour. All the television revenue is kept by the host board. If we get, say, 10 per cent of what the ECB generate for a series here, it would probably cover our expenses.'

James Anderson bowed out after that Lord's Test, reluctantly ushered off the stage at the age of 41 by the team's management with 704 Test wickets from 188 appearances. Not that many people saw it on television. The peak audience for the England football team in the European Championship in the summer had exceeded 20m. The BBC's coverage of the Wimbledon Lawn Tennis Championship came in at 2.4m. The peak audience for the Anderson farewell behind the Sky paywall, though, was 694,000. And no amount of spin can put a gloss on that, however exceptional the quality of the coverage is.

The Doomsday Clock was discussed a lot during the Cold War between the East – led by the Soviet Union – and the United States of America-led West. It represented the imminence of a human-made global catastrophe, nuclear war most likely, and made an unwelcome reappearance in 2022, sadly, thanks to Vladimir Putin's invasion of Ukraine. Test cricket could have its own clock. Every week, every month, there are new reports of how red-ball cricket is receding.

Matt Damon gave an interview explaining that the film industry is inclined to experiment much less these days. Unless you have £100m and pretty much can guarantee a return on your investment – think Martin Scorsese – forget it. So, it is generic blockbusters all the way... Marvel-ous stuff. Cricket is becoming like that, with its ever-expanding global accretion of T20 tournaments. Am I having a midlife crisis perhaps? Maybe. Stop living in the 20th century, I am told. But if you think that the world of cricket will be better in 2029 than 1989, with wall-to-wall franchise competitions and scant red-ball cricket, we will have to agree to disagree.

Perhaps if we act conservatively we will miss out on all the loot from this T20 bonanza, but the damage to county cricket and its competitions is already proving grisly. Maybe the hordes of casual cricket fans will expand, but the hearts of many traditional supporters are also being well and truly broken.

I do like a science-fiction analogy and cannot help thinking of the classic *Star Trek* episode 'The Trouble with Tribbles' (1967). The furry creatures are like T20. First there were just a few, but soon Captain James T. Kirk's ship was being overrun with them (for further research, watch the film *Gremlins* [1984]).

The impatience of our 'betters' is wearing thin. Our county clubs have been called 'heroin addicts', and we supporters have been called 'fleas on the tail', and 'Luddites'. Perhaps the moneymen will have their wish and have blanket T20 – with a bit of a T10 thrown in as variety – one day... Until then, as long as aficionados of the red-ball game can walk to the grounds, we will try to resist.

REFERENCES

Interviews I conducted for the purposes of this book are not referenced here.

Introduction

'Gideon Haigh has described as a "10th-rate IPL knock-off"': Haigh, G., 'The WTC final is cricket's lip service to a format with a clouded future', *The Australian*, 2 June 2023. Available at: www.theaustralian.com.au/subscribe/news/1/?sourceCode=TAWEB_ WRE170_a_GGL&dest=https%3A%2F%2Fwww.theaustralian.com.au%2Fsport%2Fthe -wtc-final-is-crickets-lip-service-to-a-format-with-a-clouded-future%2Fnews-story %2Fe9dff5d5165ff7ad227c97177e3b7dc1&memtype=anonymous&mode=premium&v21 =GROUPA-Segment-1-NOSCORE&V21spcbehaviour=append ·

'"I couldn't believe the schedule when I saw it"': Turbervill, H. 'Glenn McGrath: Facing up', *The Cricketer*, March 2023.

'"We can make Test cricket work if we make it more of an event,"': BBC Sport, 'Future of Test cricket could be like Wimbledon, says Rajasthan Royals owner Manoj Badale', 4 May 2023. Available at: www.bbc.co.uk/sport/cricket/65486612

'The New Zealander ... also suggested that the Ashes could become like the Ryder Cup': Martin, A., 'Cricketers' chief Lynch: "The Ashes could become like the Ryder Cup"', *The Guardian*, 26 May 2024. Available at: www.theguardian.com/sport/article/2024/ may/26/cricketers-chief-lynch-the-ashes-could-become-like-the-ryder-cup

'"Test cricket is very traditional and cricket started with that as the only format"': Dobell, G., 'Jos Buttler addresses rumours surrounding possible return to Test cricket', *The Cricketer*, 13 March 2024. Available at: www.thecricketer.com/Topics/england/jos _buttler_addresses_rumours_surrounding_possible_return_to_test_cricket.html

'The game has "democratised"': Dobell, G., 'Sir Andrew Strauss: "The rise of franchise cricket is one of the great steps forward"', *The Cricketer*, 1 February 2023. Available at: www.thecricketer.com/Topics/news/sir_andrew_strauss_rise_franchise_cricket_great _steps_forward.html

'"The Hundred is committed through to 2028"': England and Wales Cricket Board, 'High-Performance Review of Men's Cricket in England and Wales, Final Report', September 2022. Available at: https://resources.ecb.co.uk/ecb/document/2022/09/22/60de6c08 -1cb1-4ff7-a749-7a21cb4b4eb5/Men-s-High-Performance-Review-Report.pdf

"'a reduction from 14 rounds of County Championship matches a summer over my dead body'": Ibid.

"'act now to future-proof a healthy balance'": Ibid.

"'Just let global forces take their course'": Ibid.

"'I want to keep Test cricket at the forefront'": Gatting, M., 'David Gower has lunch with', *The Cricketer*, August 2023.

"'I played for Chennai in the IPL in 2009'": Flintoff, A., 'Andrew Flintoff: The IPL was a waste of time... Lancashire was my true love', *Mail Online*, 11 October 2015. Available at: www.dailymail.co.uk/sport/cricket/article-3268665/Andrew-Flintoff-IPL-waste-time-Lancashire-true-love.html#:~:text=But%20when%20I%20played%20for,not%20a%20reflection%20on%20them.

"'Lots of people are talking about how to keep bilateral cricket relevant'": BBC Sport, 'England v Australia: Cricket risks losing its relevance over packed schedule', 22 November 2022. Available at: www.bbc.co.uk/sport/cricket/63716620

'Former West Indies Cricket Board chief executive Johnny Grave said that they had little choice': Turbervill, H., 'West Indies doing their best to buck red-ball trend but Test picture is bleak outside the big three', *The Cricketer*, 23 December 2023. Available at: www.thecricketer.com/Topics/premiumopinion/west_indies_doing_best_buck_red-ball_trend_but_test_picture_bleak_outside_big_three.html?fbclid=IwY2xjawF-Efl leHRuA2FlbQIxMQABHfOP3ZuIW7002LCF0-s-XN0-n2mDw3yqQhSCoa1 KfSL7pOb-l1LDSWC7Xg_aem_reCkf07z70CIy3

'Steve Waugh slammed the move': Sports Desk, 'If I was New Zealand I wouldn't even play: Steve Waugh slams South Africa for naming second string side for Test series', *The Indian Express*, 1 January 2024. Available at: www.indianexpress.com/article/sports/cricket/steve-waugh-slams-south-africa-for-naming-second-string-side-for-new-zealand-tests-9090627/

"'If I was New Zealand cricket, I would be quite disappointed'": ZA Cricket, 'Mark Boucher Disappointed with CSA's Scheduling, Concerns about Test Cricket's Integrity', 16 January 2024. Available at: www.zacricket.com/2024/01/16/mark-boucher-disappointed-with-csas-scheduling-concerns-about-test-crickets-integrity

"'That's not really what you want to see'": Reid, A., 'Pat Cummins and Steve Smith rip rival nation's "weird" move against Test cricket', Yahoo Sports Australia, 6 December 2023. Available at: https://au.sports.yahoo.com/cricket-pat-cummins-steve-smith-rip-south-africa-weird-move-new-zealand-test-series-205736886.html?guccounter=1&guce_referrer=aHR0cHM6Ly93d3cuZ29vZ2xlLmNvbS8&guce_referrer_sig=AQAAANvOGVbxvJthgpSzjcpYoZSxpOYPGXb6fxlrB9knzINyM_ye9uEQjswJJq__qPMSs_lKjsyusuRJuWipDunrhkj7bowpORU6oQYIMucjOUFBJoVWvvnuKZQZZ YXNWiNYlm_HJdfRDOqqwwX3JmYHYdtDCTC4aRrda7uC6xqQ2rg0

"'It is disappointing ... It is weird'": Reid, A., 'Pat Cummins and Steve Smith rip rival nation's "weird" move against Test cricket', Yahoo Sports Australia, 6 December 2023. Available at: https://au.sports.yahoo.com/cricket-pat-cummins-steve-smith-rip-south-africa-weird-move-new-zealand-test-series-205736886.html?guccounter=1&guce_referrer=aHR0cHM6Ly93d3cuZ29vZ2xlLmNvbS8&guce_referrer_sig=AQAAANvOGVbxvJthgpSzjcpYoZSxpOYPGXb6fxlrB9knzINyM_ye9uEQjswJJq__qPMSs_lKjsyusuRJuWipDunrhkj7bowpORU6oQYIMucjOUFBJoVWvvnuKZQZZ YXNWiNYlm_HJdfRDOqqwwX3JmYHYdtDCTC4aRrda7uC6xqQ2rg0

"'I love Test cricket to bits'": Reuters, 'Boucher concerned for test cricket amid rise of T20 leagues', 13 September 2022. Available at: www.reuters.com/lifestyle/sports/boucher-concerned-test-cricket-amid-rise-t20-leagues-2022-09-13 'he "doesn't care" about accusations of sportswashing.': MacInnes, P., 'Mohammed bin Salman says he will "continue doing sport washing" for Saudi Arabia', The *Guardian*, 21 September 2023. Available at: www.theguardian.com/world/2023/sep/21/mohammed -bin-salman-says-he-will-continue-doing-sport-washing-for-saudi-arabia

Chapter 1

'There is an article [...] on the BBC website': BBC online, 'IPL: The batting blitz turning cricket into baseball', 24 April 2024. Available at: www.bbc.co.uk/news/world-asia-india -68872429

'"If you want to only see 350-run matches and rate only those wickets as good, then I disagree with that…"': Fernando, A.F., 'Dravid disagrees with "average" rating given to Ahmedabad and Chennai pitches', ESPNCricinfo, 21 October 2023. Available at: www .espncricinfo.com/story/icc-cricket-world-cup-rahul-dravid-disagrees-over-average -rating-given-to-ahmedabad-and-chennai-pitches-1404666#

'"The old guard … keep saying T20 is sh*te and we want more Tests…"': Available at: www .x.com/KP24/status/1751928902505648432

Chapter 2

'Kohli does indeed say that by the way': News desk, 'Test cricket is "real cricket", Virat Kohli says', *Pakistan Observer*, 4 March 2022. Available at: www.pakobserver.net/test -cricket-is-real-cricket-virat-kohli-says

'Ponting wrote about T20 in his *Ashes Diary 2005*': Ponting, Ricky and Murgatroyd, Brian, *Ashes Diary 2005* (HarperCollins Publisher Australia, 2005).

Chapter 4

'You couldn't make it up…': Littlejohn, Richard, *You Couldn't Make it Up* (William Heinemann Ltd, 1995)

'Which seems odd, as he later hinted that he was rather hamstrung by the deal…': Sky Sports, 'Richard Thompson: ECB chair on fixing cricket's schedules and Hundred private equity interest', 3 December 2022. Available at: www.skysports.com/cricket/ news/12123/12760818/richard-thompson-ecb-chair-on-fixing-crickets-schedules-and -hundred-private-equity-interest

Chapter 6

'"Can't wait to take you to the Gabba"': Townend, J., 'Tim Paine's Gabba taunt to go down in cricket folklore after India's remarkable series win', *The West Australian*, 22 January

2021. Available at: www.thewest.com.au/sport/cricket/tim-paines-gabba-taunt-to-go
-down-in-cricket-folklore-after-indias-remarkable-series-win-ng-b8817767392

'I will always be available to play Test cricket': Lavalette, T., 'Shamar Joseph Commits To
Financially Stricken Test Format After Cricket's Biggest Upset', *Forbes*, 29 January 2024.
Available at: www.forbes.com/sites/tristanlavalette/2024/01/29/shamar-joseph-commits
-to-financially-stricken-test-format-after-crickets-biggest-upset

'Michael Vaughan suggested a window for the longest game': Available at: https://x.com/
MichaelVaughan/status/1748809529595224185

'I would have maybe three two-month slots for premier leagues': 'David Gower has lunch
with… Mike Gatting', *The Cricketer*, August 2023.

'Rob Key […] agreed that such a change was needed: "Test cricket needs to have
windows…"': BBC Sport, 'Jofra Archer: Rob Key hopeful fast bowler can play
in T20 World Cup', 16 January 2024. Available at: www.bbc.co.uk/sport/cricket
/67999444

'Jason Holder […] was another proponent': *The Cricketer*, 'Change or die: West Indies' Jason
Holder issues bleak prediction for future of Test cricket', 21 January 2024. Available at:
www.thecricketer.com/Topics/international/change_or_die_west_indies_jason_holder
_issues_bleak_prediction_future_test_cricket.html

'we could add Kevin Pietersen's brainwave in early 2024': *Wisden Cricket Monthly*, 'AB de
Villiers suggests DRS calls be decided by commentator votes', 22 January 2024. Available
at: www.wisden.com/cricket-news/boundaries-drs-kevin-pietersen-ab-de-villiers
-recommend-changes-laws-cricket-todays-cricket-news

Chapter 8

'Test cricket is the ultimate': Turbervill, H. '"We have the power, we have the personnel" – Sir
Viv Richards makes West Indies T20 World Cup prediction', *The Cricketer*, 29 April 2024.
Available at: www.thecricketer.com/Topics/mens-t20-world-cup-2024-premium/we
_have_power_personnel_sir_viv_richards_west_indies_t20_world_cup_prediction.html

Chapter 9

'With a quote that should inspire us all when we are facing adversity': Spofforth, Fred, *The
Demon Speaks* (Self-published, 2015).

'Having a Messerschmitt up your arse': Balding, C., 'Miller's tale and a drop in pressure',
The *Guardian*, 17 October 2004. Available at: www.theguardian.com/sport/2004/oct/17
/cricket.clarebalding

'"Trevor was such a pain if you were playing against him"': Foot, D., 'Trevor Bailey
obituary', The *Guardian*, 10 February 2011. Available at: www.theguardian.com/sport
/2011/feb/10/trevor-bailey-obituary#:~:text=Keith%20Miller%2C%20who%20groaned
%20whenever,were%20that%20you%20would%20win

'"Bloody Bailey, stop crawling, let's see some cricket"': Foot, D., 'Trevor Bailey obituary',
The *Guardian*, 10 February 2011. Available at: www.theguardian.com/sport/2011/feb/10
/trevor-bailey-obituary

Chapter 10

'"A good deal of over-reaction by everyone except Gavaskar"': Turbervill, H., 'India in England, a Test history - PART TWO: India shock Illingworth', *The Cricketer*, 6 August 2018. Available at: www.thecricketer.com/topics/features/india_in_england,_a_test_history_-_part_two_india_shock_illingworth.html

'"It was a shock. India did it with grim determination"': Turbervill, H., 'India in England, a Test history - PART TWO: India shock Illingworth', *The Cricketer*, 6 August 2018. Available at: www.thecricketer.com/Topics/features/india_in_england,_a_test_history_-_part_two_india_shock_illingworth.html

Chapter 11

'"you have immediately the sensation of breathing a different air"': Orwell, George, *England Your England*, first published as part of *The Lion and the Unicorn: Socialism and the English Genius* in 1941. Available at: https://orwell.ru/library/essays/lion/english/e_eye

'an embarrassing entanglement with a barmaid': Williamson, M., 'Mike Gatting's annus horribilis', ESPNCrincinfo, 24 August 2005. Available at: www.espncricinfo.com/story/mike-gatting-s-annus-horribilis-141453

'"We live in a democracy, and he is allowed to say those things"': Gardner, J., 'ECB lacked "backbone" for not calling out Lord Botham's criticism of ICEC report', the *Independent*, 20 February 2024. Available at: www.independent.co.uk/sport/cricket/durham-ecb-england-richard-thompson-botham-b2499098.html

'which they rendered to the melody of "Jamaica Farewell"': Rohlehr, G., 'Calypso, Literature and West Indian Cricket: Era of Dominance', Anthurium, 18 April 2023. Available at: https://anthurium.miami.edu/articles/10.33596/anth.507

'the director cut to a banner in the crowd': *On Top Down Under* (1987) [VHS], BBC Video.

'"I'm sure they will be quaking in their boots"': Miller, A., 'No grovelling, just WInning', ESPNCricinfo, 3 February 2019. Available at: www.espncricinfo.com/story/no-grovelling-just-winning-1173567

'Steve Waugh called it an "abysmal showing"': Turbervill, H., 'Ashes Chronicles – Part 12: Botham's Brisbane blitzkrieg sets up Gatting's men for clean sweep in 1986/87', *The Cricketer*, 30 November 2021. Available at: www.thecricketer.com/Topics/ashes/ashes_chronicles_part_12_botham_brisbane_blitzkrieg_sets_up_gattings_men_clean_sweep_1986_87.html

'Gooch was "undeserving"': Gardner, A., 'The year of four England captains', ESPNCricinfo, 26 September 2015. Available at: www.espncricinfo.com/story/review-long-shot-summer-922727

'Border told his bemused counterpart': *The Telegraph*, 'The things they said', 17 July 2005. Available at: www.telegraph.co.uk/sport/2362115/The-things-they-said.html

Chapter 12

'"I want to make very clear that I love county supporters"': Farrell, M., 'Michael Vaughan suggests replacing 18 first-class counties with 10 franchise teams', *Wisden Cricket Monthly*,

18 January 2024. Available at: www.wisden.com/cricket-interviews/michael-vaughan
-suggests-replacing-18-first-class-counties-with-10-franchise-teams-england-cricket
-news-today

'"We'll not allow our club to be rendered irrelevant"': Reeves, T., 'Kent chairman Simon
Philip comments on proposals from the England and Wales Cricket Board issued by
former captain Andrew Strauss', KentOnline, 22 September 2022. Available at: www
.kentonline.co.uk/canterbury/sport/kent-chairman-says-club-wont-be-rendered
-irrelevant-amid-273892

Chapter 13

'"some fans described the concept as 'needless', 'a gimmick' and 'simply ridiculous"': '100-
ball competition plans because young people "not attracted to cricket"', BBC Sport,
14 May 2018. Available at: www.bbc.co.uk/sport/cricket/44113230

'"now contested by has-beens and wannabees," according to former Somerset and England
all-rounder Vic Marks': Marks, V., '50-over cricket is for losers – except when the World
Cup comes around', *The Cricketer*, October 2023.

'He wanted the Oval Invincibles to be called the Surrey Invincibles': Ouzia, M., 'Surrey
Oval Invincibles Oli Slipper interview', *The Standard*, 26 October 2023. Available at: www
.standard.co.uk/sport/cricket/surrey-oval-invincibles-oli-slipper-interview-b1115970
.html

'Power List of the main people in English cricket': *The Cricketer*, 'THE POWER LIST
2019: The Cricketer counts down the 50 most influential people in English cricket', 19
September 2019. Available at: www.thecricketer.com/Topics/news/the_power_list_2019
_the_cricketer_counts_down_50_most_influential_people_english_cricket.html

'"The Hundred adds a headache-inducing layer of complexity to the fixture list"':
Atherton, M., 'Tom Harrison: I'm proud of the Hundred but England's aborted Pakistan
tour hurt a lot', *The Times*, 8 June 2022. Available at: www.thetimes.com/sport/cricket
/article/tom-harrison-im-proud-of-the-hundred-but-englands-aborted-pakistan-tour
-hurt-a-lot-d6trwzpx9

'"This is the fulfilment of a dream for me…"' said Bransgrove': Hoad, A., 'Hampshire agree
"dream" takeover by IPL group', BBC Sport, 30 September 2024. Available at: www.bbc
.co.uk/sport/cricket/articles/cqjrypy1e2ko

'"three domestic competitions and an increased international schedule was already causing
problems"': Atherton, M., 'Richard Thompson: ECB chair on fixing cricket's schedules
and Hundred private equity interest', Sky Sports, 3 December 2022. Available at: www
.skysports.com/cricket/news/12123/12760818/richard-thompson-ecb-chair-on-fixing
-crickets-schedules-and-hundred-private-equity-interest

'he will support The Hundred if it did not cannibalise county competitions.': Keith, F.,
'Richard Gould interview: Surrey's chief executive on T20 Blast success, The Hundred
and the fifth Ashes Test', City AM, 2 September 2019. Available at: www.cityam.com/
richard-gould-interview-surreys-chief-executive-on-t20-blast-success-the-hundred-and
-the-fifth-ashes-test

'"It's not the tail wagging the dog but the fleas on the tail wagging the dog,"': Hoult, N.,
'How the counties fought back to win cricket's civil war', *The Telegraph*, 25 November
2022. Available at: www.telegraph.co.uk/cricket/2022/11/25/how-counties-fought-back
-win-crickets-civil-war

Chapter 15

'"Watching a guy bowling at that level"': 'That world class performance', Kaieteur News, 21 October 2020. Available at: www.kaieteurnewsonline.com/2020/10/21/that-world -class-performance/#:~:text=Desmond%20Haynes%20recalled%2C%20%E2%80 %9CWatching%20a,he%20bowled%20those%20guys%20out.%E2%80%9D

'"like a man who has his braces caught on the sight screen"': Bateman, C., 'RIP Martin Johnson, master of the withering prose...little dulled his pen', Sports Journalists Association, 15 March 2021. Available at: www.sportsjournalists.co.uk/obits/rip-martin -johnson-master-of-the-withering-prose-little-dulled-his-pen

'Steve James says he had "the sharpest brain in cricket"': 'How data and insight helped England become the best Test team in the world - and can this current crop do it again?', *The Telegraph*. Available at: www.telegraph.co.uk/cricket/supporting-england/ team-tactics

Chapter 17

'"players would come for a week of Test cricket and then go back to the counties"': 'How data and insight helped England become the best Test team in the world - and can this current crop do it again?', *The Telegraph*. Available at: www.telegraph.co.uk/cricket/ supporting-england/team-tactics

'"Before central contracts, everyone turned up as county players"': Gibson, R., 'England's contract thrillers: 20 years ago, the dawn of central deals saw our Test stars finally treated like elite sportsmen, sparking a winning spree that took them to No 1', *Mail Online*, 28 May 2020. Available at: www.dailymail.co.uk/sport/cricket/article-8367317/Englands -cricketers-began-contracted-ECB-20-years-ago.html

'"There is no comparison between the facilities that we have here and those in Australia"': Fraser, A., 'Marsh claims England lead the way with Academy', *The Independent*, 26 September 2002. Available at: www.independent.co.uk/sport/cricket/marsh-claims -england-lead-the-way-with-academy-178152.html

'"The team has to be together to beat Australia."': 'Flintoff turned up drunk, he could not throw the ball, never mind catch it. And this was our captain', *The Standard*, 13 April 2012. Available at: www.standard.co.uk/sport/flintoff-turned-up-drunk-he-could-not -throw-the-ball-never-mind-catch-it-and-this-was-our-captain-6676708.html

'"It had to be Flintoff"': 'Flintoff turned up drunk, he could not throw the ball, never mind catch it. And this was our captain', *The Standard*, 13 April 2012. Available at: www .standard.co.uk/sport/flintoff-turned-up-drunk-he-could-not-throw-the-ball-never -mind-catch-it-and-this-was-our-captain-6676708.html

'the Peter Principle': Wikipedia contributors, Peter principle, Wikipedia, 31 August 2024. Available at: https://en.wikipedia.org/wiki/Peter_principle#:~:text=The%20Peter%20 principle%20is%20a,competent%2C%20as%20skills%20in%20one

'"either Moores went, or he went"': Booth, L., 'Pietersen quit before he was sacked', The *Guardian*, 8 January 2009. Available at: www.theguardian.com/sport/2009/jan/08/ england-kevin-pietersen-andrew-strauss

Chapter 18

'"I can't let him get away with that"': Turbervill, H., 'Ashes Chronicles – Part 12: Botham's Brisbane blitzkrieg sets up Gatting's men for clean sweep in 1986/87', *The Cricketer*, 30 November 2021. Available at: www.thecricketer.com/Topics/ashes/ashes_chronicles _part_12_bothams_brisbane_blitzkrieg_sets_up_gattings_men_for_clean_sweep_in _198687.html

'"It was hard to watch"': Ibid.

'"Cricket is [the album] *Revolver* by the Beatles…"': Anderson, Jimmy, *Bowl. Sleep. Repeat.* (Cassell, 2019).

'"His pace forced my body to do things I'd spent my whole career training not to"': Ronay, B., 'Joe Root on Ben Stokes' Ashes return: "You could almost hear his smile down the phone"', The *Guardian*, 31 October 2021. Available at: www.theguardian.com/sport /2021/oct/31/joe-root-ashes-is-the-one-series-every-player-is-desperate-to-perform-in

Chapter 19

'"He's a guy who prefers to lurk in the shadows"': Miller, A., 'Meticulous Flower helps England bloom', ESPNCricinfo, 7 January 2011. Available at: www.espncricinfo.com/ story/australia-v-england-meticulous-flower-helps-england-bloom-495813

'"Stop looking for the dream ball every ball"': Booth, L., 'Graeme Swann's bust-ups that so nearly forced England's star spinner to give up', *Mail* Online, 31 December 2009. Available at: www.dailymail.co.uk/sport/cricket/article-1239705/Graeme-Swanns-bust -ups-nearly-forced-Englands-star-spinner-up.html

'"very much the sort of people we want the England captain and his family to be"': 'England's Ashes whitewash was appalling, says ECB chairman', BBC Sport, 20 May 2014. Available at: www.bbc.co.uk/sport/cricket/27466154

'"He seems to be able to do nothing about the outcome of the game"': Turbervill, H., 'The Googly: Carry On Captain! Alastair Cook Has Seriously Thick Skin', *The Cricketer*, 10 November 2016. Available at: www.thecricketer.com/Topics/globalgame/the-googly -carry-on-captain-alastair-cook-has-seriously-thick-skin.html

Chapter 21

'"responsibility for upcoming cricketers who aspire to play for England"': Turbervill, H., 'Ben Stokes wants help from the press - but his predecessors would testify that is a rare luxury', *The Cricketer*, 14 September 2022. Available at: www.thecricketer.com/Topics/ england/ben_stokes_help_press_predecessors_rare_luxury_england_bazball.html

'"get behind the team and leave the hindsight and negativity to the pundits… come on England"': Available at: www.x.com/benstokes38/status/1803852135349518492

'The headline on *The Australian* newspaper website said it all': Savage, N., 'England shredded for "kamikaze cricket"; Australian openers "absolutely bossed it"', FOX Sports, 1 July 2023. Available at: www.foxsports.com.au/cricket/the-ashes/england-shredded-for

-kamikaze-cricket-australian-openers-absolutely-bossed-it-lords-ashes-test-day-3
-talking-points/news-story/21e216b5bf9f677b0d1ff856b564e6da

'"Test revolution that has thrilled everyone bar the po-faced and one-eyed"': Booth, Lawrence, *Wisden Cricketers' Almanack 2024* (Wisden, 2024)

'"There's a form of intellectual snobbery about the game': Bloom, Ben, *Batting for Time: The Fight to Keep English Cricket Alive* (Pitch Publishing Ltd, 2024) p. 82.

'"Any cricket needs to be smart cricket"': Turbervill, H., 'Ashes Test at Lord's, 2023', Huwzat, 18 August 2023. Available at: www.huwzat.wordpress.com/2023/08/18/ashes -test-at-lords-2023

'"I'm full of admiration for Ben"': Booth, L., 'Pope is allowed to reverse-sweep a spinner first ball... in my day he wouldn't have played again for three years! Legendary former England and Ashes-winning captain MIKE BREARLEY on how Ben Stokes has banished the fear of failure', Mail Online, 28 May 2023. Available at: www.dailymail .co.uk/sport/cricket/article-12134319/Legendary-former-England-captain-MIKE -BREARLEY-Ben-Stokes-banished-fear-failure.html

'Brearley had "caveats"': Ibid.

'"You've just cost us the Ashes, that's all"': The OSM team, 'September's ten', The *Guardian*, 2 September 2007. Available at: www.theguardian.com/sport/2007/sep/02/cricket .features

'A lean spell of 242 runs in 11 Test knocks': Dobell, G., 'Joe Root still trying to discover role in England's Bazball revolution', *The Cricketer*, 20 February 2023. Available at: www .thecricketer.com/Topics/new-zealand-v-england-men/joe_root_still_trying_discover _role_englands_bazball_revolution.html

'"Root had a bloody fine record playing normally"': Sports Desk, 'IND vs ENG: Ian Chappell lambasts Root's Bazball approach, "had a bloody fine record playing normally"', *The Indian Express*, 21 February 2024. Available at: www.indianexpress .com/article/sports/cricket/india-vs-england-root-had-a-bloody-fine-record-playing -normally-ian-chappel-lambasts-bazball-9171092

'"This is the Joe Root mode that wins you Test matches"': Rediff Cricket, 'This is the Joe Root mode that win you Test matches', Rediff.com, 23 February 2024. Available at: https://m.rediff.com/cricket/report/this-is-the-joe-root-mode-that-win-you-test -matches-ranchi-test-england-tour-india-2023-24-pix/20240223.htm

'he attacked 41 per cent of balls in 2022': Turbervill, H., 'Ben Stokes wants help from the press - but his predecessors would testify that is a rare luxury', *The Cricketer*, 14 September 2022. Available at: www.thecricketer.com/Topics/england/ben_stokes_help _press_predecessors_rare_luxury_england_bazball.html

'it sparked a fiery reply from Nasser Hussain': 'Jaiswal learned from his upbringing, not from Bazball: Nasser Hussain to Ben Duckett', *The Hindu*, 21 February 2024. Available at: www.thehindu.com/sport/cricket/jaiswal-learned-from-his-upbringing-not-from -bazball-nasser-hussain-to-ben-duckett/article67868375.ece

'Kevin Pietersen posted on X after England started the first Test poorly': "If you're that person who's now blaming England for warming up in Abu Dhabi, please give yourself an uppercut!"': Available at: https://x.com/KP24/status/1750872412059775165

'"Oh f*** off @KP!"': Available at: https://x.com/abutch58/status/1750916651904647326

'"Yes, get a hundred, but actually stay there for two days, that means that you belong"': Turbervill, H., 'Whatever happened to... Mudassar Nazar', *The Cricketer*, September 2023.

' 'The point of courage is that it cannot exist without fear'": Barnes, S., 'The Ashes needs the fear factor', *The Cricketer*, July 2023.

'"I just want to get you around the group'": Macpherson, W., 'Jordan Cox: I fought back from "disgusting" finger injury to earn England Test call-up', *The Telegraph*, 12 August 2024. Available at: www.telegraph.co.uk/cricket/2024/08/12/jordan-cox-finger-injury-england-cricket-kent-essex/#:~:text=Cox%20recounts%20the%20call%20he,which %20is%20what%20you%20have

Chapter 22

'"Neither side took it too seriously"': Turbervill, Huw, *The Toughest Tour* (Aurum, 2010)

'"You'd have to have an absolute stinker not to make the quarter-finals"': Farrell, M., 'The Irishman who became captain of England', *The Cricket Monthly*, 15 May 2019. Available at: www.thecricketmonthly.com/story/1182683/eoin-morgan---england-s-irish-world-cup-captain

'"he was not too worried about meaningless matches like that"': Turbervill, H. 'Glenn McGrath: Facing up', *The Cricketer*, March 2023.

'ODIs should now be reduced to 40 overs per side': Turbervill, H., 'Whatever happened to... Doug Walters', *The Cricketer*, July 2022.

Chapter 23

'"It's my personal opinion that there shouldn't be any international cricket that clashes with the IPL," said England captain Jos Buttler.': ANI, '"International cricket should not be clashing with IPL": England captain Buttler', *The Hindustan Times*, 22 May 2024. Available at: www.hindustantimes.com/cricket/international-cricket-should-not-be-clashing-with-ipl-england-captain-buttler-101716352994225.html

Chapter 25

'"I saw history being written not in terms of what happened but of what ought to have happened according to various party lines"': Morrison, D., 'Orwell Up Close', *Time*, 22 June 2023. Available at: www.time.com/archive/6645400/orwell-up-close

'"We intend to punish them for their impertinence"': Turbervill, H., 'We need to keep earning respect', *The Sunday Telegraph*, 16 May 2004.

'Shane Warne called him "England's greatest captain"': Hughes, D., 'Ashes 2005 team: what happened to the England squad that beat Australia 2-1 in the greatest of all Test series?', *inews*, 2 August 2019. Available at: www.inews.co.uk/sport/cricket/ashes-2005-team-england-squad-vs-australia-now-what-happened-now-321091?srsltid=AfmBOoo vWHxszGSYMKNCiAqyJhqSSDDoS-IR_GP9i1TJO-zKmQTghqgR

'"When Vaughan is in charge"': *ESPNCricinfo*, 'Flintoff gives thumbs-up to Vaughan', 20 September 2005. Available at: www.espncricinfo.com/story/flintoff-gives-thumbs-up-to-vaughan-219651

'"It's time to lose a day and have four-day Tests!"': BBC Sport, 'Michael Vaughan: Four-day Tests worth a try to rejuvenate format', 4 June 2018. Available at: www.bbc.co.uk/sport/cricket/44364569

'"Replace counties with franchises!"': Farrell, M., 'Michael Vaughan suggests replacing 18 first-class counties with 10 franchise teams', *Wisden Cricket Monthly*, 18 January 2024. Available at: www.wisden.com/cricket-interviews/michael-vaughan-suggests-replacing-18-first-class-counties-with-10-franchise-teams-england-cricket-news-today#:~:text=Michael%20Vaughan%20suggests%20replacing%2018%20first%2Dclass%20counties%20with%2010%20franchise%20teams,-Jan%2018%2C%202024&text=Michael%20Vaughan%20has%20called%20for,replaced%20by%20ten%20franchise%20teams

Chapter 26

'disobeying orders; being antagonistic; showing egoism…': The Background to the Far East Campaign, Swaffham Museum. Available at: www.swaffhammuseum.co.uk/documents/FEPOW/The-Background.pdf

'He suggests cricket keeps the Northern Superchargers in The Hundred': Sky Sports, 'Joe Root: England's all-rounder among players calling for a change to cricket's busy schedule', 16 May 2024. Available at: www.skysports.com/cricket/news/12123/13128174/joe-root-englands-all-rounder-among-players-calling-for-a-change-to-crickets-busy-schedule

Conclusion

'"The world is reacting to – not England, I agree – the short form"': Turbervill, H., 'The Battle to save Test cricket', *The Cricketer*, Summer 2024.

'"the overall impression that I took away from the day was that the decline of long-form red-ball cricket is just an inevitability"': Ibid.

'Badale warned us that change was coming': Gower, D., 'Don't kill Test cricket for the rest of us', *The Cricketer*, Summer 2024.

'People will listen to the recent greats': Ibid.

'Cummins said: "Test cricket ties the cricket world together. It's where people learn their craft…"': Turbervill, H., 'The Battle to save Test cricket', *The Cricketer*, Summer 2024.

'Stokes called Test cricket "incredibly vital"': Ibid.

'"We don't make money from any home series apart from England or India"': 'Jason Holder: I broke my back for West Indies, now it's my time', *The Times*, 9 July 2024. Available at: www.thetimes.com/sport/cricket/article/jason-holder-west-indies-first-fair-earn-too-england-tour-g77vvtd5h

BIBLIOGRAPHY

Bloom, Ben, *Batting for Time: The Fight to Keep English Cricket Alive* (Pitch Publishing Ltd, 2024)

Booth, Lawrence, *Wisden Cricketers' Almanack 2024* (Wisden, 2024)

Edmonds, Frances, *Another Bloody Tour* (Kingswood, 1986)

Edmonds, Frances, *Cricket XXXX Cricket* (Kingswood, 1987)

Hersh, Seymour, *The Dark Side of Camelot* (Little, Brown & Co., 1998).

James, Steve, *The Plan* (Bantam Press, 2012)

Key, Rob, *'Oi, Key' Tales of a Journeyman Cricketer* (White Owl, 2020)

MCC Cricket Coaching Book (Heinemann, 1962)

Orwell, George, *Animal Farm* (Secker & Warburg, 1945)

IMAGE CREDITS

Introduction: The England team line up to mourn the passing of the Queen before they take on South Africa in the final home Test of 2022 at The Oval. © Gareth Copley – ECB/ECB via Getty Images

Chapter 1: Captain Paul Collingwood kisses the World T20 trophy on the beach in Bridgetown, Barbados, after they beat Australia in the final at the Kensington Oval. © Clive Rose/Getty Images

Chapter 2: Spectators queue for a ticket to see the opening day of the fifth Test of the series between England and West Indies on August 22, 1957 at the Kennington Oval. © Derek Berwin/Fox Photos/Hulton Archive/Getty Images

Chapter 3: England captain David Gower celebrates on the shoulders of Allan Lamb and Mike Gatting at Kanpur after winning the Test series in India in 1984/85, a remarkable effort after they lost the opening match. © Adrian Murrell/Allsport/ Hulton Archive/Getty Images

Chapter 4: A camera films England's Len Hutton, on his way to 364, and Maurice Leyland bat against Australia at The Oval in August 1938; that summer was the first time the BBC televised cricket. © Central Press/Hulton Archive/Getty Images

Chapter 5: Graham Gooch pulls a short ball against India at The Oval in 1979; his England Test career lasted 20 years thanks to incredibly hard work. © Adrian Murrell/ Allsport/Getty Images/Hulton Archive

Chapter 6: Coach Brendon McCullum and captain Ben Stokes want their England Test players to take the belligerent approach at all times. © Gareth Copley/Getty Images

Chapter 7: A day at the Test is not just about cricket, it's about eating, drinking, dressing up, friendship and fun, as these spectators show in the match between England and New Zealand at Headingley in 2022. © Stu Forster/Getty Images

Chapter 8: The fearless and imposing Viv Richards of West Indies, here batting against Australia at the Gabba in December 1979, was a wonder to watch. © Eric Piper/ Mirrorpix/Getty Images

Chapter 9: One imagines Geoffrey Boycott was not thrilled to be 12th man, but he seems genial enough alongside Maurice Foster during the second Test against West Indies at Edgbaston in 1973. © Allsport/Getty Images/Hulton Archive

Chapter 10: England captain Mike Denness hits out in the second innings of the first Test against India at Old Trafford; the great entertainer, Farokh Engineer, is behind the stumps. © Dennis Oulds and Leonard Burt/Central Press/Hulton Archive/Getty Images

Chapter 11: His adoring public are jubilant as Ian Botham has New Zealand Bruce Edgar caught at slip with his first ball at The Oval in 1986 after a ban for smoking drugs. © Adrian Murrell/Allsport/Getty Images/Hulton Archive

Chapter 12: With so many County Championship matches scheduled for spring and late summer now, fans are grateful when the sun comes out, as it does here in the match between Derbyshire and Surrey in late May 2013. © Tony Marshall/Getty Images

Chapter 13: Southern Braves men and Oval Invincibles women celebrate winning the inaugural Hundred; the controversial tournament has attracted some new fans, but alienated many existing ones. © Stu Forster/Getty Images

Chapter 14: Pakistan's Mudassar Nazar bats in a tour match at Northamptonshire in May 1978; he is worried that youngsters are choosing more lucrative T20 assignments over Test cricket. © Bob Thomas Sports Photography via Getty Images

Chapter 15: England duo Angus Fraser and Phil Tufnell, both of Middlesex, were often blinded by the brilliance of Australia in the 1990s. © Graham Chadwick/ALLSPORT

Chapter 16: Jack Russell has channeled all that concentration he had as England wicketkeeper/batsman into painting; but he is worried about cricket's future. © Jordan Mansfield/Getty Images

Chapter 17: England's captain Nasser Hussain watches the rain come down at Centurion Park in 2000... sadly he was about to be duped by South Africa's skipper, Hansie Cronje. © Graham Chadwick/ALLSPORT

Chapter 18: Merv Hughes befriends a pitch invader at Trent Bridge in the 1993 Ashes Test; the mustachioed pace bowler was one of Test cricket's great characters, with quite a bark of his own. © Patrick Eagar/Popperfoto via Getty Images

Chapter 19: Andrews Strauss and Flower – 'the Andocracy' – made England officially the best Test team in the world for the first and only time in 2011. © Clive Rose/Getty Images

Chapter 20: New Zealand's Richard Hadlee was Test cricket's leading wicket-taker, with 431, when he bowed out after his final Test, against England at Edgbaston in 1990. © Ben Radford/Allsport/Getty Images

Chapter 21: Ben Stokes and Brendon McCullum believe the entertaining brand of cricket that they have injected into England's DNA gives Test cricket its best chance of surviving. © Stu Forster/Getty Images

Chapter 22: Australia's 50-over World Cup win in 1999, after beating Pakistan in the final at Lord's, goes down well in the Crown Casino in Melbourne, Australia. © Stuart Milligan/ALLSPORT

Chapter 23: Reece Topley did well in the first-class game for Surrey, but the sport's unrelenting multi-format scheduling has forced him to concentrate on white-ball cricket. © Alex Davidson/Getty Images for Surrey CCC

Chapter 24: The beautiful Monkton Combe Cricket Club near Bath; there is widespread concern at the decline in the number of recreational cricketers. © Laurence Griffiths/Getty Images

Chapter 25: An unusual view of Hove... a day there is a treat, but less charracterful, concrete stadiums are threatening to squeeze such venues out. © Mike Hewitt/Getty Images

Chapter 26: Mike Gatting, Ian Botham, David Gower and Graham Gooch – brilliant players, but for a few notable series exceptions, the England team in the 1980s underachieved. © Adrian Murrell/Allsport/Getty Images/Hulton Archive

Conclusion: The urn is taken to Sydney for the Bicentenary Test between Australia and England in 1988; fortunately, the Ashes remains popular, even if lesser Test series do not. © Greg White/Fairfax Media via Getty Images

ACKNOWLEDGEMENTS

Thanks to Mum and Dad for their love, and a house full of books, newspapers and magazines. To my grandfather Ted and neighbours for reading my sports publications when I was in single digits. To Graeme Riley, Douglas Hurdley and Mike Weaver for inspirational teaching. *The East Anglian Daily Times*' Tony Garnett, for giving me my chance in Ipswich. To encouraging sports editors in Fleet Street, Jon Ryan and Scyld Berry of the *Sunday Telegraph*, the *Daily Express* team, and the *Daily Telegraph*'s Keith Perry and Dan Evans (and the not-so-helpful ones, for motivating me). For my saviour, Andy Afford, and then Guy Evans-Tipping, for support and trying to teach me about business. To Jim Hindson, James Coyne, Geoff Barton, George Dobell and my colleagues at *The Cricketer*. To Tom Maslona and Nick Pagan, who read the book for me and gave me lots of advice, and Morgan Davies and Sean Gardner, for ideas. To Matt Lowing, Caroline Guillet and their Bloomsbury team, for backing me, and Melanie Michael-Greer, for her considerable help. To David Gower, Graham Gooch, Jack Russell and the other interviewees who kindly gave me their time. Finally, to my wife Emma, children Grace, Ben and Polly, and my writing companion, Honey the cockerpoo.

INDEX

Page numbers in italics are figures.